Boston Terriers
The Early Years

Cathy J. Flamholtz, editor

OTR Publications
Centreville, Alabama

Front Cover Art by: Gladys Emerson Cook
Back Cover Art by: Harrison Fisher, 1912

Boston Terriers, The Early Years

© 1997, by Cathy J. Flamholtz

ISBN 0-940269-13-9

All Rights Reserved. No part of this book may be reproduced or transmitted in any form or by any means, electronic or mechanical, including photocopying, recording, on-line transmission or by any information storage or retrieval system—except by a reviewer to be printed in a magazine or newspaper—without permission from the publisher.

Printed in the United States of America

10 9 8 7 6 5 4 3 2 1

Although the author has extensively researched sources to ensure the accuracy and completeness of the information contained in this book, we assume no responsibility for errors, inaccuracies, omissions or any inconsistency herein. Any slights of people or organizations are unintentional.

OTR PUBLICATIONS
P.O. Box 481
Centreville, AL 35042

Dedication

To my parents, Wilson and Evelyn Vail, who never lived to see any of my books published. You are always in my heart.

Life *magazine, c. 1920. From the Flamholtz collection*

Table of Contents

Introduction *by Cathy J. Flamholtz*   7

Chapter 1   History of the Breed *by Dr. J. Varnum Mott*   11
    Early Dogs *by Fred R. Bearse*   15
    A Tribute to Mr. Barnard and the Breed *by Edward Axtell*   16
    The President and the Boston *by Cathy J. Flamholtz*   18
    Dr. C.F. "Connie" Sullivan, Trimount Kennels, *by Cathy J. Flamholtz*   20

Chapter 2   The Boston Terrier and the AKC *by James Watson*   23
    Early Breed Names *by Vinton P. Breese*   28

Chapter 3   Notable Early Stud Dogs *by H. Tatnall Brown*   33
    The Buster Family   34
    The Punch Family   35
    The Cracksman Family   36

Chapter 4   A Tribute to Robert L. Dickey *by Cathy J. Flamholtz*   41

Chapter 5   The Boston as a Show Dog *by Dr. J. Varnum Mott*   55
    Julius Fangmann   56
    The Mosholu Story *by Cathy J. Flamholtz*   58

Chapter 6   Educating a Boston *by Dr. J. Varnum Mott*   61
    Squantum Kennels   66

Chapter 7   Buying a Boston *by Dr. J. Varnum Mott*   69

Chapter 8   The Care of the Boston *by Dr. J. Varnum Mott*   75
    Sunny Hill Kennels   78
    Highball Kennels   79

Chapter 9   Breeding Boston Terriers *by Miss Emily Pomeroy*   81
    Holiday Kennels   91

Chapter 10 Breeding for Good Disposition *by Edward Axtell*   93
  The Hamil Bostons   95
  The Ringmount Bostons   96

Chapter 11 Breeding for a Vigorous Constitution *by Edward Axtell*   99
  The Shire Bostons   103

Chapter 12 Breeding for Size *by Edward Axtell*   105

Chapter 13 Breeding for Color and Markings *by Edward Axtell*   109
  Tryon Kennels   111
  Winna Kennels   114

Chapter 14 Present Day Boston Terrier Strains *by Alva Rosenberg*   117
  Heilborn's Raffles   118
  Ringmaster Bostons   119
  Alva Rosenberg   120
  Ravenroyd Kennels   121
  Reign Count Kennels   123

Chapter 15 Early Boston Terriers in Canada *by C. L. Mac Quillan*   125
  Haggerty Bostons   128

Chapter 16 Bostons in Canada Today *by C. L. Mac Quillan*   133
  Vincent Perry   135

Chapter 17 The Boston Terrier Standard Simplified   139
  Thorpe's Bostons   141
  Kingway Kennels   145

Chapter 18 Boston Terrier Type *by Vinton P. Breese*   151
  Judges and Size *by Mrs. F. E. Storer*   153
  Arroyo Kennels   155
  Million Dollar Bostons   158

Appendix 1 Glossary   164
Appendix 2 Boston Terrier Champions of Record   170
Appendix 3 First Annual Dog Show Catalogue of the Boston Terriers Breeders' Club, 1898   180
Appendix 4 Directory of Reliable Breeders of Boston Terriers, 1927   199
Index   206

Introduction

I love old dog books. The musty smell, the dog-eared pages, the margin notes penned by past readers, the photos, grainy by present day standards, the intricate cover engravings...I love it all. They afford us a chance to hold history in our hands.

Almost one hundred years ago, as the Spanish-American War began and Teddy Roosevelt led his Rough Riders into Cuba, as H.G. Wells saw the *War of the Worlds* roll off the presses in London, as the Boxer Uprising began in China and as many Americans packed up their gear and headed to the latest gold strike in Alaska, a doctor in Boston sat down to pen a booklet on his favorite breed. Dr. J. Varnum Mott poured all his delight, love and concern for "America's Dog" onto the pages of his little book. Well known in the Boston Terrier fancy, Dr. Mott was the owner of Ch. Lord Derby, who was shown under his "Presto" banner.

One can only surmise that Dr. Mott was surprised by the success of his endeavor. *The Boston Terrier* was released in a number of editions. It was filled with stories of the earliest dogs and their breeders (gleaned from that most valuable of all Boston books, *The Boston Terrier Club Book,* one of this country's first yearbooks), as well as his own personal observations and opinions on the breed. Mott's love for the Boston shines brightly from every page.

Mott's *The Boston Terrier* is one of my all time favorite breed books. I love the intensely personal way he writes about the breed. He was a man ahead of his time. Indeed, much of his socialization and training advice, with a few modern adjustments, could have been penned by someone writing in 1998, not 1898. "Make a companion of your dog," he tells us, "love him...treat him with due consideration." In an age when the authors of most dog books owned large kennels, Mott lauds the personal companion. "Boston Terriers seem to possess remarkable reasoning powers, and use them on every possible occasion. In order to develop these attributes their education must begin when they are young, and they should be so placed that without any special effort their senses are unconsciously developed. Hence it is well never to raise pups in large kennels, for the reason that their life there would of necessity be the same from day to day, and the opportunity of brain development would be materially restricted."

Mott continually likens the raising of a Boston pup to the upbringing of a child, a rare way of thinking in his age. In a time when methods of discipline were often quite harsh, Mott tells us to scold the dog, but never hit him. He uses a chain to restrict the dog for such activities as housebreaking, but one knows that, had he had a crate available, that's what he would have preferred.

Mott's commitment to the breed as a whole is also apparent in *The Boston Terrier*. He decries the trickery so often seen in turn of the century dog shows and abhors the back biting, bickering and over-commercialization that was rampant. Always, always, he appeals to owners to keep "the best interests of this most desirable little dog at heart."

In 1927, a new edition of *The Boston Terrier* was released. Fred J. Skinner, managing editor of the popular *Field and Fancy,* engaged new authors to bring Mott's booklet up to date. The breed had made many advances since the days of Dr. Mott's original work and Skinner hoped that, by calling on well known modern fanciers, he would be able to retain the charm of the original work and yet broaden it's appeal to fanciers of the 1920s. This makes the 1927 edition of *The Boston Terrier* unique. Unlike most other dog books, the revision spans a 30 year period, one that is critical in Boston Terrier history. Here we can see, before our very eyes, the evolution of the breed. From the coarse bully-type dogs with their surfeit of white, to the neat dapper dogs of today, Mott's book offers the bridge from the earliest days to the present.

It was my fondness for Dr. Mott's book that led me to approach OTR with the idea of reprinting the 1927 edition for today's fanciers. Following in the footsteps of Fred Skinner, I decided to expand the project to give current readers a better feel for this period. In selecting additional inclusions, I focused on the period up to the 1920s. I turned to my own large library of dog books, magazines, photos, paintings and prints to see what would enhance Mott's work. James Watson's *The Dog Book* (1905) gave first-hand information on the efforts to obtain recognition. Edward Axtell's *The Boston Terrier and All About It*, published in several editions in the early 1900s, added information on the early colors found in the breed, the size controversy and his unstinting opinions on temperament and vigor. His glossary gives us an idea of the terms popular in that day.

One of the most interesting items contained herein is a wonderful little booklet, originally selling for fifty cents, titled *The Boston Terrier Standard Simplified*. A better title would have been *The Boston Terrier Standard Amplified*. A series of these little books were published, around the turn of the century, on the most popular breeds.

This drawing is by well-known artist Diana Thorne. From the Flamholtz collection

Today, they are sought after collectibles. The offering on the Boston was first released in or about 1907. It was compiled after numerous discussions with all the leading breeders, exhibitors and judges of the day. In the chapter on type, Vinton Breese, one of the original authors, talks about the difficulty of reaching a consensus of opinion. *The Boston Terrier Simplified* went through at least two revisions. The copy I have is the third edition, "revised to July 1916," and compiled by C.N. Grey, then Secretary of the Boston Terrier Club of America.

I have also included a catalog from the first show given by the Boston Terrier Breeders' Club, in Boston, in November of 1898. Here we see the names of many early lights in the breed. It seemed appropriate to include this catalog as the show was held during the year when Mott's work first appeared.

I hope that readers will enjoy the tribute to artist Robert L. Dickey. Some time ago I became intrigued by Dickey's work and began to collect it. Art critics of today may fault Dickey for his highly stylized, anthropomorphic bent, but these are the very qualities that made him so popular during the early days of this century. A Boston Terrier owner himself, he infused the dogs in his work with a clownish charm and sense of humor that could only be the product of knowing the breed so intimately. The popularity of his own work helped to fuel the growth of the breed.

To give a full picture of the breed and its evolution during this critical period, I have tried to include as many photos as possible. I combed through my collection for photos from the earliest days to the 1920s. With only a few digressions, I have tried to stay true to this period. Aiding me in my search for photos, were my turn of the century dog magazines. Sadly, the quality of many of these old photos doesn't compare to today's reproduction standards. Using computers, the design people at OTR have attempted to enhance these old photos so that they may be better appreciated by today's readers. In some cases, the results are still less than we would wish for. In others, the outcome has been dramatic. My sincere thanks to all the design people who put in so many hours on this work. Deciding where to place this many photos was a difficult operation. Please refer to the Index to locate the photos of dogs mentioned in the text.

Throughout the text, you will come upon various editor's notes. It should be patently obvious to readers that much of the advice given is dated and included only for its historical significance. Still, to avoid confusion to any of those who are unfamiliar with dogs, warnings with regard to certain practices have been incorporated in this manner.

I hope that readers will enjoy this compilation of early writings, photos and artwork on the Boston Terrier. It may be the first time that you have seen some of the photos of early dogs who have since faded from pedigrees. I hope it will bring to life some of the early breeders, their dogs and their accomplishments. Most of all, I hope it will give you an appreciation for their efforts in breeding "America's Dog." Enjoy!

Cathy J. Flamholtz
September 1997

In the early 1900s, a Boston firm released a series of postcards featuring Boston Terriers. No doubt they were proud of their city's native dog. These three cards are from that series. Unfortunately, the dogs are not identified. From the Flamholtz collection

Chapter 1

History of the Breed

by Dr. J. Varnum Mott

A correct biography of this most popular and important breed cannot fail to prove of absorbing interest, and we are particularly fortunate in being able to rely on the history as given by one who certainly had ample opportunity, by his long and varied experience as a breeder, to become familiar and thoroughly conversant with all of the most important facts of Boston Terrier history. The mingling of the blood of the aristocratic English Bulldog and the pugnacious Bull Terrier occurred over forty years ago, and the result was responsible for the present Boston Terrier.

To present a correct history of this breed, application was made to Mr. Dwight Baldwin, to be permitted to use in its entirety his description of the early history of the breed. Search was made among the earlier breeders for photographs of the dogs of days gone by, and as a result of their interest and kindness photographs of dogs, who, although noted in their day, have never thus appeared before the public are in this volume.

The question is often asked: How did the breed originate? Briefly stated, it may be said to have resulted from a cross between the English Bulldog and the English Terrier, and then to have been considerably inbred.

About sixty-five years ago Mr. Robert C. Hooper of Boston came into possession of a dog named Judge. This dog, which he purchased from Mr. William O'Brien, was undoubtedly imported. Judge, commonly known as Hooper's Judge, was destined to be the ancestor of almost all the true modern Boston Terriers. He was a cross between an English Bulldog and an English Terrier, leaning in type rather more toward the Bulldog. He was a strongly built, high-stationed dog of about thirty-two pounds weight. In color he was a dark brindle, with a white stripe in the face. His head was square and blocky, and he resembled the present Boston Terrier in that he was nearly even mouthed. Judge was bred to Burnett's Gyp (or Kate). Gyp was a white bitch, owned by Mr. Edward Burnett of Southboro, Mass. She was of about twenty pounds weight, had a fine three-quarter tail and was quite low stationed. She was of stocky build, showing considerable strength in her make-up. Her head was good, being short and blocky.

From Judge and Gyp descended Wells' Eph. This dog was of strong build and, like his dam, was low stationed. His weight was about twenty-eight pounds. He was of dark brindle color, with even white markings, and, like Judge, was nearly even mouthed. Eph was mated with Tobin's Kate. This bitch was of small size, weighing only twenty pounds. She had a fairly short head, was of a golden brindle color, and had a straight three-quarter tail.

From Wells' Eph and Tobin's Kate came Barnard's Tom, the first dog in this line to rejoice in a screw tail. Tom was a dark brindle dog, with a white blaze on the side of his face, white collar,

*The famous **Barnard's Tom** is considered to be a cornerstone of the breed. He was the first dog to clearly show the characteristics of the modern Boston. He is the first dog reported to have had a screw tail, much to the horror of his owner. In fact, Mr. Barnard took Tom to a vet to see if it was possible to put his tail in splints to straighten it. Tom was a dark brindle with a white blaze on one side of his face, a white collar, white chest and white feet. Accounts of his weight vary—one listing it at 22 lbs, while another says it was 18. Tom was said to be the best Boston of his day. He was widely used at stud and proved to be prepotent.*

Atkinson's Toby *was born in 1877 or 1878. At 10 months of age, in 1878, he was exhibited at a Boston show, where he was entered as a Bull Terrier. Dark brindle and white in color, with a full length tail, Toby was more evenly marked than his brother Barnard's Tom. A popular stud, many of the best dogs trace back to Toby.*

white chest and white feet. His weight was about twenty-two pounds. This dog was a great improvement over his sire and grandsire, being the first to show that fine quality that is present in a good specimen of the modern Boston Terrier. Tom was undoubtedly the best Boston Terrier of his day, and was naturally much used in the stud. He proved very prepotent, much more so than his litter brother, Atkinson's Toby. The latter was also dark brindle and white, but differed from Tom in being evenly marked. His tail was not as good, being of full length. From Tom came Barnard's Mike, out of Kelly's Nell.

The latter was a dark brindle bitch, with uneven white markings, one side of her face being brindle, while the other was white. Her weight was about twenty pounds. The head was good, being short and blocky, while the tail was three-quarters in length and tapered well.

Mike was of rather light brindle and white, and weighed about twenty-five pounds. He was even mouthed, and had a large, full eye. His tail was exceedingly short. He, like Tom, had proved very prepotent. That this is true we have only to look at their descendants and observe the type of head, large eyes and short or screw tail that are continually reappearing; so that it can fairly be said that much more is due to Tom and Mike than to any other dogs for the establishment of the present type of the Boston Terrier.

Among other dogs that were useful may be mentioned Townsend's Sprig, a son of Tom, out of Higginson's Belle. Sprig was a very small dog, weighing about twelve pounds. From Sprig are descended most of A. L. Goode's strain of dogs, remarkable for their color and markings. Another dog was Ben Butler. He also was a son of Tom, out of Barnard's Nellie.

Other prominent stud dogs were Hall's Max, O'Brien's Ross, Hook's Punch, Trimount King, McCullen's Boxer and Ben, Goode's Ned, and Bixby's Tony; all of whom, through Barnard's Tom, or his brother Atkinson's Toby, trace their ancestry back to Hooper's Judge.

Among the earlier bitches who proved worthy may be mentioned Reynolds' Famous, dam of Gilbert's Fun; Kelly's Nell, dam of O'Brien's Ross and Trimount King; Saunder's Kate, dam of Ben Butler, Nolan's Mollie, dam of Doctor, Evadne and Nancy.

Besides the above dogs, and quite remote from them, were several imported small dogs. These served to introduce fresh blood into the line represented by Judge and Tom, which had been considerably inbred up to this time.

One of these was the Jack Reed dog. He was an evenly marked reddish brindle and white dog, and weighed from twelve to fourteen pounds. He had a straight three-quarter tail, but was unfortunate in having a rather rough coat. Another outside dog was the Perry dog. He was imported from Scotland and weighed but six pounds. He was of a peculiar blue color, having some white on him. He also had a three-quarter straight tail. Kelly's Brick was another outsider. He also came from the other side. This fierce little dog was of white color, with several black spots. His weight was from sixteen to eighteen pounds. He had a good, large skull and an unusually large, full eye. The tail was straight. A fourth outsider was O'Brien's Ben. He was a short, cobby, low-set dog, of a white and tan brindle color. His weight was about twenty pounds. His tail was straight and of three-quarters length, carried low. He had an exceedingly short head and was even mouthed. His breeding was unknown. These few outside dogs were all small, and undoubtedly helped to fix the small size of the present dog, while the continued interbreeding of the sons and daughters of Tom tended to make the type permanent. The above gives very briefly the main facts concerning the older dogs of this breed, practically bringing the line down to the present generation.

A careful perusal of the foregoing shows very conclusively that the present Boston Terrier, as he is now known (his name some thirty-five years ago having been changed from the Boston Bull), is a result of inbreeding of the most careless or happy-go-lucky sort, and as a consequence, even after a lapse of forty-five years, he continues to present himself as representing several distinct types—so that we often have an example of the English Bull, the true type of Boston Terrier and a pronounced Terrier in the same litter, despite the utmost care in breeding.

From another authority, Mr. James A. Boutelle, who is one of the oldest of the present day fanci-

Hall's Max *was a prominent stud dog who did much to influence breed type.*

Well known stud dog **Ben Butler**, *a son of Barnard's Tom, weighed about 22 lbs.*

Dr. James Boutelle was one of the earliest fanciers. Along with Mr. Bicknall, he owned Round Head Kennels, in Providence, Rhode Island. Catalogs from the 1890s show that he was a frequent exhibitor.

ers, we have the following information regarding the earlier days of the breed:

> There are many people who claim to "be in on the ground floor" in the production of these Terriers, but to Mr. John P. Barnard, Jr., of Boston, Mass., the credit is mostly, if not entirely, due. Over fifty years ago one of the famous hack stables belonging to the John P. Barnard Syndicate was situated on Myrtle Street. This was the headquarters for nearly every one "doggy inclined" in the city. John P., Jr., had in his employ the late Tom Thornton, acknowledged one of the leading authorities on Pit Dogs of his day. Over the office, on the second floor, Mr. Barnard had a nicely arranged kennel, and the walls were covered with prints and photos of all the leading canines of both countries. Truly it was a treat for the eyes to look them over. In his kennel pens were thoroughbred Bulldogs and Bull Terriers of every type and color. There were always competent men in charge. Still Mr. Barnard was frequently on hand at feeding time and usually superintended their grooming. He took a personal pride in the advancement of his one hobby, the "Bullet Headed" dog. That these round-headed dogs were the outcome from the original crossing of the Bull on the short muzzled fighting Terriers, there can be no dispute.
>
> Another gentleman who was quite enthusiastic on this breed was Mr. R. M. Higginson, and was presented by him with a pup in 1877, bred from Barnard's Tom and Higginson's Belle. He never grew tired of telling the wonderful qualities these crosses produced. She became known as Seabury's Buzz, and was the first of the breed that went into the State of Rhode Island. Her breeding may be of interest to the reader as it not only gives names of dogs and owners, but weights also, and notes made by Mr. Higginson in his own language (see pedigree below).

From the above comments my statement that the original crossing was with the Pit Bull Terrier sounds quite feasible. This point we wish to be clearly understood by the reader, the predominating influence of the fighting strains in the Boston Terrier. Any practical breeder of extensive experience must admit that frequently this pugnacious

```
              ┌ 18 lbs.        ┌ 22 lbs.           ┌ 25 lbs.        ┌ Langdon's Crib
              │ Barnard's Tom  │ Well's Elph       │ Hooper's Judge │
              │                │                   │                └ Drasy's Bitch
              │                │ 16 lbs.           │
              │                └ Barnard's Nell    └ Somris Fanny
   Buzz ──────┤
              │ 14 lbs.        ┌ 30 lbs.           ┌ 12 lbs.
              │ Higginson's    │ Hammerwell's Joe  │ The Reed Dog
              └ Belle          │                   │
                               │ 15 lbs.           │ 18 lbs.
                               └ Fall's Kate       └ McManus' Bitch
```

Remarks—In "Tom's" family all these dogs (male) I knew but "Crib," but I know the man who had him at his death. They are all superior dogs for beauty, and "Crib" was a great fighter, as was his dad, Nevin's "Steele." Langdon bred Hooper's "Judge," and he says "Crib" was the handsomest dog he ever saw. On Belle's side her father, Hammerwell's "Joe," was the noblest Bulldog I ever saw, and a great fighter. His breeding I never could find out. Fall's "Kate," Belle's mother, is the prettiest bitch living, unless it is Belle herself, and a very game dog and splendid ratter.—R.M.H. (Editor's Note: The pedigree is reproduced just as it was presented in Mott's book. While Higginson's remarks are extremely interesting, the pedigree should be taken with a grain of salt. It is incomplete and, in some instances, inaccurate. We know, for instance, that the mother of Well's Eph was Barnard's Gyp, also known as Barnard's Kate and Tom's mother was Kelly's Nell, not Barnard's Nell. The weights given also vary from those listed by other sources.)

Early Dogs

by Fred R. Bearse

The breeding of Boston Terriers is a very interesting subject..., particularly since it brings to mind the wonderful advancement which has taken place in this breed since I became interested in them as a boy.

When a youngster I was always interested in dogs, and had in mind a short-haired dog for the house. Then I first saw the Boston. His short coat and smart trappy appearance interested me greatly, and I believed that he was the dog of the future. That was over thirty years ago. At that time the Boston Terrier was more of the coarse Bull type. With successful breedings he became refined to where about ten years ago many of the breeders were claiming that the Terrier type was the proper thing for the breed. As they progressed along came the weedy, pinch-nosed, long-legged Boston, which seemed to find favor with many breeders. Judges too seemed inclined to pick this type, but not within the last five years, as new breedings developed wonderfully as to type. I believe it has been done by breeding very strong headed Bull type bitches, many of which would not win in the show ring, but when bred to a male of proper conformation produce winners. I remember a number of interesting conversations with the late John P. Barnard, the owner of Mike and Tom, the fathers of the breed. Barnard favored the strong bull type.

Then F.G. Bixby, another old owner, had a little dog called Tony Boy. Alex Good owned Buster, and bred his son Monty.

These dogs were the typical sturdy type with handsome color and markings. In the early days it was quite a practice to breed for color and markings, and also to get them down in weight. Once someone told me about a white dog owned over in South Boston, so I traveled over to see Punch, owned by Dr. C. F. Sullivan, long before he became a Veterinarian. Punch, I believe, was the sire of more nice specimens than any of the earlier ones, but to my mind the best of the old timers seem to be the bitches.

Take McMullen's Dolly, by Punch out of McMullen's Corrine. She was the best Boston I ever saw. Mr. C. D. Borden bought her as a puppy.

There was also another sweet one, Peggy S., bred by H. M. Stone, of Natick. Peggy was by Punch, from a stocky bitch out of Buster. She only weighed twelve pounds, and was too small to show at that time, as the low weight limit was then fifteen pounds. Many of the dogs to today are ancestors of these earlier ones, whose progeny have been sold and scattered to all parts of the country.

Dog News
March 1927

Fred R. Bearse bought his first Boston when he was a boy and remained a lifelong fancier. He was also a well known judge. His Massasoit Kennels were located in Springfield, MA.

Mr. Bearse's Ch. Fascination.

A Tribute to Mr. Barnard and the Breed

by Edward Axtell

J.P. Barnard, "Father of the Breed"

I was sitting by an open fire the other evening, and there passed through my mind a review of the breed since I saw it a great many years ago, when the world, to me, was young. A handsome little lad leading down Beacon Street, Boston, two dogs, of a different type than I had ever seen before, that seemed to have stamped upon them an individual personality and style. They were not bulldogs, neither were they bull terriers; breeds with which I had been familiar all my life; but appeared to be a happy combination of both. I need hardly say that one was Barnard's Tom, and the other his litter brother, Atkinson's Toby. Tom was the one destined to make Boston Terrier history, as he was the sire of Barnard's Mike.

Mr. J.P. Barnard has rightly been called the "Father of the Boston Terrier," and he still lives, hale and hearty. May his last days be his best, and full of good cheer!

I am now readily approaching the allotted time for man, but I venture the assertion that were I to visit any city or even small town of the United States or Canada, I could see some handsome little lad or lassie leading one of Barnard Mike's sons or daughters. Small wonder he is called the American dog.

The celebrated Dr. Johnson once remarked that few children live to fulfill the promise of their youth. Our little aristocrat of the dog world has more than done so. May his shadow never grow less!

characteristic crops out in a litter, and the utmost care has to be exercised to subdue it in infancy. I have seen litters of pups fall together like thoroughbred pit stock and, if not separated, would kill. Then again, I have seen, in litters of pure bred pit stock, as fine a specimen of a Boston Terrier as one might see on many a bench. The brother of the celebrated "Tanner," a many time winner in the pit, was a nice-headed, screw-tail dog, but rather over size. Another, the father of Burke's Dixie, was a small fourteen pound, screw-tail, handsome specimen, with none of the blood of any bench dog ever shown. Again, there is a record of an evenly marked, screw-tail pit dog, fourteen pounds, that was pitted, and took his death in a Buffalo pit a few years since. Many others could be mentioned.

Their appearance also indicated this. Some were "gubby jawed," and out at the elbows and shoulders. One little twelve-pounder, the ideal of the Higginson string, was Teddy, and with his kink tail, bow front and undershot muzzle was a picture for a comic artist.

As the breed increased and others became interested, the desire to have their production admitted for competition at the various bench shows grew exceedingly strong among the breeders. In 1888 the New England Kennel Club first granted them recognition by offering prizes for three classes. They were to be identified as the Round

Head Bull and Terrier, the division of weights to be over and under twenty-five pounds; both sexes to compete together for the top weight, and separately under the limit. The acknowledged founder of the breed was selected to place the first ribbon that ever denoted quality in this combination of blood lines.

Well's Eph *goes back to the very start of the breed. Of Bulldog type, Eph was low-stationed and strongly built. A dark brindle dog, with even white markings, he weighed about 28 lbs. He was the sire of Barnard's Tom and Atkinson's Toby.*

The popular early stud dog Hook's Punch.

Even at so early a date Providence was heard from in the entry of the Round Head Kennels, of that city, Boutelle and Bicknall, proprietors—their representative winning third prize. The following year the New England Kennel Club, still willing to assist its patrons, again offered classes for the Round Head Bull. This time two classes were made and the weights were over and under twenty-five pounds. Mr. James Newman was acceptable to all to place the ribbons, and again the Providence dogs had a look in at the money. These gentlemen continued to breed and show these dogs for years, until Mr. Bicknall's increased business prevented his devoting the time he personally desired to give to them, and although he always had a few about his home, he refrained from showing. Along in the '90's several of the most enthusiastic breeders around Boston conceived the idea of forming an organization, drafting a standard and seeking admission to the American Kennel Club. The question of a name was now settled for all time, that of the Boston Terrier.

The first application for admittance to the American Kennel Club was made by Mr. Power, at the May meeting, 1891. The Club was then known as the American Bull Terrier Club. At the suggestion of Mr. A. P. Vredenburgh, the Secretary of the American Kennel Club, the name Boston Terrier was adopted, the Club at once seeing the adaptability of the name, as the majority of breeders and owners were at that time in and around Boston. The Boston Terrier was finally admitted to registration in the American Kennel Club Stud Book on February 27, 1893, with the proviso that only those dogs should be accepted that had an approved pedigree of three generations.

How hard and ably this little body of men were represented only those interested can tell. The

Dr. Dwight Baldwin *was one of the earliest fanciers. We are indebted to him for recording the early history of the breed for posterity. Show catalogs of the 1890s show him as an active fancier.*

Edward Burnett, of Southboro, MA, has earned a place in history as the breeder of Well's Eph.

The President and the Boston

by Cathy J. Flamholtz

Warren Gamaliel Harding (1865-1923), our 29th President, was a confirmed dog lover. He often told friends that people were more "inhuman" and cruel than dogs.

In 1884, the young Republican purchased and served as editor of the *Marion Star*, located in Marion, Ohio. A little Boston Terrier was a frequent visitor to the newspaper's offices and, as is so typical of the breed, he charmed everyone there. When this much loved dog was poisoned, Harding penned an eloquent editorial tribute to "Hub."

In 1900, Harding began a stint in the Senate and later ran for and was elected President. He continued his ownership of the *Star* for some years. I do not have the date of this moving tribute to his Boston friend, but it appears to have been penned prior to 1900.

"He was Edgewood Hub in the register, a mark of his breeding, but to us just Hub, a little Boston terrier whose sentient eyes mirrored the fidelity and devotion of his loyal heart. The veterinary said he was poisoned; perhaps he was; his mute suffering suggested it.

"One is reluctant to believe that a human being who claims man's estate could be so hateful a coward, as ruthless to torture and kill a trusting victim, made defenseless through his confidence in human masters, but there are such....

"Perhaps you wouldn't devote these lines to a dog, but Hub was a S*tar* office visitor nearly every day of the six years in which he deepened attachments. He was a grateful and devoted dog with a dozen lovable attributes, and it somehow voices the yearnings of a broken companionship to pay his memory deserved tribute...

"Hub was loving and loyal with a jealousy that attests its equality. He was reserved, patient, faithful. He was sympathetic, more than humanly so, for no lure could be devised to call him from the sickbed of mistress or master....

"He couldn't speak our language although he somehow understood, and was eloquent with uttering eye and wagging tail, and other expressions of knowing dogs....Whether the Creator planned it so, men may learn richly through the love and fidelity of a brave and devoted dog."

doors of the A.K.C. were well hammered before admission was gained. They were finally rewarded by the recognition they well earned, and today at every eastern show it is safe to say they make the record entry among Terriers. Although that change in name was made a number of years ago, and the standard has been slightly changed a few times, still there is that unconscious leaning toward the Bull by nearly all of the older breeders.

The new club certainly had its trials in arranging its scale of points, and no doubt fancied it had absolutely covered all the ground, but time soon found differences that had to be settled, and whether or not it acted wise-ly is still an open question. At first the skull was requir-ed to be large, broad and flat, which counted fifteen points; muzzle short, wide and deep, without wrinkles, ten points; nose, black and wide, five points; eyes, dark and soft, wide apart, large and round, five points; ears, five points, and must be thin, but small and set near corners of the skull as possible. Rose ear preferred. Here we have for the head alone forty points. The mouth to be even, but not to scale a point; neck, thick, clean and strong, with five points, while legs to be straight, well muscled, and feet small, round and strong counted ten points. The tail, fifteen points, thus defined: short, fine, carried low. Coat, short, fine, bright, hard, brindle, and brindle and white in color preferred, ten points. Symmetry and body, ten points each, but specifies the body to be cobby built: loins and buttocks strong, short backed, well ribbed, but deep in chest, while a high order of symmetry is required. The standard of weights were twenty to thirty-five pounds for the heavy, and all under twenty pounds were admitted in the lightweights. Great importance was attached to causes for disqualification, principally that of docking tails, although there was decided objection to "goggled eyed" dogs, or any with a mouse black or liver colored coat. Hair lips were barred.

That the screw tail on the Boston Terrier adds to its value does not admit of question therefore every means has been resorted to for its production, while there have been scores of failures, still some even pass the most critical inspection. The writer saw a dock-tailed bitch pass judges and also the veterinarian, who was called especially to examine it. Another passed a judge with cut tail and defect in eyesight. Both cases coming under eastern judges and in eastern cities. New Yorkers have the New England fanciers "skinned a mile" in preparing a dog for the sale market. Many other cases might be mentioned.

The questions have often been asked whether the Boston Terrier has degenerated since its early admittance to the Stud Book? If the early champions had been equaled by the later productions? If the type had been preserved? If there had been a steady inclining toward the Terrier cast of muzzle, and more delicate bone substance? These and many more questions of pronounced importance are to be settled in the minds of breeders before the much mooted subject of a new standard and scale of points can be decided on. Comparison of many of the older champions with the present winners at bench shows should be a subject interesting and instructive to the novice. One must allow that it is only his personal interpretation of the faulty standard that permits him to draw any conclusion as to the merits of specimens brought before him for judgment. I have noticed two champions on the platform, both possessing wonderful quality, and of decidedly opposite type: One the broad muzzle and flat skull, large eyes, grand front, nice feet, color, most desirable marking and three-quarter tail; yet, to my idea, a trifle low in station. The other specimen, with equal quality in many points, with the orthodox screw tail, but in front of the eyes directly opposite to the first champion. I won't question the right of the award; suffice it to say, that both could not be right according to the standard.

There is no doubt that when the breed began to attract public attention, and the little handful of fanciers banded themselves together to further the interests of their choice, that they intended to breed on certain lines and aim for a specific object for admiration. They also had for their guidance some specimen from which to draft their ideal of perfection. Allowing this to be true, what dog was at that time nearest to the mark?

Dr. C.F. "Connie" Sullivan

by Cathy J. Flamholtz

Dr. C.F. "Connie" Sullivan

Dr. C.F. "Connie" Sullivan was born in Boston in 1869 and died in 1929. He became involved with Bostons in the 1870s or 1880s. It was his love for dogs that led him to become a veterinarian. Dr. Sullivan served as president of the parent club for two years and was known for his quiet manner and generosity to those eager to learn about the breed. His opinions were highly valued by both novices and veterans alike and his views were often requested. He was instrumental in guiding the breed to prominence.

Dr. Sullivan's prestigious Trimount Kennels was known nationwide. One of his stud cards read: "I have owned and made more champions during the past thirty years than any other two breeders combined. My stud dogs were the foundation of the breed. The proof—look over the pedigree of your dog for Trimount. Reference—ask or write any breeder or fancier throughout the country."

Sullivan's "Punch," a white dog with brindle head markings, was the foundation dog of Trimount Kennels. He stood at stud for 14 years and was the most noted sire of his day. An enthusiastic and successful show dog, Punch always created a stir when he was shown. The floors of early show rings were covered with sawdust. Punch would strut into the ring, stretch and then scratch with his hind legs, scattering a cloud of sawdust that covered ringside spectators.

Ch. Whisper, *a Punch daughter, became the breed's first champion. She was later sold to Walter E. Stone.*

The 14 lb. **Ch. Trimount Tad,** *sire of many eastern winners before being sold to Mrs. S.A. Beck, San Francisco, CA.*

Trimount King *was a prominent stud dog who produced many white Bostons.*

Ch. Dallen's Spider, *a son of Heilborn's Raffles, was both a prominent ring winner and an outstanding prepotent stud. Indeed, a high percentage of winners can be traced back to either Spider or his brother Trimount Star. Originally owned by Dr. Sullivan, Spider was later sold to Ben Pope.*

The posed dog is **Ch. Trimount Roman.** *The dogs in the basket are* **Peter's Little Boy** *and, on the right,* **Roman.** *A son of Ch. Dallen's Spider, the seal and brindle Roman was considered perfectly marked with an exceptional head. Roman and his litter brother Ch. Peter's King kept early show rings lively with their head-to-head competition. Though both did well, Roman was the more successful show dog. It was King, however, who would distinguish himself as the more outstanding stud. In later years, he was sold to Mrs. George E. Dresser, of Thompson, Conn.*

Many other Trimount dogs made names for themselves in the show ring. In 1893, Dr. Sullivan's dogs won every trophy given for the breed. In addition to the dogs pictured here, Sullivan bred or owned Ch. Rocks, Ch. Revilo Peach, Ch. Trimount Lida, Ch. Trimount Fairy, Ch. Trimount Countess, Ch. Trimount Harper, Trimount Duke and Trimount Star (a litter brother to Ch. Dallen's Spider). *See Chapter 3 for more information on Punch.*

Ch. Lady Dainty, *a Punch daughter, was an extremely popular show dog. Hailed as one of the best bitches of her day, she was sold to Myron W. Robinson.*

Ch. Sportsman, *a successful show dog, was originally owned by Dr. Sullivan and then sold to E.H. Kaufman.*

By the early 1900s, Boston Terriers had become so popular that they were routinely featured on postcards and advertising items. From the Flamholtz collection

Chapter 2

The Boston Terrier & The AKC

by James Watson

Although the raw material was imported from England, the Boston Terrier was "made in America," and that within the memory of men who are a far way from being in their dotage. A little over thirty years ago, Mr. Robert C. Hooper of Boston purchased a dog from William O'Brien, of that city, which became known in pedigrees as Hooper's Judge. It is supposed that this dog was imported, but nothing is known as to his breeding, though he was undoubtedly of the half-bred bull and terrier type used for fighting. He has been described as a dog well up on his legs, dark brindle, with a blazed face and weighing a little over thirty pounds. From this dog and a bitch of equally unknown pedigree, but showing more bulldog in her formation, owned by Mr. Edward Burnett of Southboro, Mass., and described as weighing about twenty-eight pounds, dark brindle, evenly marked with white on face. In type he favored his dam, being low on the legs. Well's Eph was bred to a bitch named Tobin's Kate, of unknown breeding, smaller than any of those already mentioned, her weight being given as twenty pounds. Like the others she was a brindle, the shade being a rich yellow or golden. One of the results of this mating was Barnard's Tom, who stands as the first pillar of the stud book in connection with Boston Terriers.

These dogs were not called Boston Terriers, but were first of all lumped in with the bull terriers. We have before us a copy of the first catalogue of a Boston show, that of the Massachusetts Kennel Club of 1878, and in it Class 31 was for bull terriers. There were eighteen entries, and among them appear Barnard's Nellie, white and brindle, three years, imported stock, price $75. Mr. Barnard also entered his Kate, and another entry is that of Atkinson's Tobey (sic), a brother of Barnard's Tom. Tobey (sic) was then ten months old and he was not the brilliant success at stud which his brother Tom was. Of course Mr. Prescott Lawrence had to dabble in this breed as well as every other variety of terriers in their pioneer days, and he and James Lawrence each had an entry of unknown parentage. James G. Lathrop, the Harvard professor of athletics, had three entries, one of which was by the Reed dog, as a dog owned by a man named Reed became known. Mr. Lathrop also had a white bitch of Mr. James Lawrence's breeding, being by his Crab out of his Kate.

At the third show of the Massachusetts Kennel Club it was pretty certain that white bull terriers of the English type would win, hence the entry of the short-faced ones was light. Four entries of the local sort were made, including Sandy, by Barnard's Tom out of Higginson's Belle, a bit of breeding that after a few years was a desirable foundation to trace back to. The next show at Boston was that of the present New England Kennel Club, with Mr. J. A. Nickerson as a hard-working, enthusiastic secretary. He was the first to follow the example set by the National Breeders'

In the early years, Frederick Gordon Davis was an enthusiastic and tireless worker for the breed. He served as the first president of the Boston Terrier Club of America. During the 1880s and '90s, dogs owned and bred by him were frequently seen in shows and routinely sold for high prices. His dogs were often priced at $500-1,000.

show at Philadelphia in November, 1884, of which we were manager, of a catalogue with the printed awards. After that all shows of any prominence had to do likewise. Mr. Nickerson had little use for crossbred dogs and as the show bull terrier was then well represented the local brindle dogs were crowded out almost entirely. Finally, as the numbers increased and the wished-for opportunity to exhibit became more frequently expressed the Boston show committee opened classes for "Round-headed bull and terriers, any color," and the response was so good that the classes became fixtures. In keeping with the name there was a kennel at Providence called the Round Head Kennels, and the proprietors, Messrs. Boutelle and Bicknell, were very successful. Starting with a third prize record in 1888, they managed by good judgment to buy and breed Mike II., Sir Vera and two bitches named Topsy, and win with them four firsts at Boston in 1890, and two seconds with Jack and Gladstone.

Very shortly after this the Bostonians got together and formed a club, the idea being to get recognition of the dog they were developing. Early in 1891 an application was received from the "American Bull Terrier Club" of Boston for membership in the American Kennel Club and recognition of the breed they represented. At that time we filled the position of active working member of the Stud Book Committee and had a good deal of correspondence with the club at Boston. We suggested that as their dog was not a bull terrier at all and

Ch. Autocrat *was much admired for his type.*

was only bred at Boston that it would be better for the club to take the name of Boston Terrier Club. The result was that although the application had been made in the name of the American Bull Terrier Club, Mr. Power, who had come on from Boston to state personally what he could in favor of the application when it came before the American Kennel Club, said, in conformity with our suggestions, that on behalf of his club he desired to avoid all conflict with the Bull Terrier Club or any other club and his fellow members were desirous of changing the name to Boston Terrier Club, and in that name he made application for admission. The club, however, did not admit the Boston applicants until 1893. There is nothing of any great moment in this information, but as we have seen it stated that another person made the suggestion of the name Boston, the facts might as well go on record.

Ch. Captain Monte *was considered the best show dog of his era and was widely admired for his type. The authors of the original standard were said to have based their descriptions, in large part, upon him. He was widely used at stud and the sire of champions.*

Ch. Oakmont Gent, *owned by Oakmont Kennels.*

Ch. Stubbie, *owned by Mrs. W.G. Harding*

Mr. Dwight Baldwin in his early history of the breed published in the Boston Terrier Club book mentions some other importations which assisted in forming the breed. Among them was the Reed dog already mentioned, a dog of about twelve pounds, reddish brindle and white, rather rough in coat. Another was the Perry dog, which was blue and white and came from Scotland. This was possibly one of the Blue Paul terriers bred down the Clyde, which were great fighting dogs. This one, however, was said to have been but six pounds weight, so that rather knocks the Blue Paul theory. Another dog from England was Brick, known as Kellem's Brick, a black spotted dog of eighteen pounds and a most determined fighter. Another of the same sort was O'Brien's Ben, a short-backed white dog with brindle markings. These later importations were smaller than the Hooper's Judge style of dog and tended to lower the size, so that in the 1890 Boston classification there was a division of weight of under and over twenty pounds for dogs and eighteen pounds for bitches.

As can be readily understood, there was no great regularity in the type of these early dogs. Some favored the bulldog, while others were more of the terrier order. It was this lack of uniformity which led us to oppose the admission of the club in 1893, and thereby recognize the breed. The official report of our position is thus recorded in the *American Kennel Gazette* when reporting the fact that the three members of the Stud Book Committee each held a different view: "For my own part I cannot bring myself to favor admitting the dog. I would like to admit the club, but it appears we have to take the dog too. The question for this club is, is it a proper breed to admit to the stud books, and I cannot say I am in favor of admitting it."

Ch. Lord Direct, *owned by Myron W. Robinson.*

That that position was not altogether wrong we quote from the *Gazette* of December, 1894, the case being the canceling of a registration of a Boston Terrier which had a bulldog as a sire. The breeder of this combination was Mr. W.C. Hook, who was also the person who passed upon and approved pedigrees of the breed for acceptance in the stud book. He was asked to explain, and in his answer said: "It is a well-known fact that on account of inbreeding certain very important points of the Boston Terrier have become almost obsolete, namely, the broad, flat skull, rose ears and short tapering tail, all bulldog characteristics, and to my mind the only way to again bring them into prominence is to infuse the original bulldog blood into our stock, which is now too strongly terrier...At the next Boston show we shall offer a premium for the best *rose ears* on a Boston Terrier, to encourage the breeding of the same. Very few indeed have any approach to a rose ear, and as it is a bulldog characteristic I do not see any other way to get it than to breed to the bulldog." As chairman of the Stud Book Committee we thus commented upon Mr. Hook's letter, first referring to the fact that the committee had not previously endorsed the admission application: "The gentlemen representing the Boston Terrier Club assisted their arguments most materially by producing the photographs of two or three generations of breeding, and other photographs to prove the thorough establishment of type in the breed, and were most positive in asserting that the Boston Terrier could not be produced as a first cross. Within a year we have Mr. Hook, so much of an authority on the breed as to be chosen by the club to act as pedigree supervisor, informing us that 'certain very important points of the Boston Terrier have become almost obsolete by inbreeding.' In contradiction to that peculiarity breeders will be more apt to claim or admit that only by inbreeding can points be established, and that if this has already become necessary in the case of the Boston Terrier it is not an 'established breed' in the sense used by the American Kennel Club." The result was that the Stud Book Committee was put in charge of the matter and they arranged with the Boston Terrier Club that only one cross should be permitted to a bulldog or terrier and that only in the third generation. We can very well recall that at the meeting at which the solution of the difficulty was accepted, February,

Hollander's Peter *was a very successful stud.*

Weiner's Bessie *did much for the breed.*

Zizel's Hold 'Em, *owned by Zizel Kennels, Reg., weighed 16 lbs.*

1895, we unconditionally surrendered and stated that in no breed then being shown at Madison Square Garden was there more uniformity of type or such as advance in that direction within two years, and that the Boston Terrier deserved all the encouragement the American Kennel Club could give it.

We have introduced the foregoing for present-day exhibitors, who imagine that the cropped-eared, screw-tailed terrier we now show is the original type of Boston Terrier. Remember that it is little more than ten years since all that we have now recounted took place. Mr. Hook was one of the oldest exhibitors of the round-headed bull and terrier and personally knew the characteristics of all the old dogs. Following up this line we give a copy of an updated letter of Mr. John P. Barnard's which we have had in our possession for many years. It was, we think, written about the time of the Hook episode, and is addressed to Mr. William Wade of Pittsburgh, who sent it to us at the time:

Dear Mr. Wade:

There have been no bulldogs or bull terriers used in breeding the Boston Terrier for the last twenty-five years. The original dog, Hooper's Judge, was a small dog, about thirty pounds weight, and was very similar to my dog Mike. Well's Eph was a son of Judge, and was bred to a bitch of a kind very common here twenty years ago. They were brought out of England by men employed on English steamers. Their weights ran from ten to twenty pounds, and they were round-headed with short, pointed noses. Dr. Watts of Boston has several old paintings of this breed of dogs that was surely forty years old.

Rex Americus, *owned by Dr. C.A. Howell.*

My old dog Tom was bred from Eph out of one of these bitches and he was the first dog to be put to stud. I bred him to a number of his daughters, and by so doing established a breed that would breed to a type.

Hooper's Judge was the only dog that could possibly have had any bulldog blood in him and none since will be found in the Boston Terrier.

I exhibited Tom in a show given by John Stetson before the Massachusetts Kennel Club shows were held, and before a bulldog or bull terrier had ever been in Boston.

The Boston Terrier in my mind should be very close in appearance to a small bulldog, with the exception of the lay-back of the bull. I differ in this with the Boston Terrier Club, and claim that in trying to make the breed fine they will lose skull and bone and the characteristics of the breed.

Very respectfully yours,

John B. Barnard

Mr. Barnard was not quite correct in saying that at the time he wrote there had been no introduction of bulldog blood. That there was no genuine bull terrier blood introduced we readily admit, for that would have ruined the muzzle entirely, but quite a few of the dogs registered up to 1898 showed bulldog lines. These we have got rid of so far as anything in the record of registering with the Kennel Club is concerned.

We have, however, two of the best informed of the old breeders and exhibitors, men who assisted most materially in the formation of the breed, both asserting that it is a dog of bulldog type as opposed to that of the terrier, yet the dog has been changed altogether from what they said

Early Breed Names

by Vinton P. Breese

Speaking of the history of the breed, particularly its origin and earliest records, the reader is referred to Dr. J. Varnum Mott's book, *The Boston Terrier*...It is an absorbing brochure to any one of a historical turn of mind and a fact or two gleaned from it together with some reminiscences of the present writer may be of interest. It gives the first show at which the breed received recognition as the New England Kennel Club event at Boston, April, 1888, where open classes for dogs and bitches over and under twenty-five pounds were offered for "Round headed Bull and Terrier Dogs." Under this name the breed continued to be shown for a number of years when in 1891 a coterie of its sponsors in Boston organized what they called the "American Bull Terrier Club," and made application for membership to the American Kennel Club. Upon the suggestion of the late James Watson, who was at that time connected with the Stud Book Committee of the governing body, and to avoid conflict with the Bull Terrier Club, it was thought advisable to change the name to the "Boston Terrier Club." However it was not until 1893 that admission was granted and the breed recognized owing to the wide diversity in type of the dogs and their mixed breeding, but from that year on the breed was officially known as the Boston Terrier. However, such names as Round Head, Boston Bull Terrier and Boston Bull remained in common usage among the rank and file of the fancy for several subsequent years.

About that time Hugh Coyne, a blacksmith of Arlington, N.J., had succeeded fairly well in establishing a strain of dogs which he called Jersey Terriers. They were in reality a low set, round headed, short muzzled Boston Terricr of about twenty-five pounds weight and chiefly of a brindle body coloration with white heads. I recall that he informed me it had taken him many years to produce these dogs from an intermingling of Bulldog and Bull Terrier blood and that he was so jealous of his success and the name he had coined he would never exhibit them under any other and he never did. He found ready sale at good prices for all he could produce and I was one of his many customers. A number of these dogs were mated with Boston Terriers and near Boston Terriers of a probable Bulldog and Bull Terrier extraction in the vicinity of Newark and New York and doubtless their blood has come down to some of our present-day Boston Terriers. There were probably other cases similar to this and I merely mention it as evidence that not all of the earlier progenitors of the breed were confined to Boston or the New England section, as many people are led to believe.

...insofar as the actual origin and establishment of the breed is concerned it may undeniably be termed purely American. Furthermore, as it was chiefly due to the perseverance of fanciers around Boston in breeding these dogs, organizing a club to foster them and finally gaining recognition for them from the American Kennel Club it is indeed fitting that the breed bear the name of that city.

Ch. Ellsworth Fi Fi, *a daughter of Ch. Revilo Peach, was owned by Mrs. J.N. Champion.*

Teddy IV, *owned by Mrs. Hiram.*

it should be. Mr. Hook was using the reversion to the bulldog to get back the rose ear, and was advocating it in September, 1894. In May of the following year the American Kennel Club Committee on Constitution and Rules proposed the abolition of cropping dogs, yet no club more bitterly opposed that than the Boston Terrier Club, because of interference with the practices of its members, and that club and its members assisted materially in defeating the measure. We are not giving this information with the idea of taking sides as to whether the Boston Terrier should be of bulldog type of more terrier-like. That is for those interested in the breed to decide. Our object is to state facts of history, and in this case to show that as late as twelve years ago old members were regretting the change that was being made in the breed. How good a dog would have turned out if the effort for improvement had been along the lines of the bulldog front and body, with rose ears and level mouth no one can say, but all will admit that if the dog was not to belie its name it should not be a bulldog in general character, but a terrier, and that it is to-day in the main, with a lingering touch of the bulldog here and there.

There yet remain some missing terrier attributes to which attention should be directed. More regard should be paid to perfecting the legs and feet. The fore legs should not only be straight in bone but look straight. There is a tendency to too much spring in fetlocks and with that the usual attendant flatness and openness of feet. These are decided objections in a terrier. It is almost heretical, perhaps, to say anything against the twisted and deformed apology for a tail which is considered such an absolute essential in this dog, but we cannot stand that in any terrier, when it comes to a personal opinion. Mr. Hook in 1894 bred back to the bulldog to get some disappearing properties, one being the "short tapering tail"...As a deformity we will always regard it, though judges have to bow to the ruling power of the Boston Terrier Club. The members will permit us to recall the fact that it is not more than ten or twelve years ago such double dewclaws were as much an es-

Dick Turpin

sential in St. Bernards, but a few then took up the cry that they were deformities and not the essential which had been held by their advocates. It was actually claimed that these loose, dangling claws on the hind legs assisted the dog in walking on snow. Common sense prevailed and we hear no more of them, so that perhaps when a new generation of Boston Terrier breeders realize that screw tails are a deformity they will also be bred out, and the short, straight tail substituted. Even if the gnarled tail was not a deformity it is not a terrier tail by any means. Lead in a long-tailed terrier with the tail that is being bred in the Boston Terrier and how long would the judge keep it in the ring?

Mrs. Frank M. Van Orden's **Peggy IV.**

We thus have ears changed from the rose ear of the bulldog to the cropped ear of the terrier and the short, straight tail of the early specimens to the gnarled tail of the extreme flat button type of the bulldog. In the matter of color there have also been some changes, and punctuation has played a conspicuous part in published standards. We have books in which it reads, "Any color, brindle, or brindle and white, etc." The late Dr. Varnum Mott's brochure on the breed renders it thus: "Any color; brindle, evenly marked with white strongly preferred." The official standard reading is, "Any color brindle, evenly marked with white, strongly preferred." Finally Mr. Dwight Baldwin wrote to the American *Stockkeeper* that he was the member of the standard committee who drew up the color clause and that the committee agreed that a Boston Terrier might be any color and that the standard should read: "Any color; brindle, evenly marked with white, strongly preferred." By and by some mighty man of Boston will arise in his strength and we will have this sentence correctly punctuated.

On the subject of size the tendency of late has been to a decrease until we have got far too close to the regulation toy size of other terriers. At first the club bitterly opposed this innovation, and it cannot be beyond the memory of the youngest member of the club that the case of a club having provided classes under fifteen pounds was carried before the American Kennel Club, with a view towards having such classes prohibited. That was done so recently that it is difficult to account for the club having already changed the standard weight so as to admit the very dogs the American Kennel Club was so urgently requested to prohibit from all shows. Of course the American Kennel Club took no such action, basing the decision on the ground that it did not recognize standards, that being a matter with the show-giving club to do in its published schedule and conditions.

Recently we wrote somewhat in support of this reduction of weight on account of the adaptability of the small size for pets, for which we were taken to task by some breeders of influence on the ground that the Boston Terrier is a man's dog and not a ladies' pet. Most readily do we admit that it originally was so, but the trend in this breed has been altogether a mercenary one. Entirely fictitious values were created for these terriers some years ago, and it will be remembered what a mixture of type was the result of the rush of the Boston fancy to New York shows to reap the golden harvest. Very naturally buyers picked out attractive and pretty dogs and the smaller Bostons have always been the ones that sold best,

O'Brien's Rossie, a well known brood bitch.

so that those who were in the fancy only for what they could make out of it bred selling dogs. Some came too small to show at the fifteen-pound limit and these breeders were the ones who got the low-weight classes complained of as above stated. Other shows put them on as well and finally the wish to legitimize these good-looking dogs and render them eligible for Boston Terrier Club prizes became so strong that the low limit was put at twelve pounds.

That these changes were made with any idea of benefiting the breed no one will attempt to maintain, the object being purely mercenary. That we will admit to the advocates of the Boston being a man's dog. On the other hand, however, the advocates of this claim make no use of the dog in any way except as a house pet. To come down to the hard-pan truth the dog was originally a pit terrier. That was his only vocation as a man's dog, and it would be impossible to find one man in the club who would now make use of him in that way. That day is past entirely, and the only thing to consider if the future of the dog. The present limit is not likely to be the final one unless some very decided action is taken, for the same causes which brought about the extra classes outside the former limit will be likely to develop again, and dogs as low as ten pounds will soon be plentiful enough to permit of guaranteeing classes and, unless restricted, shows will give them. Those opposed to any further reduction in standard weights should now take action looking to that end, while they can get sufficient support in their own club, otherwise a gradual change of opinion will put them in a position similar to what they were in when they were outvoted at the recent change.

Walter E. Stone poses with Ch. Whisper, *the first female champion.*

It is somewhat singular that just as we had concluded the foregoing paragraph the mail brought us a letter from one of the sound members of the Boston Terrier Club, a gentleman for whom we entertain the highest opinion, not only for his knowledge of the breed, his prominent connection with it as an exhibitor, but the excellence of his judgment. He writes as follows:

Upon the horizon of the Boston Terrier world the cloud no larger than a man's hand has appeared and surely it is increasing in size. More and more clearly we are beginning to feel the pressure of the popular demand for a smaller Boston Terrier. The judges in the ring, the show classifications, the very standard itself are each and all gradually yielding to the demand. Can it be possible that at no distant day the market value of a specimen may be inversely in pro-

This grainy photo, from 1906, shows the brood bitch Lady Dimple.

Another 1906 photo, this one of Sunlight.

Gordon Boy *was just one of several studs owned by Mr. Kimball.*

Remember, *born in 1925, was one of the studs at the Stroller Kennels, in New York City.*

portion to its size? Let us trust not, and yet we are beginning to hear of abnormally small specimens selling for fabulous prices.

This matter of size is in my opinion the pitfall which awaits the Boston Terrier unless there is a change in the direction of our p r o g r e s s. Surely we ought to keep the division wide enough between the dog as we have known him for ten years of more, and the tiny, shivering, bloodless creatures we occasionally come across in other toys. Great reduction in size means injudicious inbreeding, with the loss of intelligence, loss of stamina, loss of reproductive powers which follow that course; in fine, the loss of all that we most value in the breed.

This question of size seems to be the burning one at the present time, but it is a matter in the hands of the club members, and if the majority are breeders for the market and the purchasers want small dogs the reduction will not stop where it is at present. If the majority as it now exists insist upon no further reduction in the future it will be perfectly feasible for legislation to that effect to be enacted by the club whereby the weight scale can only be altered by such a large majority, say three-fourths of the members, and only after due notice of such proposed change. Then the heavyweight members should get up special prizes sufficient to induce breeding for a larger dog. Club specials can also be withheld from shows giving classes for dogs outside the limits of weight laid down by the club.

Chapter 3

Notable Early Stud Dogs

by H. Tatnall Brown

When after many applications the breed had been acknowledged as established by the American Kennel Club the opinion of many of the leaders differed, and these individual tastes and ideals naturally resulted in the production of dogs dissimilar in characteristics, but the differences were never carried to the length of anything approaching families or strains. That calls for years of breeding with certain objects as of paramount importance till they were established. But in all breeding, even where the foundation does not seem secure for any dog, there will always be found one or more gifted by a prepotency which lifts his progeny above the average, and in scanning the history of the Boston Terrier we find that four dogs stand out pre-eminently in this respect. These are Buster, Tony Boy, Sullivan's Punch and Cracksman. If compelled to make a selection of one we should feel inclined to say that the greatest of all was Buster, that grand old dog which will ever be associated with the name of Mr. Alexander L. Goode of Boston.

Buster, from a show standpoint, had many faults, being by no means a typical Boston Terrier, but the list of winners produced by him and his progeny is phenomenal. Champion Monte, winner of seventy first and special prizes and perhaps the greatest show dog of this breed that ever lived, was a son of Buster, and he in turn demonstrated his ability to pass on the blue blood of his sire by producing a long list of good ones, including Champion Butte and Champion Colonel Monte, the former a sire of wonderful prepotency and the latter one of, if not the greatest of present-day winners. Among the many other splendid dogs sired by Buster we may mention Champion Stephens' Rex, Spotswood Banker, Maxine's Boy, Broker, Sqantum's Criterion, Dazzler, Pat G. and Rattler II. The last named two are both sires of champions, Pat G. having produced Champion Patson, while Rattler II. was the father of Champion Boylston Reina, considered by many sound judges to be the best Boston Terrier bitch of today. Following in this line we might go further and show that a remarkable number of typical dogs have Buster's name in their family tree. Cracksman, the present-day sire of champions, is himself a grandson of Champion Monte, hence a descendant of old Buster.

Almost contemporary with Buster was Tony Boy, owned by Mr. Franklin G. Bixby of Boston. This dog stands at the head of what perhaps came nearer than any other to being a distinct strain. Tony Boy sired Tony Boy, Jr., Tony Girl, Benny Boy, and Dandy Boy, and after them in the next generation came Champion Miss Phyllis, Tony Boy IV., Benny Boy, Jr., Teddy Boy, Dandy B., The Duke, The Monk and Bobs. While not so prominent in the show ring as the offspring of Buster, yet this group of dogs laid the foundation for a stock excelling in color, rather small in size, and with the much desired tail properties;

The Buster Family

Founder of a famous strain, **Goode's Buster** *was described as a sound, but ordinary dog. The dark mahogany dog proved, however, to be extremely prepotent.*

The rich mahogany brindle **Ch. Monte** *was owned by Alexander Goode.*

Ch. Colonel Monte, *a Ch. Monte son and Buster grandson, was a top show dog. Throughout the 1890s, he was said to be "invincible." A prominent sire himself, he was owned by Mrs. Mortimer Brooks.*

These two photos are of **Ch. Boylston Reina,** *a Buster granddaughter, described as the most famous show bitch of her era.*

The Punch Family

Ch. Lord Derby, *a Punch son, was a very successful show dog and a widely used stud.*

In the early days, when white bodied dogs could still win in the show ring, the Punch daughter **Ch. Lady Dainty,** *often triumphed. She was owned by Myron W. Robinson.*

The Punch daughter, **Ch. Opal,** *was one of the foundation bitches of Mark Knipe's Revilo Kennels. She produced many prominent Bostons, including champions.*

For more information on Punch and his descendants, see Chapter 1.

The Cracksman Family

Ch. Oarsman *was one of the most memorable of the Cracksman offspring. These dogs were responsible for moving the breed away from the bully-type dogs.*

Ch. Sportsman *was one of the "top notch" sons of Cracksman. Originally owned by Dr. Connie Sullivan, of Trimount fame, he was later owned by E.H. Kaufman.*

The Cracksman daughter, **Ch. Remlik Bonnie,** *was owned by Willis S. Kilmer.*

Ch. Captain Kinsman *was one of the most popular scions of the Cracksman line.*

A lovely headstudy of the outstanding Cracksman daughter, **Ch. Remlik Bonnie.** *This bitch was so successful, in her day, that she was considered the "queen of her sex."*

qualities that had a marked and beneficial influence upon the breed.

No remarks concerning Boston Terrier sires would be complete without mention of that grand dog, Sullivan's Punch. In spite of the handicap of his color—white with brindle head markings—he has proved himself truly a marvel as a sire. From him we have had Champion Opal, Champion Lord Derby and that popular favorite, Champion Lady Dainty, besides a host of lesser lights, such as Sherlock Holmes, General Cronje, Spike, Dude S. and Remlik D'or. And now let us speak the magic name of Cracksman the last of this great quartet of sires.

What are the achievements that entitle him to place in the Boston Terrier Hall of Fame? Like Buster his laurels have not been gained in the ring, but by his remarkable ability to produce descendants of the sound, clean terrier type now so eagerly sought after. His early honors came to him through the phenomenal success of his deservedly renowned daughter Champion Remlik Bonnie, in her day and generation the queen of her sex. Since then he has produced Champion Sportsman,

Champion Oarsmen and Champion Eastover Lancelot, all top notchers. Another of his sons, Kinsman, has made a reputation for the Cracksman blood by siring Kinsman's Belle and Champion Miss Kinsman; the last named gaining her championship in record time by gaining first in her winners class at two successive New York shows.

A comparison of the immediate descendants of Buster with those of Cracksman show some marked differences in the characteristics of the two groups. The offspring of Buster were noted for their richness of color, their markings, their good tails and general style. They were all of good courage and possessed the ability of showing well under the judge's eye. The Cracksman dogs, on the other hand, are mostly lighter in color, running more into the golden brindles, but they excel in softness and size of eye and in general expression. They are clean headed and clean limbed dogs of great quality, but usually seem to lack the fire and vim that belong to the Buster stock and form so attractive a part of Boston Terrier character. The legacy left breeders is the crossing of these four great producing lines of blood to produce a resultant race of Boston Terriers possessing the best qualities of each and superior to all.

Bixby's Tony Boy *was a direct descendant of Hooper's Judge and a most influential stud dog. The author of this chapter says he belongs in the Boston Terrier "Hall of Fame."*

Edwin Megargee, born in 1883 in Philadelphia, is recognized as one of America's premier dog artists. He served as an AKC Director and, for many years, was a judge. He also managed the AKC's library. The drawing at the top comes from his book **Dogs** *and the bottom drawing is from a special supplement he did for a Philadelphia newspaper. From the Flamholtz collection*

Chapter 4

A Tribute to Robert L. Dickey

by Cathy J. Flamholtz

We usually attribute the rise in popularity of a breed to the many breeders and exhibitors who toil so diligently on its behalf or found a famous strain. Occasionally, it's a dog who appears in movies that is responsible for catapulting a breed to national prominence. In large part, the meteoric rise in the popularity of the Boston Terrier, in the early years, was due to the work of an artist.

Robert L. Dickey was a highly successful commercial artist. He drew the promotional ads for The American Tobacco Company's newly released brand of cigarettes, as well as doing other work for companies. His highly stylized drawings of Bostons appeared in the most successful magazines of the day. A contemporary of Norman Rockwell, Dickey's work, usually drawings of Bostons and other breeds, appeared regularly in *The Saturday Evening Post, Life* and other popular magazines of the day.

Art critics will, no doubt, fault Dickey's work. He was not known for strict accuracy, rather he infused his dogs with human-like qualities. This is particularly apparent in his drawings of Bostons. And, it's no wonder. Dickey's own dogs, Beans and Violet, provided an on-going source of inspiration. They ruled his house, living with him for most of the year in New York City, and traveling with the family to St. Petersburg, Florida for the winter season. The drawings reflect the charm, curiosity, mischievousness and intelligence of the Boston Terrier. They could only have been made by someone who knew the breed so intimately.

While the critics may have scoffed at Robert Dickey's drawings, the public loved them! Confirmed readers of the most popular magazines fell in love with the clownish dogs seen in the pages of their favorite publications. They wanted one of these dogs and they bought "America's Dog" in large numbers. Soon, Boston Terriers were one of the most popular breeds in the country. Robert L. Dickey helped to make the Boston Terrier a hit.

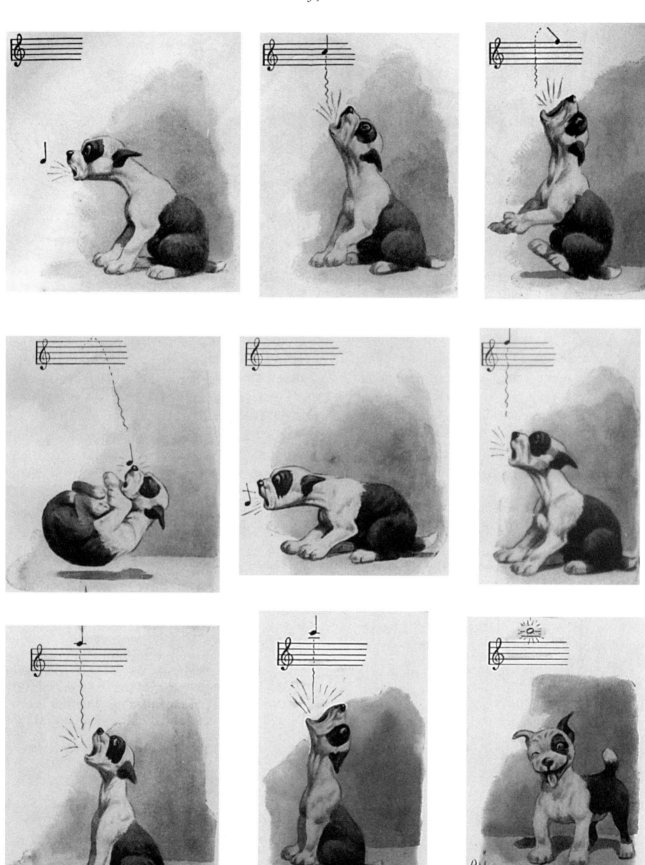

"The Satisfaction of Achieving The C in Alt" Robert L. Dickey, Life magazine, c. 1920s. *From the Flamholtz collection*

Noted artist and illustrator Robert L. Dickey. On the left, are two advertising cards featuring Bostons. These may have been cigarette cards, released in 1906, by The American Tobacco Company. Dickey's drawings from early in the century show Bostons with much more white and more of a bully appearance. He kept up with the times, though, his later dogs clearly showing the evolutionary changes that occurred in the breed. From the Flamholtz collection

"Presto! Kreutzer Sonata, Opus 47, Beethoven," Life magazine, c. 1920s. *From the Flamholtz collection*

Mr. Dickey's beloved Violet poses with a litter of her puppies. In a departure from his stylized drawings, Dickey drew realistic portrayals of Beans and Violet for the turn of the century newspaper Popular Dogs. *When the magazine printed a photo of Violet's pups, Dickey made the drawing on the right, picturing the dogs reading the magazine. The drawing on the left accompanied a short story by Miss Josephine Z. Rine, who later went on to author a number of dog books, including one on the breed.*

"The Boston Terrier: These class distinctions make me ill. Had she been born on Beacon Street I couldn't love her more." **Life magazine, c. 1920s.** *From the Flamholtz collection*

"Oh, Mother! Wasn't Santa Claus good to Peggy?" **Life magazine, c. 1920s.** *From the Flamholtz collection*

"Gee, this has been a rotten day, everybody gone and I haven't pulled anything rough yet."

"I have it. I'll try the kitchen."

"Here's where I get a start, cook's forgotten to put away the milk."

"Disgusting! I can't reach it."

"I'm afraid I'm a failure."

"No, not yet. One more chance. I'll scramble every bed in the house."

"Stung! They've closed every bedroom."

"Oh! The Big Idea!"

"I'll wait until they've all gone to bed, then I'll howl all night."

HIS TRUMP CARD

"FRIENDLY ENEMIES" **Life magazine, c. 1920s.** *From the Flamholtz collection*

"Gee, Fellas! That's a tough guy! He says there's no Santa Claus!"

"Tough, did you say? And no Santa Claus? Oh, boy!"

THE UNSPEAKABLE TRUTH

"Did you hear of the latest horrible effects of Prohibition?
"No, what are they?"
"Mrs. Boston Terrier's new pups were all born without corkscrew tails."

I never did like beans;

codfish in any form nauseates me and while I admit Literature and Art occasionally afford me a certain relaxation

I contend I get as much satisfaction out of any old newspaper as I do from the Transcript

and can enjoy life as fully in a Wichita barber-shop as I can on the Back Bay

THE REFLECTIONS OF A BOSTON TERRIER

"Oh brother! Ain't Nature wonderful?"

"This must be Spring!"

"Let us gambol abroad in the glorious sunshine"   *"And listen to the little birdies carolling"*

"But brother! This chill! This sudden change!"

"OOH! 'Tis but Nature being still more wonderful!"

SPRING, SPRING, BEAUTIFUL SPRING!

He was just an amateur
"Like everything else, chasing cats needs practice."

"Now keep close together, children, while Mother pays the fare."

Both from Life *magazine, c. 1920s. From the Flamholtz collection*

Gladys Emerson Cook was particularly adept at portraying the Boston Terrier. In her 1945 book, **American Champions,** *she drew depictions of actual champions. This is* **Ch. H.M.S. Kiddie Boots Son.**

Chapter 5

The Boston as a Show Dog
by Dr. J. Varnum Mott

The Boston Terrier holds a position in doggy America that is particularly unique. It is a breed, the only breed, that is distinctively American and consequently there is no importing from England. As it has been impossible to import winners, it has been necessary for someone to breed them and while there are some who still follow the buying game so popular in other breeds, the vast majority of the Boston fancy are breeding their show stock. The success that has attended the efforts of the Boston Terrier men and women along these lines shows very plainly that it is possible to breed good dogs in America and the fanciers devoted to other varieties will do well to take the hint.

Another peculiar thing about the Boston as a show dog is that although there are many big and very successful kennels continually showing fine strings of dogs, still the small breeders are also very active exhibitors. In most cases, when half a dozen big kennels enter a breed they temporarily hurt it, for small owners find that it is hopeless for them to show against such competition and becoming discouraged drop out. This lasts till the big kennel owners either discover that they have themselves killed the goose that was laying their golden egg or else break up their kennels. Then the small men re-enter the fancy only to be forced out in a few years by a new lot of "big 'uns," and so it goes on in an endless chain. With the Boston Terrier, however, this is all different for, although there are many big owners, still the "kitchen kennels" are also benching. The explanation of this is to be found in the youth of the breed and its consequent inability to breed true to type. This has made it impossible for the wealthy fanciers to gobble up all the good breeding stock. The present popularity of the breed seems to foretell that by the time they do breed with accuracy there will be so many good dogs in the country that a man would have to have the wealth of the Indies to even start a Boston "corner."

The hardest class to judge at any show, and the ones from which the vast bulk of kicking comes, are those where the Boston Terrier competes for bench honors. At a first glance the conditions that exist in these classes seems to be the outcome of the vast popularity of the breed, which always guarantees good large classes. While, of course, this is a factor in the dissatisfaction that runs riot among Boston Terrier exhibitors, there are other features that should not be overlooked. It is a very regrettable, but, nevertheless, true fact, that the Boston fancy is the most materialistic one in the entire game. Nine out of ten of the breeders of the "American dog" are in the fancy not for sport, but for the money that there is in it. Of course, there is nothing criminal in being a breeder of dogs for the money that is to be made out of the sport, nor does this stamp a man as dishonest; but it does tend to cause kicking over judges' decisions. This is but natural, for if your dog is thrown down he loses in value, and to those who are continually trying to sell their dogs at as high prices as possible, it is a considerable blow. The Boston Terrier people feel that each peg lower their dog is placed in the prize list is just so much money out of their pockets, and, naturally, they complain.

This very materialistic view of their dogs has other bad effects upon the Boston Terrier fancy and is conducive to many little "tricks" that are certainly, to put it in its mildest form, a little bit off color. There are many in the fancy who would scorn to deal in any but the most upright manner, but there are also many who do not scruple to resort to shady methods to make a sale. As is always the case, the just suffer with the evil, and unless there are some very radical changes the men who are supposed to have the best interests of this most desirable little dog at heart will kill the breed.

The diversity in opinion as to just the correct thing in Boston Terriers is another question that causes considerable complaint. There are several other features which, in a way seem to justify the complaints that are daily heard among the breeders of this dog, but it seems that there is a great deal of this sort of thing that could very well be gotten along without. The continued squabbling, scrapping, charges and countercharges that are indulged in hurt the dogs far more than the men, and if it continues will seriously and pre-eminently injure the Boston Terrier.

—Courtesy Newark Evening News

Julius Fangmann

Julius Fangmann, of New Rochelle, New Jersey, was an extremely enthusiastic fancier in the early days of the 1900s. Originally a French Bulldog fancier, he switched to Bostons in 1916. He was a hobby breeder, never having a large kennel. He adopted the prefix Monte Carlo. Fangmann bred the important dog Ch. Captain Haggerty, whom he sold to the Rosenblooms, of Haggerty Kennels.

Born in 1924, Ch. Fangmann's Sandra was bred and owned by Mr. Fangmann. This dark seal bitch began her show career by capturing Winner's Bitch at the National Specialty from the puppy class and was never defeated by another female.

Though shown, Monte Carlo Billy never completed his championship. He was a son of Ch. Ace of Aces.

In the early days, all dog shows were "benched." Dogs were required to be on display during the hours that the show was open to the public. Both clubs and individuals often went to elaborate measures to decorate the benches. In the heyday of the breed, Bostons were often the most numerous breed entered in a show. The Boston Terrier Club of Hollywood elaborately decorated, in red, white and blue, the several rows of benches featuring the breed.

The Mosholu Story

by Cathy J. Flamholtz

Madeline McGlone and some of her favorites.

Madeline C. McGlone grew up in a home surrounded with pets. Her father bred French Bulldogs, but it was the Boston Terrier that caught young Madeline's eye. She obtained her first Boston in 1905, but it was several years before she became heavily involved with the breed. In 1906, she finished her first champion and there was no looking back. In the next 10 years, she finished 15 champions. Mrs. McGlone established a large kennel which at one time housed 90 dogs. She owned more than 30 champions and campaigned her dogs far and wide. No breeder of her time had so many generations of homebred champions.

Madeline McGlone had her own vision of the ideal Boston Terrier and it differed dramatically from the majority of dogs seen in the show rings of the day. While the breed had moved away from the "bully" type, Bostons were still essentially very substantial, square dogs. Mrs. McGlone liked a more elegant dog with what she called a more "finished," or polished look. She did not, initially, meet with great success. Though her dogs were well marked and sound, they were just too radically different for many judges. But she persisted and finally broke down the conventional barriers. Soon her own dogs and those of her breeding were topping shows and the Mosholu pups were in great demand.

A tireless advocate for the Boston, Madeline authored the breed column in *Popular Dogs* for many years. She became a highly sought after judge. Most of all, though, she remained a staunch lover of the Boston Terrier.

Ch. Mosholu Beau

Ch. Mosholu Brigand

Ch. Mosholu Blink *is considered one of the pillars of the breed. This son of Hawkes Peter (a son of Ch. Peter's King) was originally registered as Elbanna Derby King. Mrs. McGlone bought him from his breeders Mr. & Mrs. C. Annable. A golden brindle, Blink did not have an easy time in the show ring because he was so different. Despite his obvious quality, it took him two years to complete his championship. Finally, he triumphed. In 1921, he topped the breed at Westminster. More importantly, he revolutionized the breed and started a wave of enthusiasm for this new "look."*

Blink's true value, however, was as a stud. He proved to be extremely prepotent, siring nine champions and many grand and great grandchildren who became champions. He was Best Stud Dog in Group, at Westminster (when such awards were still given) a record three times. His weight has been variously listed at 14 lbs. and 17 lbs.

With other dogs, Blink was aggressive and it was said that he loved a fight above all else. He would strut into the ring with fire in his eyes and it was hard for even those who didn't care for his type to take their eyes off him. With people, however, he was extremely gentle and known as a perfect gentleman.

Ch. Mosholu Blink

Ch. Mosholu Buddie Blink, *owned by Mrs. W.E. Potter, Kingway Kennels.*

The mahogany brindle 12 1/2 lb. Ch. Mosholu Tommy Blink *finished and was then sold to Graymar Knls.*

Ch. Mosholu Bad Boy

The Blink son Ch. Little Tommy Tucker *was bred by Mrs. C. Holmstrom and purchased by Mrs. McGlone. It was a wise buy. A successful show dog, he teamed with his father to win Best Brace in Show at Westminster. He was much in demand as a stud and sired several champions. One buyer was so impressed with a Tommy litter that he purchased all the pups at six weeks for $1,000. Tommy died at seven years old of a heart condition.*

Ch. Mosholu Bearcat *won BB at several specialties and was a Group winner and sire of champions.*

"Impressions," by British artist G. Ambler

Chapter 6

Educating a Boston Terrier

by Dr. J. Varnum Mott

The special characteristics of the Boston Terrier may be summed up by stating that for a loving, faithful and all-round companion he cannot be excelled. He is a small, short-haired dog, of a decidedly sporty appearance, intelligent to a very marked degree, kind and affectionate, yet fully capable, should occasion require, of taking not only very good care of himself, but also of his master or mistress.

Some years ago the idea was credited among misguided and misinformed persons that the Boston Terrier, although he was a handsome and an expensive dog, could not be taught like other dogs. In other words, that he was naturally stupid, and could only look pretty when on dress parade. At first the author did not give the matter any special consideration, for he did not own one, but within a year he saw a pup a little over six months old, and the degree of intelligence that was manifested in his beautiful eyes prompted him to purchase the little fellow and deciding to test the matter as to his ability of absorbing knowledge. He was a son of Ch. Monte, ex-Murphy's Lottie. He was named Muzzie Dee, and at once introduced into the home, breaking him to the house, which, as is usual with this breed, was very easily accomplished, for they are naturally cleanly in their inclinations. By easy stages he was taught various tricks and accomplishments, and it was amazing the facility with which he became proficient. Before he was nine months old he could perform some of the most difficult feats, and was always ready and anxious to display his knowledge.

Boston Terriers seem to possess remarkable reasoning powers, and use them on every possible occasion. In order to develop these attributes their education must begin when they are young, and they should be so placed that without any special effort their senses are unconsciously developed. Hence it is well never to attempt to raise pups in large kennels, for the reason that their life there would of necessity be the same from day to day, and the opportunity of brain development would be materially restricted. A far better plan is to find a small family, who for a consideration, will take them to board, and who will permit them ample opportunity of exercising around the house and playing with the children.

In this way they develop mentally and physically. Pups under such conditions virtually grow in grace, and when six or eight months old are housebroken, affectionate and in full possession of their mental faculties, ready to be further educated in the higher branches of canine learning, and shortly are fitted to take their rightful position as an important member of the family in one of the homes of the "Four Hundred."

When a purchaser seeks a dog probably the first query will be, "Is he housebroken?" Generally the reply is, "Perfectly." Now, this may be correct so far as the experience of his previous owner is concerned, but it is not the proper reply to give unless we know positively that the prospective owner thoroughly appreciates the correct handling and care necessary when introducing a dog into a new home. It is, therefore, much better to modify the reply and to give explicit directions, which, if carried out, will often save much trouble and annoyance for both parties. Let us suppose, as an example, that you have just purchased a pup five or six months old, and that he has no special recommendations as to cleanliness. You naturally desire, as quickly as possible, to break him to the house. The directions given below will apply to a greater or less degree to every breed of dog you may take into your home. It will depend upon his previous habits as to how long you will be obliged to exercise a strict supervision.

In the first place he should have had a good run before being brought into the house, where of necessity everything will prove strange and will tend to make him more or less nervous. The strangeness of a new home, new people, etc., will often make an old and ordinarily well-trained dog forget himself, so the rule holds good in all cases. After fondling and petting him to a limited extent take him to a corner of the room previously prepared with a rug or pillow, and tie him up with a fairly short leash or chain. Remain with him for some time until he has tired of gazing around and has of his own accord laid down, apparently to sleep. If, when you leave him, he should cry, or even be inclined to be noisy, appear suddenly and reprove him by speaking quickly and sternly, telling him to lie down or keep quiet. He will quickly obey, for the same words have been frequently used in his early training. In about two or three hours you should ask him, "Do you want to go out?" and when at the length of his chain he has manifested his willingness, take him on the chain to the door leading to the yard, and if enclosed, let him loose to remain out as long as may be necessary. When you take him in he can be allowed to follow you through the house without a chain, and for a gradually extended time be kept free to frolic about. He should be taught that his corner belongs to him, and that when you say, "Go to your corner," he must obey. Prompt obedience should be demanded on all occasions and if this rule is enforced much care and trouble will be avoided.

The housebreaking of a dog will be greatly facilitated and simplified if one,

Mr. Mott's beloved **Fuzzie Dee.** *(In Axtell's book, he spells the name Muzzie Dee.)*

Ch Halloo Prince

Rockydale Junior

Editor's Note

Mott's love for the breed and regard for the Boston's intelligence is clearly visible in this chapter. Many of his attitudes and much of his advice are surprisingly current. Modern breeders would, however, clearly object to confining the dog on a short chain or leash, in the house, as was the custom in Mott's day. They would, in all likelihood, advise the use of a crate or a puppy gate as aids in training. It's not likely that breeders today would place tobacco, which might prove poisonous, on spots where a dog had a housebreaking accident.

Mott cautions vigilance when exercising a dog on city streets, but does not place a great deal of emphasis on this point. We must remember that when Mott penned his original work, the automobile had not yet been invented. Dogs were more likely to be trampled by horses. The car had come along by the time later revisions were published, but was still a rarity. In the interest of safety, today's Bostons, even well trained ones, should be on leash when not in the house or a fenced enclosure.

and only one, member of the family assumes the whole charge of the dog, and when that person is not present the dog should be tied in his corner. This methodical care should be persevered in for several days, and the result will never fail to prove perfectly satisfactory.

Remember one thing, namely, always let your dog out the FIRST thing in the morning and the VERY LAST thing at night. Have his chain quite short at night, and he will be much less likely to offend. Once he learns the way out and the habits required of him he will very quickly adapt himself to them, and should he then offend in the house in any way it will be due either to his not being well or to negligence on the part of the one having him in charge. Regular exercise and opportunity to relieve himself will prevent a repetition. If caught in the act he should be punished not with a strap or a cuff, but severely scolded. Bear in mind that a Boston Terrier is a very affectionate animal, and hence exceedingly sensitive. Speak quickly, looking very stern, straight in his eyes, and he will feel it most keenly; strike him and you will either cow him or he will, if old enough, resent it by becoming surly. It is seldom necessary to admin-

Ch. Sonnie Punch

The famous mystery writer, Mary Roberts Rinehart, author of more than 60 books, stops to pose outside her Washington, D.C. home on the way to her office. Rinehart carries one of her favorites. She owned several Bostons.

Worthwhile Watchme, *owned by Mrs. A.R. Bollard, Worthwhile Kennels, Reg., Akron, OH.*

Ch. Little Bo Peep Forbes *and her daughter* **Ch. Lady Babbie Forbes** *represented several generations of the breeding of Mrs. E.A. Forbes, Hollywood, CA.*

ister other than a rebuke in order to convince him that he has offended and displeased you, and he will show his sorrow most decidedly. Having convinced him of his wrong doing, send him to his corner and make him remain there in disgrace for a short time; then call him to you, and, after again expressing your surprise, but more mildly, gradually make up to him, and you will be greatly pleased at his attempts to regain his former position in your affection. After he has been a member of your household for a couple of weeks he will of his own accord make known his desire to go out, should occasion require oftener than is his usual custom, by going to the door and by otherwise making the fact known.

Make a companion of your dog, study his peculiarities of temperament the same as you would a child you were about to instruct; talk "dog talk" to him and he will all the more quickly learn what you mean. For the information of novices I would state that "dog talk" resembles very closely the same vocabulary you would employ when speaking to a babe in the arms, coupled with endearing terms, and with a rising inflection of the voice, the combination forming a language of its own, peculiarly adapted and very intelligent to the canine race.

If for any reason you think your dog has offended in any place or places in the house it will be well to place a little tobacco or pepper at these spots, and you can be assured that he will avoid them in the future.

To sum up the requirements of housebreaking and tabulate them in rule form:

First—Let your dog have one master or mistress who will keep the dog under supervision during a reasonable period of probation.

Born in 1925, **Ch. Deanhurst Stanzalone** *was bred by Mrs. I. Duchene and owned by Mr. & Mrs. J.R. Dean, Deanhurst Kennels.*

Second—Fasten him up when it is not convenient to watch him.

Third—Always take him out immediately upon letting him loose, leading him through the house the first few days.

Fourth—Let him out at regular intervals during the day, and always the first thing in the morning and as late as possible at night.

Fifth—Tie him up at night with a short chain or leash.

Sixth—If you would have your dog cleanly in his habits love him. Treat him with due consideration, and do not expect or try to exact impossibilities.

When we consider what grand watchdogs Boston Terriers are when properly handled, it is more than surprising that they are not kept in every house where valuables are at hand and where the lives of the occupants are often at the mercy of midnight prowlers. When we desire a dog to be watchful it does not necessarily imply that he is to be savage and tear strangers promiscuously to pieces, but that he should simply be on the alert when we are sleeping the sleep of the just. Here is where the discrimination and discernment of this breed is clearly exemplified, for when properly trained your dog will not arouse the whole household should perchance, a member of your family remain out rather late at his club for the dog will recognize him even though the step be a little off at times and will simply welcome by quiet manifestations the pilgrim's safe return. If you leave your dog loose at night he will show his breeding and good sense, and working on the principle that "the best is none too good," will select a soft pillow on the sofa, coiling himself up and thus invite Morpheus to reign supreme. On the contrary, if you will fasten him by a fairly short leash in the hall at the head of the stairs, obliging him to sleep on an old piece of carpet, he will quickly consider himself on duty, and will promptly notify you of any unusual or strange sounds that may emanate from below. This post of vantage fairly controls the advance of any burglar, for a small dog's bark or baby's cry is most dreaded by Bill Syke's fraternity, and they will quickly seek another house. This is also the proper place for the dog when the family is down in the dining-room at dinner, and the doors of the rooms are left open you need have no fear of second-story artists.

It is natural for Boston Terriers to be watchful if given half a chance, consequently you must not overfeed your dog, for we well know that a glutton sleeps soundly. If you wish him to prove a faithful and thoroughly reliable guardian give him a hearty meal for breakfast and only a tidbit for supper. In other words he should indulge his sleeping ability at odd times during the day, so that at night, with an empty stomach, his brain will be clear and his senses acute.

Ch. The Bat of Buffalo, *owned by Mrs. Albert Tumser, of Buffalo, N.Y., was a controversial dog. His scant white markings were a rarity among show dogs of the time, but his conformation was so outstanding that he could not be held back. It is interesting to note that his victories were largely under breeder/judges.*

The best way to quickly develop these watching propensities is to test them from time to time. Begin the very first night by providing an entertainment for him, and never fail to respond by appearing in the hall should he bark as if he had reason to do so. One plan is to have a string run from the bedroom down through one of the openings of the banisters and attached to the other end a piece of wood, which should be concealed in a closet or behind a door. When all have retired and stillness reigns supreme give the cord a few pulls, just enough to make a slight noise in the hall below. If your dog jumps up and barks, go out and let him loose, and he will run down stairs to the seat of the disturbance. Go down with him

Squantum Kennels

Squantum Kennels, owned by Walter G. Kendall, Atlantic, MA, was one of the largest Boston kennels, though it was not always held in high repute. Pictured here is **Squantum Criterion,** *a son of Goode's Buster, a winner at several shows.*

Squantum His Nibs *was sold to J. Pierpont Morgan for $1,000.*

A painting of **Squantum Rags** *and a French Bulldog friend. Exhibited in shows around Boston, Rags had several wins.*

Squantum Squanto *won several classes.*

Squantum Shawmut *did a good deal of winning as a puppy.*

Squantum Punch

Ch. Mister Jack

Ch. Caddy Belle

encouraging him and showing him that he is doing right by saying, "Go for him, find him boy," etc. After a few minutes you can both return, reward him with praise and petting, and then, after fastening him up, retire to your room. This can be repeated very late the same night, should you chance to wake up, and the program continued each night for a week, various changes being made from time to time.

If you will promptly jump out of bed when he sounds an alarm and listen with him for a few minutes he will quickly catch on to the idea that if he wants you he has simply to bark. There is a marked distinction between a bark and a whine, and while the former demands an immediate response the latter should be as quickly suppressed by a good scolding and by calling out, "Lie down," or "Be quiet, sir."

We will now suppose that you have tested your dog quite thoroughly with the cord and wood, and that he is quick to respond. If you desire to continue this method vary it by having the cord on the outside of the house so that the wood will serve as a "tick tack" on one of the windows of the lower floor, and when this method has been exhausted ask the night watchman once or twice a week to shake the front or back door just to make sure that your dog is wide he can eat at any one meal, for his digestion would very soon he seriously impaired. Avoid sweets of every kind, for there is nothing you can give him that will tend more quickly to cause acute gastritis, foul breath and decayed teeth.

In purchasing a dog buy from a reliable party, and be sure that your dog comes from a healthy atmosphere. Remember that you cannot find absolute perfection in the points of any dog, particularly in Boston Terriers; therefore, be prepared to sacrifice some show excellencies for true merit, unless you are prepared to pay a very high price. A good specimen always commands a fair value for the demand far exceeds the supply, so you must

The popular artist Diana Thorne captures the curiosity of a young Boston.

be prepared to pay something for your pet. Always buy a good one, rather than to purchase a dog of doubtful breeding, whose chief recommendation is his low price. In the former instance you will have a dog that from the beginning will prove a handsome, valuable and sporty acquisition to your household, while in the latter case you are bound to daily become more and more dissatisfied with him, and, acting upon the advice of your friends, will eventually either relegate him to the stable or dispose of him at a loss.

Purchase one from nine to eighteen months old, and one that has had the distemper. He is then old enough to at once become a true companion, and the liability of serious illness would be reduced to a minimum. A finely bred Boston Terrier, with proper care, should live to the age of ten or twelve years. Some live much longer without becoming infirm, but the above statement as to their longevity is a fair average. Through carelessness or indifferent training many are killed by accident. This factor should always be borne in mind when exercising your dog in the city streets, and he should have special training if you live in a large town.

Boston Terriers are not aggressive to other dogs, hence the injuries sustained as a result of fighting are very few and far between. As a companion for ladies they are peculiarly adapted, being very easy to get under perfect control, able to enjoy no end of petting, and are always ready, should the occasion require, to prove their true allegiance to their mistress.

Chapter 7

Buying a Boston

by Dr. J. Varnum Mott

The query is often heard, "Why are Boston Terriers so sought after as household pets, and why are they so expensive?" In the first place as stated in the previous pages, being a very handsome and sporty looking short-haired dog, they are peculiarly adapted for our homes. Coupled with this, they are of a very affectionate disposition and possess an even temperament. As an all-round companion they appeal most forcibly to all lovers of dogs, for whilst they are not aggressive, still should circumstances so require they are fully capable and willing to take care of themselves and their masters.

As to the second query, it is readily answered by stating that the demand for well-bred and house-broken Boston Terriers far exceeds the supply. The reason for this is not only because they are so highly appreciated, but because they are very difficult to raise. It may seem a strange statement to make, but it is none the less true, that about 65 per cent die at birth or prior to reaching maturity, and generally the best in a litter are the ones that are lost. This, however, is not an exclusive peculiarity of the breed for all dog fanciers know that "the good die young" and it is always the best of the lot that passes away. Hence their very scarcity keeps up the prices. It is true that poor specimens are often sold for the proverbial "song," but the writer is dealing in this little volume with only the correct type of pedigreed stock, and has no use for "Yah Hoo's" and "Mutts."

It has already been stated that this breed is not readily raised, particularly when the attempt is made to rear puppies in a kennel, so it may truthfully be stated that the Boston Terrier is in no sense a kennel dog, hence only small kennels are needed; for until a pup is twelve months old he must be boarded with a family who is paid to raise him. This information may be used when buying by remembering that the best dispositioned dogs are in the smaller places.

As a general rule purchasers are advised not to buy other than full grown dogs, for the reason that, despite the best care, so many pups die before they are one year old. Whilst it is true that all dogs do not have to go through distemper in one of its many forms it is equally certain that Boston Terriers are peculiarly liable to contract it in its most fatal phase and quickly succumb to its ravages. Although a grown dog naturally costs more money, you will be amply repaid for the outlay if you know that it has had the distemper, is thoroughly house-broken under good command and ready to prove a boon companion. Only those who have been through a siege of distemper can know what it means, and if buyers realized this they would not get a dog who has not had the disease.

Each dog has his special characteristics and individuality, so when about to make a selection, always choose the dog that appeals to your eye and seems responsive to your advances, for he will give you the best satisfaction, all other details, such

Born in 1925, Ch. Joy O'Valentine, *was part of an outstanding litter sired by Woodward Captain and bred by P.J. Kane. Valentine's litter sister took Winner's Bitch at Westminster, in 1927. She was owned by Mrs. Nellie M. Lawrence, Columbus, OH.*

Bantam Ace of Aces *was a son of the famous Ch. Ace of Aces. Born in 1925, the 14 1/2 lb. dog was bred and owned by A. Messing, New York City.*

as price, age, etc., being equal. Reference is not being made to show dogs, but to highly bred dogs suitable for household pets. Naturally, the breeding of the dog should be considered, for "like begets like," and as intelligence is a most important factor we can only be certain to obtain it when the record of the ancestors justifies the expectation.

A perusal of the foregoing leads us very naturally to realize the importance of dealing with only the most reliable parties, who have dogs to sell, otherwise no dependence can be placed upon the pedigree, personal history or habits of the dog. Again, it is very essential, if you desire to avoid unpleasant consequences, to secure a dog that has been brought up under good sanitary conditions, and not one that has been neglected and only "conditioned" to sell at a bench show. As to the best markings, that is simply a matter of preference; the same will refer to the kind of tail; these two features often govern or regulate the price, and if you want a dog with perfectly even markings and just the correct kind of screw tail you must be prepared to pay a good round price. These two are very hard points to get in perfection and consequently dogs possessing them command good prices. Remember this one essential fact in selecting a dog namely, that it is almost an utter impossibility for a man to find a dog as near perfect as any of the great cracks, but should you do so he will command almost any price. Therefore, seek not perfection, for one is almost unattainable, for when you examine a number of dogs you will discover that some are strong in the head, others nice in the tail; some a good deal off in

Prince Lutana

Ch. Fosco

In her inimitable style, Diana Thorne captures the aspects of the Boston puppy.

markings, others decidedly bully in shoulders, etc., etc. Your search should result finally in acting upon the advice already given, namely, to take the dog that attracts you, and nine times out of ten you will have made no mistake, for very quickly the affinity that led you to making the choice will have developed and both dog and owner will be more than satisfied. If you are looking for a bench specimen it will be wiser to take a good judge, whom you trust, and let him pick for you, for no book can teach the fine points of a breed. Would-be purchasers, owing to living in a distant city, cannot always exercise this choice, and must depend upon this duty being performed by a friend

Ch. Auburn Happy Jr., *owned by C.H. Mower, Auburn Kennels, Burlington, VT.*

The early dog **Ch. Fascinator.** *Note the older type.*

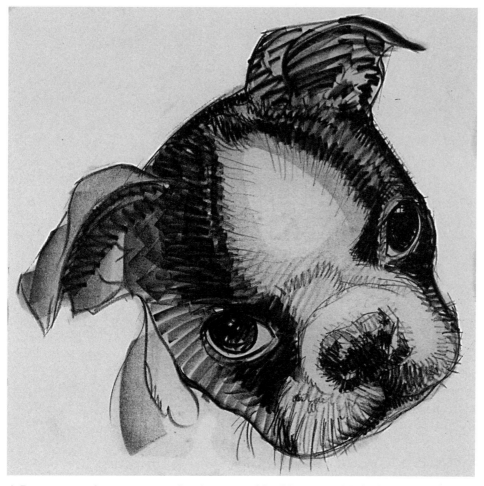

A Boston puppy's sweet expression is captured in this pen and ink sketch by Walter T. Foster. From the Flamholtz collection

or rely entirely on the honesty and judgment of the parties who offer the dog for sale. Here again rises the importance of dealing with a reputable kennel, one whose prestige, already secured through honest and reliable methods, would prove a certain guarantee of satisfactory treatment.

It is a safe statement to make that a Boston Terrier who has had distemper is worth double at eight months old what one is who has the disease in anticipation. Like scarlet fever among children distemper is very liable to prove disastrous to the dog, even though it is not actually fatal. Deafness is one of the sequels to be dreaded; chorea, similar in its manifestations to St. Vitus dance; partial or total blindness, various skin diseases and other after effects, any of which might very properly prompt you to put the dog out of his misery often follow this dreaded illness. When selecting a dog, unless you have perfect confidence in the seller try and verify his statement if he states that the dog really has had this disease. Unfortunately, however, distemper will sometimes afflict the dog twice, and although the second attack is not generally as severe, still in exceptional cases it is very acute and more likely to become associated with pneumonia, with which complication it is generally fatal. These second attacks naturally tend to discredit the statement of the seller, therefore it is best, when possible, to have his claim investigated and confirmed. The seller labors under another disadvantage, for if the dog is taken sick a month or so after being sold, and a veterinary, well-posted on horses and cattle, but never having had any experience with Boston Terriers, is called in, at once proceeds on general principles to proclaim the dreaded fact that the dog has distemper, when in reality he has only a slight cold or his digestion is for the time being somewhat impaired. You will need not only the best "vet" you can obtain, but one who is thoroughly honest and above the contemptible

Am. & Can. Ch. Playfair Let's Go *was one of the most successful show dogs of the late 1920s, defeating many champions. He won five Bests in Show, including one from the classes. He was owned by Playfair Kennels, Reg., Portland, OR.*

Ch. Prince Conde *was one of the breed's most important sires. The 16 lb. dog was bred by A.A. Appel, of Philadelphia, and later sold to Mrs. Edward J. Graves, Fascination Kennels, Detroit, MI. Prince sired eight champions.*

practices of some who adorn (?) that profession. It has been the custom of some of these latter to share or limit their responsibility by stating emphatically that the dog was undoubtedly a sick dog when purchased, although several weeks or even months have elapsed since the animal changed hands. Some will go further by declaring that the dog had always been an invalid thus discrediting the seller regardless of his reputation for honest dealing. Possibly they think that such an occult demonstration will add to their importance, when, as a matter of fact, an intelligent person will quickly realize that it is a subterfuge pure and simple, and although prompted by profound ignorance is none the less disquieting to the purchaser and unjust to the seller. Men of this stamp have done much harm to reputable kennels and have spread abroad the idea that all dog men are robbers.

It would be a boon to all parties concerned if the custom to have every dog regularly examined and certified to by a competent "vet" prior to a sale being consummated, the would-be purchaser to select the veterinary, were in vogue.

Fortunately, however, there are in most of our large cities a number of very competent and honest veterinaries, who have made a special study of the dog and are fully capable to render prompt and efficient aid in time of need. Should your dog be ill and really need the services of a "vet" try and secure one of these, so that the proper diagnosis can be made. The treatment in most cases is so simple that it is a secondary consideration. First and foremost you want to know what the trouble is, and nursing, proper nourishment, with a modicum of drugs, will do the rest.

Now, to sum up, purchase as good a Boston Terrier as you can possibly afford; use good judgment in selecting him; buy only from a responsible party, and once obtaining the dog take good care of him by exercising common sense in regulating his eating and habits.

Persons often write to know how much cheaper a bitch is than a male dog. The reply is that if they possess the same degree of excellence, as to show points there is practically no difference in the market value as applied to the Boston Terrier, but when they are champions, naturally the dog is of greater value. Again, we are asked which sex is best for a house pet. This is a very hard question to answer when the query is made about Boston Terriers, for they cannot help being of a most affectionate disposition, but there is no denying the fact that the females are the most trusting and clinging, possibly not so pronounced in their enthusiasm or open in their manifestations of affection, but have a way all their own of showing their deep love for their owner. It is true that when kept simply as pets they must be cared for twice a year. This is the only objection that can be urged against them, and that is readily provided for by sending them to pass those weeks at some well-appointed kennel, where they will not only receive the best of care, but be absolutely safe. We all know that a dog will often wander beyond certain prescribed limits in the company of other dogs, whilst his sister could not be coaxed out of the yard. Accordingly there is less likelihood of your losing a bitch. If you desire to breed, always select a bitch that is rather long in the body, whose breeding is of the best, and mate her along sensible lines.

Boston Terrier drawings by two famous dog artists. The headstudy on top is by British artist Arthur Wardle; on the bottom is a drawing by Edwin Megargee.

Chapter 8

The Care of the Boston
by Dr. J. Varnum Mott

As it has been the aim and purpose to make this little book practical and useful to all classes of Boston Terrier owners, we will give briefly a few directions, for the benefit of the novice, as to the care of a house dog. The foundation of health, in dogs, as well as humans, is the stomach, and we will therefore first consider the cardinal principles of feeding. It is safe to say that a vast majority of dogs kept as household pets are overfed, and as a natural result they take on a superabundance of flesh and become lazy and indolent. In order that the dog should always be "up and coming" he should be fed lightly. In other words, he should be kept in a condition to relish anything that is put before him. Dogs are proverbially like children in that they will eat until they absolutely cannot take in another mouthful, then lie down and in the blissful ignorance of sleep patiently awaiting the pain of colic and its attendant sorrows, which, however, do not deter them from repeating the same folly the very next time that opportunity affords. They lack discretion and method and you must therefore use discretion for them, acting much as you would if trying to raise a child. Regulate carefully the amount of food given by the amount of exercise that the dog has taken, varying each day to fit the needs of the moment.

It is a good idea to weigh your dog from time to time, and having ascertained what his weight ought to be to increase or decrease the quantity of food given, so as to keep him in the best possible condition. In hot weather, or after a day when rain and storm has forced him to loll around the house, do not feed him as much as you would under other circumstances. If, on the other hand, it is the dead of a cold winter, or you have had the dog out for a long walk and he has other hard work or exercise, increase his portion slightly. His ribs are a very good indication of the condition that he is in and they should be just visible, not noticeable. In order to secure this condition, or even good health, your dog's stomach must be in perfect order and the best way to keep his stomach in order is to watch carefully what goes into it.

Table scraps, while they are not the best food in the world, still they will keep a dog in good health if they are carefully attended to. Nine out of ten of the dogs that are kept in the city are used as a sort of vulture to clean up what is left on the plates after each meal. In all the big kennels of the country the dogs receive but one meal a day and if that is enough to keep these dogs, who get a great deal of systematic exercise, in the pink of condition it is certainly sufficient to keep a house pet in the same state. With some owners it is the custom to feed a big meal at night, while others do this in the morning, which seems to be the better time. The morning meal may consist of scraps, cut up fine and well mixed. This should be done for a double purpose of preventing bolting and affording a chance to have the food when it reaches

A drawing of **Prince Walnut** *by famous artist Muss Arnolt.*

the stomach of being already mixed. It will also be found a good cure for those dogs who are in the habit of picking and choosing their food. Meat, fish (carefully boned), cereals, vegetables (except potatoes), and bread all make good things to feed. Soups and gruels alternated with dog biscuits should make up the evening meal or lunch. There are half a dozen different kinds of dog crackers on the market and any of the reliable brands are good.

The one thing that above all others causes sorrow, sickness and pain to city dogs is the feeding of sweets. The publishers of this book should have printed in bold type the warning, "Don't feed candy." There are more dogs that die and suffer from candy eating. Candy destroys the desire for real, good, nourishing food, it ruins the stomach and digestion, and it rots the teeth. Here again a dog's similarity to a child may be seen, for they all dearly love candy, and once given a taste of it will never cease to beg for it.

I would not for a moment have my readers think, as they may after reading the foregoing pages, that the Boston Terrier is a difficult dog to feed properly, as they are not, for what has been advanced will apply equally well to any breed of dogs. All that it has been my intention to do is to make a plea that the dogs be fed along common sense lines. Another thing that should be brought up while we are on the subject of feeding is that of giving a bone to the dog. Nearly every author who has dipped his pen in ink to write on doggy matters has advised that a bone be given to the dogs to play with and gnaw on, but many of them have failed to warn that not all kinds of bones are

High Hat, *owned by A.E. Littig, Mt. Joy Kennels, Davenport, IA.*

First registered as "Step Lively III," this dog was later known as **Ch. Captain Moody.** *Dubbed "The Little Wonder Dog," the 13 lb. dog was purchased for $2,300 by John S. Trotzke, of Chicago, IL. He sired four champions.*

good for this purpose. Chicken bones should never be given to a dog, for they are easily cracked with the teeth and a splinter swallowed may do a world of harm. A bone splinter in the stomach or the intestines has often caused a good dog's death and the chances of such an accident are too great to make it advisable to give chicken bones. A big shin bone, with the joint attached to it makes a very good thing to give a dog to chew on and play with. There is absolutely no virtue in an old soup bone that has all the good boiled out of it, besides these are soft and can be broken by a strong dog.

By nature the Boston Terrier is a playful dog, if he were not he would not enjoy that popularity that is his, and it is well that he be given something to play with while in the house. For this purpose there is nothing in the world so good as an old shoe. Let him have this and see that it is always kept in a certain place and you will have little difficulty in training him to use that and that alone for his frolics. If he should happen to take a fancy to a rug or some other article around the house, take him away from it and give him the shoe. A few repetitions of this will teach him the purpose of his plaything and generally you will have no further trouble with him. If, however, he persists in his wrongdoing, tie him up on a short chain when he is caught in mischief and it will not take him many weeks to come to associate the confinement with the destructiveness. In extreme cases a little tobacco or tobacco sauce placed on the articles he plays with will prove an effective cure. Do not place too much of the punishment on the things for you do not want to make him sick, only to afford a surprise that will prove lasting.

Next to food the most important thing in the well keeping of a dog is exercise. A dog's exercise may be divided into two classes, the first a simple airing to give a chance for the animal to relieve himself. For this purpose a closed-in yard is all that is needed. It is not sufficient, however, to let your dog out in the yard to play all by himself, for as soon as the necessities of nature have been complied with, he will come to the door and crouching down wait to be admitted. In the warm months this may cause

> **Editor's Note**
>
> The information contained in this chapter is inluded for its historical content only. Check with your veterinarian before following any of the advice.

Ch. Bayside Chauncey

Ch. Yankee Doodle Pride

Mrs. William Kuback poses with her **Ch. Lady Sensation.**

Sunny Hill Kennels

Born in 1924, Ch. So Big of Sunny Hill was a tremendous winner. The 15 lb. dog earned his title with seven Bests of Breed. He was campaigned extensively, capturing 200 Bests of Breed in 1926 alone. Esteemed breeder/judge Alva Rosenberg said of him: "A dog whose conformation, color and markings adhere as closely to the standard as any dog alive."

Mrs. E. A. Rine with her beloved **Ch. So Big of Sunny Hill.** *Mrs. Rine was one of the earliest breeders in New Jersey.*

Ch. Flash of Sunny Hill

no harm, but in winter, with ice, rain and snow, the climatic conditions, he quickly becomes chilled, catches a cold and becomes a fit subject for pneumonia or other ills. Another reason why the owner should watch the dog while he is out in the yard is that by observing his passages a very good idea of his condition may be formed. In no other way can you so quickly detect that something is not quite right than by this observation should he be constipated or unduly relaxed, a slight change in diet may remedy the trouble and avert a serious illness.

In addition to this airing your dog should have at least an hour's walk in the open each day. This is an important part of his life, not only as an aid to digestion and exercise, but also as a pleasure to you for you will come to enjoy the walks with your canine friend and the benefit that it will do your health will also be considerable. If you are to enjoy to the fullest extent this feature of your dog you should get a dog weighing somewhere between fifteen and twenty-two pounds. If you get a dog that is smaller than that you will naturally have to lift him in and out of cars and carriages and, unless you want to risk the chance of having him maimed or killed, you will have to keep him on a lead. If, on the other hand, he is a big dog he will be too large to go on the cars or in your brougham, and on many other occasions you will find that he takes up too much room. Therefore, so as not to have him burdensome, select a medium sized specimen, a good all-around dog, capable of taking care of himself in any company or under any conditions.

The first thing that you must teach your dog if you would take him walking in the crowded thoroughfares of a city is prompt and strict obedience to your whistle. Select some distinctive call of one,

Oarsman's Anthony

Ch. Roxie

two or three notes, but always use it so that he will readily distinguish your call from the others, but only use it when you really want him, as he soon learns the moral of the story of the boy who called "Wolf!" and he will think you are only fooling him. It is necessary that he should be taught to obey your call before you venture on the streets. The best way to teach him is to whistle the desired notes, encouraging him to come to you, and when he obeys pet and make much of him. Half an hour will generally be all that is needed to teach this lesson, and when once you are sure that he knows what is expected of him punish him if he does not come. The next step is to have him trained to walk right beside you. This is an important part of his training and will be found to be invaluable many times. It is the best preventive for fights, and will be found a great convenience in a crowd or crossing streets. Call the dog to you and saying the words, "To heel," or something similar, make him walk beside you. Always give the command the same way, using the same words and the same tone of voice and gradually increase the distance that you have him walk near you till he is perfectly trained in this respect. You can let him run ahead with the words, "All right," or "Go on," but care should be taken not to allow him to leave you till you give your permission. It is a good plan to always call your dog to heel on crossing a street and a week or so of this will often find him coming to you of his own accord. If he should do any-

Highball Kennels

Am. & Can. Ch. Highball's Let's Go, *a 16 lb. dark seal brindle owned by W.N. McCoy, Middletown, OH.*

The 17 lb. **Highball's Sensation** *was owned by J.J. Barrett, New York City.*

Excel Glenwood King *was a son of Can. Ch. Highball Kid. The 16 lb. mahogany brindle was owned by Mrs. Ira McBride, Maymac Kennels.*

Ch. Willowbrook Glory

Ch. Silk Hat King, *a son of Sigourney King, was owned by Dr. D.J. Van Velsor, Pittsburgh, PA.*

thing directly contrary to your commands, scold him severely and put him on the leash. This is one of the best ways of punishing a dog and if you notice the down-hearted and contrite way in which he walks along while under this disgrace you will yourself be convinced that it is an effective reprimand. It is a good plan to always carry a lead with you, for if that is the way in which he has been punished you will find that a mere sight of it will often cause him to mend his ways. When your dog has been trained perfectly in this wise he will indeed be a companion, a comfort and a protection, and you will soon grow to enjoy your walks with him. There is nothing more humiliating than having a poorly trained dog on the streets and those unfortunate ones who have not taken the trouble to train their dogs are to be pitied. How foolish a person looks vainly calling after a dog that is running riot all over the streets and how much danger there is in such a course for the dog.

The secret of success in exercising a dog, as in pretty much everything in the world, is common sense and moderation. Be humane in the amount of exercise, making it enough to keep him in health, but not so much as to take the flesh off his bones.

Gladys Emerson Cook illustration

Chapter 9

Breeding Boston Terriers

by Miss Emily Pomeroy

It is safe to assume at the very outset that there is no occupation that presents a more interesting, complex and, at the same time, uncertain proposition than the breeding of Boston Terriers. Those of us who have tried the experiment can cheerfully testify that the Boston Terrier is a law unto himself and seems adverse to complying with the rules and regulations that govern the breeding of dogs in general. Experience alone qualifies a man to advise others, irrespective of the length of time he has been engaged in breeding Boston Terriers, for one often attains a lot of experience in a few years, particularly if he has conducted his breeding along liberal and progressive lines.

The chief end and aim with most breeders of Boston Terriers has been to breed and raise a winner. This is certainly a very commendable ambition, but one very seldom realized in both desires, for the temptation to sell a fine pup for a high price before it reaches maturity is very great, and as a rule typical specimens pass into other hands before they are a year old. There are certain laws that must be observed in breeding the Boston Terrier if we wish to obtain even partial success.

We cannot, in breeding the Boston always bank on the fact that "Like produces like," for in producing the little Yankee dog this is far from a certainty. I am afraid that too many of us have taken for granted that if we breed a high class bitch to a champion stud we were sure to get a litter of flyers. Just think the matter out for yourselves, and it will not appear so very strange to you that so many have failed while only a few have obtained success. According to the way most of us breed is it any wonder that we draw so many blanks and so seldom the prize puppy, and when we do is it not in most instances but a chance creation?

Did we, before we mated the pair, have in our minds exactly what type we wished to produce and did we know the true ancestors of the dogs, or, in other words, did we have a mental picture of the ancestors and know that the pair were suited to each other?

If we have a bitch that we know is well bred but weak in head, but is otherwise good, she should be bred to a stud dog that has a strong head. If the most noticeable fault is in the bitch's eyes, body, legs, back or markings, seek a dog that is ideal in those qualities which your bitch is weak in. Of all you do look further back into the stock than just the individual you are selecting to breed to. He may be a superb dog in the particular point you wish to strengthen in your bitch, but if you were to know or see his ancestors for several generations back it might be that they were weak in the very point you wish to improve and that the dog you have selected is only an accidental production. He would more than likely produce puppies that would "throw back" to his ancestors that were faulty in the very point your bitch is faulty in and that you are so ardently seeking to improve. Seek a sire that is strong himself in the point you wish

Broker

to improve and that comes from a family that is noted for being strong in this particular point. Do not consider just individual excellence or you will fail nine times out of ten in producing what you want.

Do not expect your male Boston when seven or eight months old to get you a litter of puppies. He, if well grown, will without the least trouble serve your bitch when at that age but he will not get you any pups. If you have an older stud dog and wish to educate the youngster a bit, when he is under a year old let him serve the bitch, but use your mature stud dog the following day or in all probabilities, if you trust to getting pups entirely to the youngster, you will lose the use of your bitch until she comes in season again. *(Editor's note: It would be taboo among modern breeders to ever use more than one stud dog on a bitch during a season.)* A dog that has some age on him will get larger litters than a real young dog. A young dog will keep getting larger litters as he grows older until he reaches the limit.

Do not allow your stud dog to try to serve great leggy bitches that he has to stand on first one leg and then the other to reach. Have a bench with legs that you can raise and lower. He will serve her far easier if he stands up higher than she does. I have seen dogs try to serve bitches much taller than themselves until they would bruise their feet until they would bleed around the nails and be so sore in the muscular part of their backs that they could scarcely move for days.

Editor's Note

The information contained in this chapter is inluded for its historical content only. Check with your veterinarian before following any of the advice.

The 15 1/2 lb. **Pomeroy's Trimount Billy** *was owned by Miss Emily Pomeroy, of Dushore, PA, author of this chapter.*

Ch. Dean's Lady Luana *was the first Boston champion in Michigan.*

Ittsawood Direct *was Best of Breed at Westminster in 1926 and topped the Detroit Specialty. He was owned by Mrs. I.G. Wood.*

Ch. Dick Turpin

Feed your stud dog good nourishing food, eggs, some milk, raw beef cooked meat and, of course, vegetables, but give him a rather concentrated food if you work him hard at stud. Do not have him burdened with a lot of soft fat but muscled up and as hard as a race horse. Give him all the exercise, in a gentle manner, that you can induce him to take. Take him with you when you go any place where you can. A stud dog does not want a few moments a day of violent exercise that makes him sore in every muscle, but he wants an unlimited amount of gentle exercise.

Try to breed dogs true to type and what the standard asks for. If you are breeding Bostons and have a bitch of the Whippet type, select a dog of stocky type, one that has plenty of bone and muscle, but always keep in mind that if you wish to permanently improve your stock you must mate with a dog coming from a family strong in the points you wish to correct or improve.

If you have a bitch, I will assume, that is weak in muzzle herself, but comes from a family of *strong headed Bostons,* do not seek a sire with a great massive head and that comes from a strain that is very strong in head, for if you do the puppies will be far from your liking. Your bitch, even though a bit weak in this point herself, coming from a strong headed family will be able to do her share in putting good heads on the puppies.

When selecting a sire find out if he gets puppies that strongly resembles himself or if he has a tendency to throw back and get pups that strongly resemble some remote ancestor. Some sires never reproduce themselves but sire puppies that strongly resemble some particular ancestor. Therefore, a champion stud dog may prove to be a very poor stock getter. While a stud dog with a very noticeable defect may prove himself to be a producer of elegant puppies.

We do not necessarily have to have prize winners in order to produce good stock but we do want dogs that the fault that keeps them from being prize winners has not been present for generations. A good stud dog if bred to what might be considered rather an inferior bitch, providing she comes from the right stock, may produce ideal puppies. Many of our noted prize winners are out of bitches that would not get a "look in" at a real show.

If we inbreed our dogs in order to establish some desirable point we will have to use the greatest amount of intelligence and make certain that the individuals do not in any way possess the same faults or we will greatly intensify the fault in the puppies while we are trying to establish the desirable point. If say the bitch is by chance defective in some particular point and she had a brother or half-brother perfect in that point and they both appeared in a high state of health and vigor then it would be permissible to breed them. By doing this we have reason to expect we will correct, in the puppies, the fault existing in the bitch.

Visit all the kennels that are producing typical Bostons that you can and study the dogs. Form an idea of what type of Boston you wish to produce and then "go to it" and do not allow yourself to grow discouraged. Select a sire that is large enough to produce a litter of four, five or six puppies and a sire that can breed a bitch naturally. One that does not require too much help. One that has plenty of vigor.

If a Boston Terrier female is well nourished and cared for, as a rule, at about nine months of age nature asserts herself and we discover the bitch to be in season. The time varies, however, in different strains and individuals. Some strains do not mature as early as others even though kept under the same conditions. It is noticed that a young bitch that is fed on highly concentrated food and left to exercise unrestricted with several of her own sex and a stud dog will come in season earlier than the young bitch that is retained as a pet and is rarely if ever allowed to romp and play with other dogs. A bitch kept largely on starchy food will not come in season as early as will the bitch that is fed on a liberal diet of meat, eggs and milk.

The length of time between the periods of season has frequent variations and this is caused much by the same conditions and influences that delay the first occurrence in some bitches. A good rugged bitch, with a good liberal nourishing diet and happily surrounded, will come in season at least

A basket of puppies from the 1920s.

twice a year and some about every five months.

Some fanciers breed their bitches at the first time in season if it by chance happens to be as early as seven and a half months. This is very wrong for the bitch is little more than a puppy herself and needs her food, etc., to finish rounding out her own body and equipping her with a vigorous constitution so that she may be a useful and lasting bitch after she attains the age to be bred, produce and rear puppies. If for any reason you breed your bitch before she is fully mature keep in mind the enfeebling influences this has on her constitution and try as far as possible to counterbalance it by a most generous nourishing diet, gentle and systematic exercise, good ventilation and clean and happy surroundings.

When some bitches are about to come in season there is marked change in their behavior. They are more affectionate toward their attendants and wish to frolic violently with other dogs. Some appear unusually restless and nervous. The sign that cannot be mistaken is the appearance of a sanguinolent *(tinged with blood, ed.)* discharge from the vagina. This discharge gradually deepens in color until it becomes bright red. The color remains about the same for five, six, seven or more days then it begins to gradually disappear. The mucus membrane lining the vagina is more or less congested and appears red. In most cases there is a marked swelling or puffiness of the vulva and surrounding parts. With young bitches the swelling seems more pronounced than with older bitches or bitches that have produced abundantly. In fact, there are bitches that the swelling is so slight that if one were depending upon appearances only to tell whether or not the bitch were in season she could easily pass by the full period unnoticed.

When a bitch is swollen to any marked degree this swelling appears hard and tense and remains so for a week or so. Then the parts begin gradually to soften and become more yielding to the touch. At the end of two weeks, in most instances, the swelling has fully disappeared.

The period of season generally lasts about three weeks but only for a few days of this time will the bitch permit the advances of the dog. I have known bitches that could be served for fourteen days and would permit the approach of the dog any day during that length of time and, then again, there are bitches that to breed successfully they would have to be looked after within two days or breeding would be impossible.

When a bitch is swollen and the swelling is tense and hard it would be utterly impossible to breed her but when the swelling softens and begins to subside you will notice the bitch is extremely anxious to court the society of the male. At this time the bitch can be successfully bred and the male will fasten without trouble. Most bitches can be mated on the eleventh or twelfth day while I have seen bitches that could be successfully bred on the second day and others that it was impossible to breed before the twentieth or twenty-first day. One can not always figure on this for the same bitch is vastly different at different seasons. If she could not be bred until the twentieth day at this particular time do not take it for granted that the next time it will be the same for she may fool you and if she is not bred by the eleventh or twelfth day, perhaps earlier, she may refuse service entirely until the next period.

A bitch may act frightened and shy in the presence of the stud dog but if the dog is properly broken and obeys his handlers' commands the bitch need not be pounced upon and mauled around but her attitude toward the stud dog can be ascertained in a careful manner.

In a few moments after the pair are introduced if the bitch is ready she will be noticed to frisk and flirt around the dog assuming peculiar poses, elevating her tail and possibly putting her paws up on the dog. Under such conditions take hold of the bitch's collar and hold her securely and command your stud dog to advance. If she stands, go on with the breeding but if she snaps and struggles severely do not annoy her further with the dog's attention but take him away until the following day when he may again be taken into her company and her attitude toward him will determine whether or not breeding will be possible.

It is a fact that if some bitches are successfully served they will go out of season almost immediately. Many people who send bitches to be bred will say "Now breed this bitch as often as you

A pair of puppies drawn by the talented artist Morgan Dennis from his **The Morgan Dennis Dog Book.**

can as long as she stays in season." It is unnecessary to say on such cases use your own judgment. I am sure one service is as good as two if it is a complete service and in every way successful.

Many people ask the question if it hurts bitches to breed every season. That greatly depends on the kind of a bitch she is and her care. If a good big vigorous bitch that is well nourished and perfectly healthy I do not find that it hurts to breed her every season providing the puppies are taken from her when little over three weeks old and she well wormed, given something to cool her blood and then a good tonic to put her into the best of health and condition. Puppies up until three weeks of age do not put much of a strain on a brood bitch and if you want a continuous and regular producer the pups should be removed at about three weeks.

The greatest help to a bitch is to be given Kal-Fos in her food from the day you breed her until you wean her pups. I know bitches that without the use of Kal-Fos could not produce a litter of puppies that one could make live to weaning time. Where with the use of it these bitches have fine pups that can be easily raised with other proper care considered. Kal-Fos also positively prevents acid milk which so many fanciers and breeders are claiming kills off their puppies. Do not be a tight wad but buy Kal-Fos and after you buy it do not be too neglectful to put it in the matron's food. Just take the puppies from an old bitch that has produced many litters and rub your hand over the top of the pup's skull and feel the big soft spot. Give the same bitch Kal-Fos and then examine the skulls of your puppies and note the difference.

It is not unusual to find a great big nice bitch that cannot be mated with the dog at all. Although she will stand like a post while the stud puts forth every effort to serve her. Upon examination you find it impossible to even introduce your finger into the vagina more than two or three inches. In other words she is not open enough for the dog to enter her far enough for the glans to enlarge and hold. You will find upon inquiry that probably bitches of this kind have had two or more litters but that they have had difficulty in whelping and that force has been employed and that combined with ignorance has lacerated the delicate mucus membranes and when the abrasions were undergoing the process of healing they were not carefully looked after and strong adhesions and scar tissue was formed until the vagina is practically closed or closed to such an extent as to make breeding impossible. Sometimes these adhesions can be broken loose by careful and intelligent use of the finger well lubricated while in other cases the conditions are such that it requires narcotizing the bitch and opening her with suitable instruments. Such cases, however, are scarcely ever very profitable or successful as future brood matrons. It is far better that a condition of this kind is not caused by an ignorant attendant than remedial measures taken after the mischief is done.

Ch. Gloria Silk *finished her championship by taking Best of Breed and going on to a Group One. She was owned by Mrs. William Irwin, Winchester, VA.*

Pages could be written on the proper care of a bitch about to whelp, and even then the subject would not be fully covered. In the first place, plenty of exercise must be given whilst in whelp, and it is a good custom to give a small amount of raw meat every other day during the last two weeks. When in whelp they crave all kinds of carnivorous food, and it is to gratify them that it should be given, and also with the hope that by satisfying this craving to a certain extent that they will not find it absolutely necessary to devour their pups. One week before due she should have her bed arranged, for it is very common for them to whelp several days ahead of time. It matters not whether she has a very little broken straw, excelsior or an old piece of carpet in the bottom of her box, for when she has finished whelping it must be cleaned out, and then a permanent covering can be substituted, according to the preference of the breeder.

It is best to select a roomy box and tack around the three sides a strip of wood about one inch deep and about two inches from the flooring —the object is to prevent the bitch lying close to the sides of the box. If properly adjusted, there will always be a space just large enough to permit a pup to crawl through in the event of its getting behind her. This little expedient has prevented many pups from being crushed or smothered by the bitch lying on them. The box should be placed in a reasonably warm place and where the bitch can be free from interference.

If the process of labor goes on satisfactorily, do not disturb her, but keep her under careful supervision. If, on the other hand, after several hours of pain nothing is accomplished, prepare at once to aid her by securing the services of a competent "vet," if you yourself are not able to render prompt and intelligent assistance. Many fine Boston Terrier bitches have been lost through delay, and valuable litters of pups are often destroyed. If, on the other hand, one pup is taken from them before their strength is depleted, they will often be able to have the rest of the litter without further aid. The period of whelping greatly varies with bitches, and it is very important to be assured that each pup soon after being born is able to secure nourishment, otherwise it should have one of the teats placed in its mouth and held there until able to work for itself.

Bitches will seldom take any nourishment until all is over, then plenty of warm milk or soup seems very grateful. It is well when the bitch is undershot or too tired to cut with a pair of scissors the navel cord, leaving about three inches attached to the pup's abdomen. This operation must not be done too soon after birth for the cord contains blood vessels and if these aren't allowed to dry up the pup will bleed to death. Bitches generally eat the afterbirths when allowed to do so; but to my mind it is just as well to limit the supply, pro-

Bramello Skeeter, *owned by Mrs. Harry W. Cassedy.*

Ch. Ketoson's Worthy Maid

viding it is a fairly large litter, by burning most of them.

After the lapse of twenty-four hours the bitch can be fed with strong soup and well-soaked stale bread; meat in small quantity can be gradually given. If the litter is large or the milk supply seems inadequate, oatmeal and milk should be freely given. On the second day the bitch should be taken out for a short time, but not kept long from her pups, lest they become chilled. If the pups are quiet and nurse well, it is a very good indication that matters are progressing nicely, but if they are continually crying it is an evidence that they are either cold or hungry. In the former case more heat must be supplied, and in the latter the milk supply must be increased. When possible, it is an excellent idea to have two bitches due to whelp within a day or so of each other, in such an event, if the service of a foster mother, even temporarily, should be indicated, you have one at hand. Some bitches have plenty of milk the first twenty-four hours, whilst with others the full supply is very slow in coming. The former condition is more apt to exist when the bitch has gone her full time, and the latter when somewhat previous.

About the ninth or tenth day the pups will begin to open their eyes, and much trouble is obviated if they are kept in a place guarded from the rays of the sun, so that they may become gradually accustomed to the light. Some breeders declare that if their pups live to be three days old they never have further trouble, but it is the experience of all others that the pups will require careful watching; that does not mean handling, for there is nothing so injurious as lifting them up for inspection and for the admiration of one's friends. Leave them severely alone until they are able to trot around and thus exhibit themselves.

I am going to try to tell you how I raise my own and how you can raise practically every puppy that is whelped at your kennels, providing it is whelped without any deformities. If pups should be whelped with "harelips," soft palates, or any other deformity do not bother with them but put them out of the way as soon as you make the discovery.

The early male, Rossie Richards *(sometimes listed as Ross Richards), c. late 1800s. Here you can see the dramatic evolution of type.*

It seems to be quite a frequent occurrence to have a puppy come with a harelip and other deformities of the mouth. Some pups will come fine healthy looking specimens but will have great difficulty nursing. If you take the pup to the light and carefully open its mouth you will find way back in the roof of its mouth a small hole, in some instances, not larger than a small shot. This seems to make it impossible for the puppy to secure sufficient nourishment to keep it alive for more than a few days. As soon as you discover this, one had better kill it and give the other pups that are all right a better chance.

A good healthy puppy will take hold and nurse in less than five minutes after it is whelped. As soon as the puppy is born or as soon as the pulsation of the naval cord ceases, cut it off about a half-inch from the body. Do not cut too quickly or the puppy will bleed too much. If the placenta (after birth) comes with the pup do not allow your bitch to eat it as it is a filthy thing at best and will physic (*Editor's note: cause to have a bowel movement*) the bitch more than she should be. Burn it up. Hold the pup in your hand and let the bitch lick out its mouth, and around the abdomen. Put your pup to the nipple and if it does not take hold, gently open its mouth by pressing with your first finger and thumb on each side of the mouth, and with the other hand place the nipple in its mouth and it will immediately begin to tug for eats. After the pup once takes hold good, it will help itself afterward unless it is very weak and tiny and the bitch's nipples large, then it has to be held to the breast while it nurses and this part must be looked after to make sure it gets sufficient nourishment. If the other pups in the litter are large and strong it will crowd the weak one out, and it will soon die from starvation unless care is taken to place it on the breast and hold it there until it is satisfied. The bowels of the puppy will move when it first nurses and the bitch will clean up the secretion. Have your bitch in a very warm place when she whelps no matter if she does pant and appear to be too warm. Better too warm than too cold. I find if in a real warm place the bitch will relax better. I have my bitches whelp in a room heated to about 80 degrees. When the next pup is about ready to be whelped take the first born and put it in a basket in a warm cloth with a hot water bottle. Do not take the pup from the bitch until you see that another is about ready to be born, for if you do it frets the bitch and does her more harm than it does the pup good. Keep tucking a little dry warm straw under the bitch so that her box does not get wet and cold. After the pups are all whelped milk a small amount of milk from her and test it for acid with the use of Litmus Paper. If the test shows acid in the milk do not let your pups nurse her, but nourish them with a little artificial food until the acid has disappeared, then they can be placed back with her in perfect safety. If the bitch is treated with teaspoonful doses of Bicarbonate of Soda dissolved in a half-cup of milk every couple of hours the acid will be eliminated in a short time. If she will not drink the milk dissolve the soda in milk sufficient and force her to take it. Milk out all the milk you can, frequently while giving her the soda, and until it shows by test that the acid has disappeared. If you give your bitch Bicarbonate of Soda a couple of times a day in milk for a week before she is due to whelp you will find her milk will be without acid and her digestion the best. After the bitch has her pups you will often see her lying all curled up and her puppies trying to get under her to nurse which she seems reluctant to allow. Most always bitches acting that way are suffering from gas and indigestion. Give her two grain doses of Pure Pepsin together with about three grains of Subnitrate of Bismuth every two or three hours. Just open her mouth and put the dry powder back on her tongue and hold her mouth shut for a minute or two.

In four or five hours after the pups are whelped I take the bitch out of her box and give her a good douche of about two quarts of fairly warm water to which is added a teaspoonful of Creolin (Pearson). I douche her each evening for three or four days. When I douche her the first time I change the straw in her box before letting her go back. You will find by doing this that her box will stay free from odor. If you do not do this the discharge coming from the bitch pollutes the box and straw and causes a very bad odor throughout the room in which she is confined. The douche thoroughly cleanses out the bitch and disinfects and helps heal any abrasions. If this is done you will have no cases of blood poison and your bitch will come in season promptly the next time due and be far more sure of getting in whelp.

If you want to raise your pups keep the mother and pups in a box enclosed on all sides with a hinged top and a hole cut in the front plenty large enough for her to easily pass in and out. Do not allow a bit of draft to strike the pups. Have this box in a room that does not drop below 75 or 80

This delightful drawing of a Boston pup comes from Diana Thorne's **Your Dogs and Mine.**

degrees day or night until your pups are a week old, then you can gradually cool off the room to a temperature of 70 and it should stand at that temperature until your pups are old enough to be weaned.

I allow my bitches to take all the nourishment they will after they whelp the pups. Don't be afraid to give your bitch plenty of raw fresh beef. It is the best milk maker you can give them. It is a good idea not to have your bitch too fat when you breed her or too fat while carrying her puppies, but after she has whelped you want to feed her, so she gains in flesh instead of allowing her to grow thinner as the pups grow older. My bitches are all much higher in flesh when the pups are weaned than when they whelp them. By feeding your bitch well it increases the flow of milk and puts the nourishment into the milk for the pups. After the first day or two I give my bitches a teaspoonful of Kal-Fos in their food once a day. This furnishes bone-making material for the pups and saves the bitch from having her system drained from substance she needs herself as a producer.

When your pups are 18 or 20 days old commence feeding them; twice a day is sufficient to offer each puppy for educational purposes. I have all my pups weaned and away from the bitch by the time they are four weeks old. Feed your pups little and often. I feed them about every four hours and always feed them separately. By doing this you know exactly how much each puppy is getting and the strong ones are not taking more than their digestive organs can take care of and the smaller ones getting such a small amount that they can just keep alive on it. When your pups are six weeks old have them eating puppy biscuit ground very fine. Give them some finely chopped lean beef once a day and some finely ground lean cooked meat will do them good. Do not feed your pups too much at one time and never feed enough to distend their abdomens or make them dumpish and sleepy. Gradually begin feeding them vegetables mixed with the ground pup biscuit and meat slightly moistened.

Do not feed sloppy feeds. When you give liquids such as milk give it to them for one meal, do not make the food sloppy with it. I buy the head meat from beef and boil it together with carrots, cabbage, turnips and in fact all vegetables with the exception of potatoes. Take these vegetables out of the broth when they are very well done, put them through your vegetable grinder and use them in connection with the broth poured over the ground pup biscuit, making all just moist enough to have the pups eat it readily. Grind your beef and add a small amount to each pup's portion When the pups are two months old I give each pup a little raw Linseed Oil in his feed once a day and watch their bowels and increase the oil until each pup is getting a teaspoonful of oil a day. If you do this you will have no extra care to give your puppies when you want to show them for you will find you have them in show shape all the time. If at any time your pups should begin to physic (*Editor's note: cause to have a bowel movement*) and you are sure the disturbance does not come from worms give them the Pepsin and Bismuth the same as advised for the brood bitch. When you notice your pups' bowels are disarranged do not wait thinking the matter will correct itself, but attend to them at once.

Just as soon as you take your pups from the bitch worm them, even though their condition may appear to be perfect. You will be surprised at the hundreds of threadlike worms they will pass.

Do not allow your puppies to become infested with fleas, lice or other pests. You cannot raise good dogs and have them infested with troublesome pests. A good washing if properly dried does your pups good and keeps them in prime condition.

Never feed your puppies or grown dogs chicken bones or bones of any kind that will splinter. Keep before your pups at all times a good supply of cool, fresh drinking water.

Now we will assume that you have grown your puppies up to the time for them to commence to breed. If it is a female you have and she comes in season when seven or eight months old or under 11 months of age, let her skip breeding unless she is an extremely well developed specimen. If you breed a female much before she is matured you certainly will have disastrous results. When she comes in season place her by herself, give her just the same care as before, but do not feed her too heavily. When she is ready to be bred try her, and

Holiday Kennels

The Boston Terriers housed at Mrs. Hilda M. Ridder's Holiday Kennels were fortunate dogs indeed. Mrs. Ridder lived in one of New York City's most fashionable neighborhoods. It was "only a stone's throw from the Hudson River and only two blocks from Broadway." An apartment which adjoined Mrs. Ridder's house was remodeled especially for the dogs. It contained luxurious kennels and opened onto beautifully landscaped gardens, equipped with diversions for the dogs, so that it served as their personal "playground." In the hot summer months, the entire kennel was packed into Mrs. Ridder's car for the journey to Baldwin, Long Island.

Mrs. Ridder became involved with Bostons in 1924 and would be classified as what we call a "hobby breeder." She loved to exhibit her dogs and they were frequently seen at shows in the Northeast and Canada. In addition to the dogs pictured here, she owned Ch. My Nominee.

Am. & Can. Ch. Rockaby Dempsey *and his brother, Ch. Rockabye Tunney were whelped on the night of the famous championship boxing match.*

The mahogany brindle **Am. & Can. Ch. Rockabye Dempsey** *was Mrs. Ridder's pride and joy. She purchased him from Dr. Gustav Brandle, of Chicago, for $1,500. It was a good buy. Dempsey became a Group Winner and a very popular sire.*

Ch. Friendship *was a multi-Group and Best in Show winner.*

Am. & Can. Ch. O'Glo's Midgie, *Best in Show winner.*

Mrs. Ridder and the gang pack up for their summer trip to Long Island.

if she stands for the dog let a couple of days pass before you allow him to serve her, and before doing this lubricate your first finger on your right hand and insert it in the vagina, opening the bitch up thoroughly. After this is attended to allow the dog to serve her at once. I breed my bitches twice. Sometimes after a lapse of 24 hours and at times allow a day between the service.

Believing that many, like myself, breeding Bostons, live in localities where a competent "vet" is unobtainable, I am writing the following: I have bred Bostons exclusively for a number of years and during that time have lost from whelping, or rather trying to whelp, two valuable young bitches. It seems to be a peculiarity of Boston matrons to suffer from inertia of the uterus. The labor pains not being strong or frequent enough to force the puppy down to even the brim of the pelvis where it may be safely secured in the grasp of a suitable pair of forceps and thus brought into the world.

I determined to find, if possible, a remedy whereby I could afford a bitch relief, save her life, her puppies, and still retain her usefulness as a brood matron. Being a trained nurse and having worked under some of the best M.D.'s in New York City, Jersey City, Philadelphia and other large cities, I knew that medicine could be given the human mother to greatly help her by strengthening pains and therefore promote labor. I had used Ergot on bitches and it did more harm than good. I promised myself to try the medicine successfully used on women on my Boston Terriers. I looked well into the matter and upon making inquiry among my medical friends, Parke, Davis & Co., I determined when the next opportunity presented itself to try use of "Pituitrin."

Within a few days after I had satisfied myself that "Pituitrin," prepared by the old and reliable firm of Parke, Davis & Co. of Detroit, Michigan, was the proper remedy, I was called upon to do what I could for a very small Toy Boston bitch. I found the bitch had been laboring for several hours, was greatly exhausted, heart fast and irregular, palpitating so it could be plainly heard to thump when standing by her whelping box. She was so weak from her prolonged and fruitless efforts to whelp that she fell over exhausted and almost prostrated in her box. Pains had entirely ceased. I gave her per hypodermic, in the muscles of her shoulder, eight minims of "Pituitrin." In a few moments she passed urine very freely, her heart action greatly improved, gradually becoming regular and strong. She took some liquid nourishment and in twenty-five minutes labor recommenced. In the course of an hour a strong, healthy puppy was born. She was allowed to rest one and a half hours and given some milk which she drank with a relish.

After a short interval I gave her a second hypodermic injection, in the muscles of the opposite shoulder, of eight minims of "Pituitrin," and she labored hard and frequently, but with little success. Up to this time I had not given the bitch a vaginal examination, but now as the pup did not seem to be descending as it should, I examined her and found one hind leg of the unborn pup in the vagina After several moments of gentle but persistent manipulation I succeeded in turning the puppy and a few moments later she whelped a very large living puppy. Soon after this, without any further help of medicine or digital interference, she whelped a very lively but small puppy.

She was given a rest of a few hours, during which time she took considerable milk to which was added a small amount of bicarbonate of soda. During this interval of rest, slight, infrequent pains, with practically no force, continued. After another lapse of a couple of hours pains were noticeably growing still weaker. The bitch appeared to be exhausted and heart somewhat irregular. I gave her a third hypodermic of about 10 minims of "Pituitrin." Pains soon became strong and frequent. Upon examination I found the pup's head, seemingly caught, under the brim of the pelvis. I carefully shoved the pup back and gently raised its head during her next pain and with the two following pains she whelped her fourth and last puppy.

The bitch was tired but otherwise in the pink of condition. The vaginal examinations were no more frequent than absolute necessity demanded and having used the utmost care she was free from lacerations and but slightly swollen.

Chapter 10

Breeding for Good Disposition

by Edward Axtell

This, to my mind, is the most important feature in the breeding of the dog that demands the most careful attention. If the disposition of the dog is not all that can be desired, of what avail is superb constitution, an ideal conformation and beautiful color and markings? Better by far to obtain the most pronounced mongrel that roams the street that shows a loving, generous nature if he costs his weight in gold, then take as a gift the most royally bred Boston that could not be depended upon at all times and under all circumstances to manifest the perfect disposition.

A short time ago I went to visit a noted pack of English Foxhounds. One beautiful dog especially, took my eye, a strong, vigorous, noble looking fellow, and on my asking the kennel man, a quaint old Scotchman, if he would let the dog out for me to see, he replied: "Why, certainly, Mr. Axtell, that dog is Dashwood, he is a perfect gentleman," and this is what all Boston Terriers should be. Of course, I am speaking of the well bred, properly trained, blue blooded dog, not the mongrel that so often masquerades under his name. Still, as there are black sheep in every family, a dog showing an ugly, snapping, quarrelsome disposition will occasionally be met with which, to the shame of owner, is not necessarily put out of the way and buried so deep that he can not be scratched up, but is allowed to perpetuate his or her own kind to the everlasting detriment of the breed.

How many a one has come away from a dog show utterly disgusted with perhaps one of the best looking dogs on the bench, after admiring its attractiveness in every detail, discovers on too near an approach to him that he possesses a snappy, vicious disposition?

I am perfectly well aware that due allowance must be made for the unnatural excitement that surrounds a dog, perhaps for the first time shown, away from all he knows, and surrounded by strange noises and faces. Yet I consider it an outrage on the public who give their time and pay their money, to subject them to any risk of being bitten by any dog, I care not of what breed it may be. At a recent show in Boston, in company with three or four gentlemen, I was admiring a very handsome looking Boston, a candidate for high honors, when his owner called out to me: "Mr. Axtell, do not go too near him or he will bite your fingers off." I replied: "You need not advise an old dog man like me; I can tell by the look of his eye what he would do if given a chance. You have no right whatsoever to show such a dog." Since then I went to the kennels where a noted prize winner is placed at public stud, and he showed such a vicious disposition and attempt to bite through the bars of his pen that the attendant had to cover the bars over with a blanket. Such dogs as these should be given at once a sufficient amount of chloroform and a suitable burial without mourners. If a man must keep such a brute,

Edward Axtell, owner of St. Botolph Kennels, in Cliftondale, MA., and author of **The Boston Terrier and All About It.**

Ch. Haynes' Midgie *was a large deep seal brindle bitch. She was owned by Mrs. Haynes, of Cleveland, OH.*

St. Botolph's Mistress King, *one of Edward Axtell's bitches.*

Born in 1924, **Ch. Lyon's Gold Top** *was a son of Woodward's Captain. He was bred by John Lyons and owned by Mrs. F.S. Wadman. Later he was sold to Walter Saunders.*

then a strong chain and a secure place where his owner alone can visit him is absolutely imperative.

Boston Terriers, of all breeds, must possess perfect dispositions if they are to maintain their present popularity; and yet, how many unscrupulous breeders and dealers are palming off upon a confiding public dogs which, instead of being "put away" (I think that is the general term they use) should be put under so much solid mother earth that no one would suspect their interment. I know it takes considerable grit and force of character to cheerfully put to sleep a dog for which perhaps a large sum of money has been paid, that has developed an uncertain, snappy disposition, yet it pays so to do; honesty is not alone the best policy, but the only one. In my experience as a dog man I could give many personal incidents concerning the sale of vicious dogs, but for space sake one must suffice.

Last year a Chicago banker sent me an order for a dog similar in style and disposition to the one I had sold him a few years previously, to go to his niece, a young lady staying for treatment at a large sanitarium in southern Massachusetts. I replied that I had not in my kennel a large enough dog to suit, but that I knew a dealer who possessed a fairly good reputation who had, and I would get him for him if he would run the chances. This was satisfactory, and I bought the dog. He was guaranteed to me in every way, but I felt somewhat suspicious, as the price was very low for a dog of his style. I kept him with me for a week and saw no outs whatever about him, and practically concluded my suspicions were unfounded.

A litter born at Holiday Kennels, in New York City. These fine pups are sired by Mrs. Hilda M. Ridder's Group winning Am. & Can. Ch. Rockabye Dempsey (Ch. Introduce Me x Ch. My Rockabye Baby).

Upon taking the dog personally to the young lady in question, I told her his history as far as I knew it, and also that while I could not give her the dealer's guarantee of the dog I could not, of course, endorse it, but then if she cared to run the risk she could have the dog on approval as long as she wished. I said in warning that there was something about his eye that did not altogether strike my fancy and that if he showed the least symptom of being anything but affectionate, to ship him to my kennels in Cliftondale immediately. As he was a handsome dog, with beautiful color, I could see she wanted him at once, and the dog seemed to take to her in an even greater degree. I received a letter from her in a week's time, saying how perfectly satisfactory the dog was in every way, and what a general favorite he had become with the lady patients there, several of whom would like me to get one like him for them. I need not say how pleased I was to hear this, but what was my surprise to receive a letter the next day asking me to send at once for the dog, as he had bitten the matron. You may depend that neither she nor any other of the inmates there would ever want to see a Boston again, and who would want them to? Of course I lost money, but that is not worth mentioning. The

The Hamill Bostons

Rajah's Premium, *a dark seal brindle 16 lb. dog known for his perfect markings. Premium was owned by Mrs. John Hamill, of Los Angeles, CA.*

Small, but mighty. The 10 lb. Group winner, Ch. Hamill's Minstrel Boy, a dark seal brindle, was Best of Breed at many large California shows.

Tannery Town King *was one of the last sons of Ch. Peter's King. The dark seal brindle dog earned points on both the east and west coasts. Owned by Mrs. Hamill.*

The Ringmount Bostons

The 13 lb. **Ringmount Tiny Tim,** *a son of Ringmount Tiny King, did a good deal of winning on the east coast.*

13 1/2 lb. **Ch. Ringmount King O' The Avenue,** *born in 1924, was bred by Patrick J. Healy and owned by Mrs. Roger H. O'Brien. King was one of the best known champions in the Boston area.*

Born in 1923, **Amulet Bobbie** *was a daughter of Ringmount Tiny King. She was bred by John S. Cute and owned by Amulet Kennels, New Haven, CT.*

sorrow I felt stays by me today. I sent for the dog and kept him at my kennels for five months, taking care of himself myself and never letting him out of my sight, during which time he was as gentle as a kitten, until one day a young dog man came down into the yard, and the dog, for some unaccountable reason, as in the case of the matron, jumped on him and took hold of his sleeve. The man, being accustomed to dogs, was fortunately not scared. This explained the low price of the dog, and it is needless to add, he ornamented my kennels no longer. I can only state in connection with this that that dealer has sold very few dogs since. I never purchase a dog now, unless I know the man from whom I buy.

The pointed dog **Rickenbacker Kid,** *owned by Mrs. Chester R. Young, Durand, MI*

How to breed dogs possessing an ideal disposition is an all-important question, and I give the rules as followed in our kennels with complete success. Breed only from stock that you know comes from an ancestry noted for this particular feature. Many dogs are naturally of an affectionate nature, but have been made snappish by ill treatment, or teasing. This can be bred out by judicious care, but where a vicious tendency is hereditary, look out for trouble ahead. Damages for dog bites come high, and he must be either a very rich man, or a very poor one, that can afford to keep this kind of stock.

Ch. High Point Toodles *was a multiple Specialty winner. This small, dark mahogany dog was owned by Norma Schlenker, of Cincinnati, OH.*

Escape, *owned by A.M. Sherwood, Joliet, IL, 1901.*

Ch. Noel's Bebe, *bred by J. Fanchon and owned by J. Noel, of Brockton, MA, was born in 1924. This 17 1/2 lb. dog was a dark brindle.*

Use only thoroughly healthy stock; disease is often productive of an uneven, sullen disposition. See that the bitch especially never shows a tendency to be cross or snappy. The male dog usually controls the shape, color and markings, and the dam the constitution and disposition. Hence it is, if anything, of more importance that the female should be strong in this feature than the male, although the male, of course, should be first class, also. So well known is this physiological fact that breeders of standard bred horses, particularly hunters and carriage horses, will never breed a vicious mare to a quiet stallion, and yet they are generally willing to risk breeding a quiet mare to a stallion not as good in this respect.

The education of the puppies should begin as soon as they can run around. Very much depends upon a right start. We are admonished to "train up a child in the way he should go," and this applies with equal force to the dog. Treat them with the utmost kindness, but with a firm hand. Be sure they are taught to mind when spoken to, and never fail to correct at once when necessary. A stitch in time save many times nine. A habit once formed is hard to break. Never be harsh with them; never whip; remember that judicious kind-

Gladys Emerson Cook's depiction of the breed from **All Breeds, All Champions.**

ness with firmness is far more effective with dogs, as with children. Be sure to accustom them to mingle with people and children, and introduce them as early as possible to the sights of the street, to go on ahead and to come at your call. Prevent the pernicious habit of running and barking at teams, etc., and other dogs. The time to check these habits as aforesaid is before they become fixed. If, after all these pains, you see a dog show the slightest disposition to be vicious, then do not hesitate to send him at once by a humane transit to dog heaven. By thus continually breeding a strain of dogs with an affectionate nature and the elimination of any that show the least deviation from same, in a short time kennels can be established whose dogs will not only be a source of supreme satisfaction to the owner, but will be the best advertisers of said kennels wherever they go.

It will readily be admitted by all who have given the matter any consideration that a dog of an affectionate nature, whose fidelity has always been constant, and whose devotion to its owner has always under all circumstances been perfectly sincere and lasting, makes an appeal to something that is inherent in human nature. The fact of the case is that the love of such a dog is imbedded in the soul of every normal man and woman who have red blood in their veins. I think it is instinctive, and has its foundation in the fact that from the beginning of time he has ministered to man's necessities, and has accompanied him as his best friend on man's upward march to civilization and enlightenment. "There may be races of people who have never known the dog, but I very much question if, after they have made his acquaintance, they fail to appreciate his desirable qualities, and to conceive for him both esteem and affection."

Chapter 11

Breeding for a Vigorous Constitution
by Edward Axtell

I think there never has been a time in the history of the breed when this particular feature needed more thoughtful, systematic and scientific attention devoted to it than now. For the past few years breeders have been straining every nerve, and leaving no stone unturned, to produce small stock, toys, in fact, and everyone realizes, who has given the question thoughtful consideration, that this line of breeding has been at the expense of vigor, and indirectly largely of a beautiful disposition, of the dog, to say nothing of the financial loss that must inevitably ensue.

Said an old Boston Terrier man (Mr. Barnard) at a recent show: "Mr. Axtell, if they keep on breeding at this rate, it won't be long before they produce a race of black and tans."

In my estimation, it will not be black and tan terriers, but nothing. It will be productive of a line of bitches that are either barren, or so small that they can not possibly whelp without the aid of a vet. One does not have to look very far to discover numbers of men who started in the breeding of the American dog with high hopes and enthusiastic endeavors to success, who have fallen by the wayside, owing largely to the fact that proper attention was not paid to the selection of suitable breeding stock, especially the matrons. Said a man to me last year: "Much as I love the dog, and crazy as I am to raise some good pups, I have given up for all time trying to breed Boston Terriers. I have lost eight bitches in succession whelping." We have all of us "been there" and quite a number of us "many a time."

In order to obtain strong, vigorous puppies that will live and develop into dogs that will be noted for vigorous constitutions, we shall simply, and in language that can be readily understood by the novice as well as the established breeder, lay down the rules that a quarter of a century has demonstrated to be the correct ones for the attainment of the same as used in our kennels. As all puppies that leave our place are sold with the guarantee of reaching maturity (unless shown, when we take no risks whatever in regard to distemper, mange, etc.), it will readily be seen that they must have a first class start, and must of necessity be the progeny of stock possessing first class vigor and the quality of being able to transmit the same to their offspring. An ounce of experience is worth many tons of theory, and it is, then, with pleasure we give the system pursued by us, feeling certain that the same measure of success will attend others that will take the necessary pains to attain the same, and they will be spared the many pitfalls and mistakes that have necessarily been ours before we acquired our present knowledge. It has been for a number of years (starting as we did when the breed was in its infancy, and only the intense love of the dog, coupled with an extensive leisure, which enabled us to devote a great deal of attention to important and scientific experiments, have enabled us to arrive where we are),

Minqua's Spark

an uphill road, the breeding problems have had to be solved at the outlay of brains, patience and considerable money. Unlike any established breed, there was practically no data to fall back on, no books of instruction to follow, but if the pioneer work has been arduous the results obtained have far outbalanced it, and the dog today stands as a monument to all the faithful, conscientious and determined body of men who would never acknowledge defeat, but who, in spite of all discouragements from all quarters, and from many where it should have been least expected, have pressed forward until they find the object of their unfailing endeavors the supreme favorite in dogdom the continent over.

In the first place, in the attainment of vigorous puppies, we state the bitches selected are of primary importance, in our view, as already stated, far more so than the sire. For best results we choose a bitch weighing from fifteen to twenty-five pounds. If they happen to weigh over this we do not consider it any detriment whatever, rather otherwise. Always select said matrons from litters that have been large, bred from strong, vigorous stock, thoroughly matured, and that have been bred by reliable (we speak advisedly) men for several generations if possible. If one can, obtain from kennels that while perfectly comfortable, have not been supplied with artificial heat. There is more of this than appears on the surface. Dogs that have been coddled and brought up around a stove rarely have stamina and vitality enough to enable them to live the number of years they are entitled to, and fall a ready victim to the first serious trouble, whether distemper, or the many and one ills that beset their path. Intelligent breeders of all kinds of stock today recognize the value of fresh air and

Ch. Wampagne Buddy Boy

Edward Axtell, Jr. with one of the St. Botolph Bostons.

unlimited sunshine, and if best results are to be obtained these two things are imperative....

The reason for choosing bitches that come from dams noted for their large litters is this: the chances are (if the dog bred to comes from a similar litter) that they will inherit the propensity to give birth to large litters themselves, and the pups will necessarily be smaller than when only one or two pups are born. The bitch that has but that number runs an awful risk, especially if she has been well fed. The pups will be large and the dam has great difficulty in whelping.

If toy bitches are bred, look out for breakers ahead; only a very small percent live to play with their little ones. A toy bitch, bred to a toy dog, will frequently have but one pup, and that quite a large one in proportion to the size of parents. When a toy bitch is bred, attend carefully to these three things. See that the dog used is small in himself, comes

The 14 lb. Ch. Suni Blink was the sire of a Best in Show winner. He was owned by Mrs. J.A. Dick, of Lincoln, NE.

The multi-Breed winner and sire of champions, **Ch. Our Sammy.** *He was owned by Mrs. E.J. Graves, Fascination Kennels, Detroit, MI.*

from small stock, and does not possess too large a head. Secondly, be sure the bitch is kept in rather poor condition, in other words, not too fat; and thirdly, and this is the most important of all, see that she has all the natural exercise she can be induced to take. These conditions strictly and faithfully adhered to may result in success.

In the next place, the consideration of the dog to be used is in order. Whether he be a first prize winner or an equally good dog that has never been shown (and the proportion of the best raised dogs that appear on the bench is very small) insist on the following rules:

Be sure that the dog is typical with first class constitution, vigorous, and possessing an ideal disposition, and what is of the utmost importance, that he comes from a line of ancestry eminently noted for these characteristics. Breed to no other, though he were a winner of a thousand first prizes. I prefer a symmetrical dog weighing from sixteen to twenty pounds, rather finer in his make-up than the bitch, and possessing the indefinable quality of style, and evidences in his make-up courage and a fine, open, generous temperament. Do not breed to a dog that is overworked in the stud, kept on a board floor chained up in a

kennel or barn, and never given a chance to properly exercise. If you do the chances are that one of three things will happen: the bitch will not be in whelp (the most likely result); the pups, or some of them will be born dead, and one runs an awful risk of the bitch dying; or, if alive at birth, a very small percent only of the pups will live to reach maturity. I think Boston Terriers are particularly susceptible to worms or distemper, and it is absolutely imperative that they should not be handicapped at the onset.

One other very important factor is natural exercise for the bitch. Unless one is willing to take the necessary pains to give her this, give up all expectation of ever succeeding in raising puppies.

...Were I asked the three most important essentials for the success of the brood bitch, I should say, "Exercise, exercise, exercise." By this I do not mean leading by a chain, running behind a horse or team, but the natural exercise a bitch will take if left to her own devices. Nature has provided an infallible monitor to direct the dog the best amount to take, and when to take it. One of the best bitches I ever possessed was one weighing fourteen pounds by the original Tony Boy (one of the best little dogs that ever lived) out of a bitch by Torrey's Ned, by A. Goode's Ned. Her name was Lottie, and she had thirteen litters and raised over ninety percent. Those who have read that interesting little book, *The Boston Terrier,* by the late Dr. Mott, will readily recall the genial Doctor speaking of the first Boston he ever owned, named "Muggy Dee," and how intelligent he was, and what a number of tricks the Doctor taught him, will be interested to know that Lottie was his great-grandmother, and she was equally intelligent. We had several bitches by the celebrated Mr. Mullen's "Boxer" out of her (this is going back to ancient history), one of which, "Brownie," was, to my fancy, the nicest dog we ever had. She, with the rest of the litter, had the run of several hundred acres, and many times I did not see them for days together. They went in and out of the hayloft at pleasure, and spent the greater part of their time hunting and digging out skunks and woodchucks which were quite thick in the woods back of us at that

I'm The Boy *was said to be a duplicate of his father, Ch. I'm The Guy. This 15 lb. dog was a mahogany brindle. He was owned by W.R. Flitton, Grand Ledge, MI.*

Ch. Patterson's Ted Bustler *was never defeated in the show ring. The 15 lb. dog was owned by Mary Masters Patterson, of Nashville, TN.*

A grainy old photo of **Ch. Crown Prince III,** *owned by Ralph J. Cahen, of Bayonne, NJ.*

time. I remember the first time Brownie was bred to that king of sires, "Buster," owned by Alex Goode (than whom a more loyal Boston Terrier man never lived), and I was rather anxious to see the litter when it arrived, as from the mating I expected crackerjacks. I had not seen her or her mother for two or three days, but the time for whelping having arrived, was keeping a close watch on the stable. About dusk she came in with Lottie, and in a short time gave birth to four of the most vigorous, perfectly formed little tots I had ever seen. Each one proved to be good enough to show, although only one was sold to an exhibitor, Mr. G. Rawson, the rest going into private hands. "Druid Pero" was shown in New York in 1898, taking first prize and silver cup for best in his class, but I think his brother "Caddie," beat him, his owner, a Boston banker, being offered a number of times ten times the sum he paid for him.

The day after Brownie whelped she and her mother went off for an hour or so, and they finished digging out Mr. Skunk (which the attention to her maternal duties necessitated a postponement of), the old dog dragging him home in triumph. I attribute the success these dogs, in common with the rest of the bitches in the kennels who had similar advantages, had in whelping and the rearing of their young to the fact that they always had unlimited natural exercise. I can enumerate scores of cases similar to these attended with equally good results, if space permitted.

In regard to mating, one service, if properly performed, is usually enough, if the bitch is ready to take the dog. If a bitch should fail to be in whelp I should advise the next time she comes in season two or even three visits to the dog, and where convenient I should suggest a different dog this time. In case this time these services were un-

The Shire Bostons

Mrs. Emily Shire, an enthusiastic Boston Terrier fan, appears here in her flapper dress cuddling two of her favorite dogs. She often wrote articles for dog magazines during the 1920s.

Mrs. Shire's best known dog was the multiple Breed winning and Group winner Ch. E. Delilah. The 14 lb. bitch was born in 1925. She was a dark mahogany brindle. Bred by L.W. Terhune, she was a consistent winner.

successful, then I should suggest the course that breeders of thoroughbred horses pursue, viz., to let the female run with the male for three or four days together. There are many things connected with breeding that we do not understand, and frequently going back to nature, as in this case, is productive of results when all else fails.

One very important factor in the production of strong, rugged pups that live, is good feeding. Do not imagine that feeding dog biscuits to the bitch in whelp will give good results, it will not; she needs meat and vegetables once a day. Biscuits are all right as a supplementary food, but that is all. Meat is the natural food for a dog, and it is a wise kennel man that can improve on nature. Be sure the meat is free from taint, especially at this time and when the bitch is nursing pups. The gastric juice of a dog's stomach is a great germicide, but there is a limit.

Be certain the dogs have a plentiful supply of good, pure water. This is of far more importance than many people imagine.

Do not administer drugs of any description to your dogs, except in the case of a good vermifuge, if they are harboring worms, and a proper dose of castor oil if constipated. If the dog at any time is sick, consult a good veterinary accustomed to dogs, not one who has practiced entirely on horses or cows. If a bitch, at the time of whelping, is much distressed and can not proceed, get a veterinary and get him quick. When the pups arrive, if all is well and they are able to nurse, let them severely alone. If they are very weak they will have to be assisted to suckle—do not delay attention in this case. Be sure the box the bitch whelped in is large enough for her to turn around in, and do not use any material in the nest that the pups can get entangled with. My advice to breeders is, if the bitch is fully formed and grown to her full proportions, to breed the first time she comes in season. She will have an easier time whelping than when she is older. If delicate or immature, delay breeding till the next time. Do not use a dog in the stud until he is a year and a half old for best results; they will, of course, sire pups at a year or younger, but better wait. To those people who live in the city, or where a kennel can not be established for want of adequate room to give the dogs the necessary exercise, an excellent plan to follow is one adopted by an acquaintance of mine, and followed by him for a number of years with a good measure of success. He owns one or two good stud dogs that he keeps at his home, and he has put out on different farms, within a radius of ten miles of Boston, one bitch at each place, and pays the farmer (who is only too glad to have this source of income at the outlay of so little trouble and expense) one hundred dollars for each litter of pups the bitch has, the farmer to deliver the pups when required, usually when three months old. The farmer brings in the bitch to be bred, and the owner has no further trouble. The pups, when delivered, are usually in the pink of condition and are, in a great measure, house broken, and their manners to a certain extent cultivated. He has no trouble whatever with pups when ordered, as he simply sends the address of customers and the farmer ships them. This, to me, is a very uninteresting and somewhat mercenary way of doing business, as one misses all the charm of breeding and the bringing up of the little tots, to many of us the most delightful part of the business. To those breeders who have newly started in, do not get discouraged if success does not immediately crown your efforts; remember, if Boston Terriers could be raised as easily as other dogs, the prices would immediately drop to the others' level.

Chapter 12

Breeding for Size

by Edward Axtell

When I joined the Boston Terrier Club in 1895, there were two classes for weight—the light weight, from 15 to 23 pounds, and the heavy weight, from 23 to 30 pounds, inclusive. This, of course, has been changed since to three classes—the light weight, 12 and not to exceed 17 pounds; middle weight class, 16 and not to exceed 22 pounds, and heavy weight, 22 and not to exceed 28 pounds and a class for Toys, weighing under 12 pounds, has been added. The Boston Terrier dog was never intended, in the writer's estimation, to be a dog to be carried in one's pocket, but such an one as the standard calls for, and which the oldest breeders have persistently and consistently bred. To my mind the ideal dog is one weighing from 15 pounds for my lady's parlor, to 20 to 25 pounds for the dog intended as a man's companion, suitable to tackle any kind of vermin, and to be an ideal watch dog in the house should any knights of the dark lantern make their nocturnal calls.

During the past few years we have had (in common, I suppose, with all large breeders), a great many orders for first class dogs, typical in every respect, weighing from 30 to 40 pounds. The constant tendency among men of wealth today is to move from city onto country estates, where they stay the greater part of the year, and in many cases all the time. They are looking for first class watch dogs that can be kept in the house or stable, that are thoroughly reliable, that do not bring too much mud in on their coats, that do not cover the furniture with long hairs, that are vigorous enough to follow on a horseback ride, and which will not wander from home. I was in the company of a party of gentlemen the other day who had bought a number of estates in a town twenty miles from Boston, and the subject of a suitable breed of dogs for their residences was under discussion. All the fashionable breeds were gone over, some were objected to because they barked too much, others because of their propensity to rush out at teams; some that their coats were too long and they brought a great deal of mud, etc., in, and still others that their fighting disposition was too pronounced, but they all agreed that a good-sized, vigorous, good natured Boston Terrier just about filled the bill. Said the nephew of Senator Henry Cabot Lodge to me last week: "Edward, I want a Boston big enough to take care of himself if anything happens, and of me also, if necessary, weighing about 35 pounds." A Boston banker, who has a large place in the country, would not take two dogs weighing under 35 pounds. Last week I received a letter from a Mr. W.B. Bogert, of the firm of Bogert, Maltby & Co., commission grain merchants, Chicago, ordering a "very heavy weight dog of kindly disposition and good blood. I can get out here any number of light weight dogs, but I do not like them. Kindly send me what you

In the show ring, the trend was toward smaller dogs. Many pet owners, however, preferred larger dogs, often in the 35 to 40 lb. range.

think will suit me." These are only a few sample cases, and I can say that my orders today call for more first class heavy weight dogs than for any other size. This is, of course, a comparatively new feature, but all up to date breeders will see the necessity of being able to fill this class of orders.

This grainy photo shows **Moody's Play Boy,** *born in 1925, bred by Jacob Cohen. This dark seal brindle dog, weighing in at 15 1/2 lbs. was first owned by Fred W. Heinzer and later sold to William Sullivan, Cincinnati, OH.*

The small sized toys will always be in demand, as they make ideal little pets, suitable eminently for a city flat or apartment house, to be carried by the lady in her carriage, or to accompany her in her walks, and they make first rate playmates for children. This class is by far the hardest to breed. For best results mate a bitch weighing about fifteen pounds, that comes from a numerous litter, to a twelve pound dog that comes from small ancestry. Some of the pups are bound to be small. One important feature in the production of small pups is this: Bitches that whelp in the fall, the smallest pups are raised from, especially if the pups are fed a somewhat restricted diet, whereas pups that are raised in the spring, that are generously fed, and have rigorous exercise in the sunshine, attain a far greater size. A great many breeders underfeed their young stock to stop growth, which I believe to be a grave mistake. There is no question whatever it accomplishes the result wished, but at the expense of stamina and a fine, generous disposition.

A posed shot of **Shenandoah Pal,** *a 14 1/2 lb. dog, owned by Mrs. William Irwin, Winchester, VA.*

A dark old photo of **Ch. Forsythe's Velvet.** *It is said that this photo did not do the dog justice. A successful show dog, Velvet went Best Puppy in Show at his very first outing and went on to complete his championship in four shows. A seal brindle, this dog was owned by F.F. Forsythe, Stoughton, MA.*

The pups from stock advanced in years, or from bitches excessively fat are very apt to run small, as are also the offspring of inbred parents. One very important fact in regard to breeding for large sized dogs to be considered is this: While a great many breeders always select for the production of large pups, large bitches and dogs, yet experi-

A lovely headstudy of **Shenandoah Pal.**

ence has proven that the majority of big ones have been the offspring of medium sized dams that were bred to strong, heavy-boned dogs of substance. I bred a bitch weighing twenty pounds to a large bull terrier that weighed forty-five pounds for an experiment, and the pups, five in number, weighed at maturity from thirty-five to forty pounds, with noses and tails nearly as long as the sire's, and his color, but were very nice in disposition, and were given away for stable dogs. Progressive up-to-date kennel men will see that they have on hand not only the three classes called for by the standard, but the fourth class, so to speak, that I have mentioned above, those weighing anywhere from thirty to forty pounds. Quite a number of breeders in the past have put in the kennel pail at birth extra large pups that they thought would mature too large to sell, but they need do so no longer. This precaution must always be taken where there are one or two of these large size puppies, viz., to look out that they do not get more than their proportionate share of the milk, or later the food, as they are very apt to crowd out the others.

Remember that the Boston Terrier of whatever size will always hold his own as a companion, a dog that can be talked to and caressed, for between the dog and his owner will always be found a bond of affection and sympathetic understanding.

Morgan Dennis illustration

Chapter 13

Breeding for Color and Markings
by Edward Axtell

Every one who has a Boston Terrier for sale knows that a handsome seal or mahogany brindle with correct markings, with plenty of luster in the coat, provided all other things are equal, sells more readily at a far higher price than any other. When one considers the number of points given in the standard for this particular feature, and the very important factor it occupies in the sale of the dog, too much attention cannot be given by breeders for the attainment of this desideratum. I am, of course, thoroughly in sympathy with the absolute justice that should always prevail in the show ring in the consideration of the place color and markings occupy in scoring a candidate for awards. Twelve points are allowed in the standard for these, and any dog, I care not whether it be "black, white, gray, or grizzled," that scored thirteen points over the most perfectly marked dog, should be awarded the prize. But be it ever remembered that the show ring and the selling of a dog are two separate and distinct propositions. In the writer's opinion and experience a wide gulf opens up between a perfect white or black dog comporting absolutely to the standard, and one of desirable color and markings that is off a number of points. I have always found a white, black, mouse, or liver-colored dog, I care not how good in other respect, almost impossible to get rid of at any decent price. People simply would not take them. Perhaps my experience has run counter to others. I trust it may have done so, but candor compels me to make this statement.

I find this condition of things is somewhat misleading, especially to beginners in the breed. They have seen the awards made in the shows (with absolute justice, as already stated), and have naturally inferred that in consequence of this, breeding for desirable colors was not of paramount importance after all. Only a month or two ago an article appeared in a charming little dog magazine, written evidently by an amateur, on this question of color and markings. He had visited the Boston Terrier Club show last November, and speaking of seal brindles, said: "If this color is so very desirable it seems strange that so few were seen, and that so many of the leading terriers were black and white, and some white entirely," then follows his deduction, viz., "the tendency evidently is that color is immaterial with the best judges, so that a breeder is foolish to waste his time on side issues which are not material." I can only state in passing that if he had a number of dogs on hand that were of the colors he specifies, "black and white, and some white entirely," it would doubtless "seem strange" to him why they persisted in remaining on his hands as if he had given each one an extra bath in Le Page's liquid glue. Pitfalls beset the path of the beginner and this book is written largely to avoid them. When one reads or hears the statement made that color and markings are of sec-

Druid Merk *was a rich mahogany brindle, Dr. Mott says that this is "one of the strains that threw true to type."*

Ch. Druid Vixen, *one of the best of the Druids.*

ondary consideration or even less, take warning. The reader's pardon will now have to be craved for the apparent egotism evidenced by the writer in speaking of himself in a way that only indirectly concerns canine matters, but which has a bearing on this very important question of color, and partially, at least, explains why this feature of the breeding of the Boston Terrier has appealed to him so prominently. My father was a wholesale merchant in straw goods, and had extensive dye works and bleacheries where the straw, silk and cotton braids were colored. As a youngster I used to take great delight in watching the dyers and bleachers preparing their different colors and shades, etc., and was anxious to see the results obtained by the different chemical combinations. When a young man, while studying animal physiology under the direction of the eminent scientist, Professor Huxley, whose diploma I value most highly, I made a number of extended scientific experiments in color breeding in poultry and rabbits, so that when I took up breeding Boston Terriers later in life this feature particularly attracted me. I was "predisposed," as a physician says of a case where the infection is certain, hence I offer no apology whatever for the assertion that this chapter is scientifically correct in the rules laid down for the breeding to attain desirable shades and markings.

When we first commenced breeding Bostons in 1885, the prevailing shades were a rather light golden brindle (often a yellow), and mahogany brindles, and quite a considerable number had a great deal of white. Then three shades were debarred, viz., black, mouse and liver, and although years after the Boston Terrier Club removed this embargo, they still remain very undesirable colors.

The rich mahogany brindle next became the fashionable color (and personally I consider it the most beautiful shade), and Mr. A. Goode with Champion "Monte" and Mr. Rawson with the beautiful pair, "Druid Merke" and "Vixen," set the pace and every one followed. A few years later Messrs. Phelps and Davis (who, with the above mentioned gentlemen, were true friends of the breed), sold a handsome pair of seal brindles, Chs. "Commissioner II." and "Topsy," to Mr. Bordon of New York, and confirmed, if not established, the fashion for that color in that city. I think that all people will agree, from all parts of the country, that New York sets the style for practically everything, from my lady's headgear to the pattern of her equipages, and the edict from that city

Tryon Kennels

The 12 1/2 lb. **Ch. Lento's Handsome Boy,** *owned by Tryon Kennels, was the sire of champions and winners. He was responsible for reducing size in his litters.*

One of the Tryon bitches, **Ch. Vallery Belle.**

Ch. Tryon's Doreen *was one of Mrs. Tryon's homebreds.*

A very grainy photo of the elegant breeder and judge Mrs. F.M. Tryon, of Hollywood, CA. In the early days, she was one of the few West Coast breeders. She bred and owned a number of champions.

Sons of Ch. Lento's Handsome Boy were much in demand on the West Coast. On the left is his smallest son, 9 1/2 lb. **Brewer's Marionette.** *The headstudy is of* **Sunny Boy Beck.** *This frequently used sire was owned by Mrs. S.A. Beck, of San Francisco, CA.*

has decreed that the correct color in Boston Terriers is a rich seal brindle, with white markings, with plenty of luster to it, and all sections of the continent promptly say amen!

I have taken the pains to look up a number of orders that we have recently received, which include (not enumerating those received from the New England states, or New York), three from Portland, Oregon, one from California, one from St. Louis, one from Mexico, four from Canada, two from Chicago, and one from Texas, and with the exception of the two who wished to replace dogs brought from us ten or twelve years previously, they practically all wanted seal brindles.

These orders are nearly all from bankers and brokers, men who are supposed to be en rapport with the dictates of fashion. It goes without saying that what a public taste demands, every effort will be made to attain the same, and breeders will strive their utmost to produce this shade. Many who do not understand scientific matings to obtain these desirable colors have fallen into a very natural mistake in so doing. In regard to the mahogany brindles they say, why not breed continuously together rich mahogany sires and dams, and then we shall always have the brindles we desire. "Like produces like," is a truism often quoted, but there are exceptions, and Boston Terrier breeding furnishes an important one. A very few years of breeding this way will give a brown, solid color, without a particle of brindle, or even worse, a buckskin. If the foundation stock is a lighter brindle to start, the result will be a mouse color. The proper course to pursue is to take a golden brindle bitch that comes from a family

These are two cigarette premiums from the turn of the century. Made out of silk, these beautifully colored items are highly sought after by collectors.

noted for that shade, and mate her with a dark mahogany brindle dog that comes from an ancestry possessed of that color. The bitch from this mating can be bred to dark mahogany brindles, and the females from this last mating bred again to dark mahogany males, but now a change is necessary. The maxim, "twice in and once out," applies here. The last bred bitches should be bred this time to a golden brindle dog, and same process repeated, that is, the bitches from this last union and their daughters can be bred to dark mahogany brindle dogs, when the golden brindle sire comes in play again. This can be repeated indefinitely. A rule in color breeding to be observed is this: that the male largely influences the color of the pups. If darker colors are desired, use a darker male than the female. If lighter shades are desired, use a lighter colored male.

If a tiger brindle is wanted, take a gray brindle bitch and mate to a dark mahogany dog. Steel and gray brindles are in so little demand and are so easy to produce that we shall not notice them.

In regard to seal brindles. A great many breeders who do not understand proper breeding to obtain them have fallen into the same pit as the others. In their desire to obtain the dark seal brindles they have mated very dark dogs to equally dark bitches, which has resulted in a few generations in producing dogs absolutely black in color, with coats that look as if they had been steeped in a pail of ink. A visit to any of the leading shows of late will reveal the fact that quite a number of candidates for bench honors are not real brindle, except possibly on the under side of the body, or perchance a slight shading on the legs. A considerable number are perfectly black, and are called by courtesy black brindles. As we call the ace of spades by the same name. A serious feature in connection with this is, that the longer this line of breeding is persisted in, the harder will be the task to breed away. In fact, in my estimation it will be as difficult as the elimination of white. One important fact in connection here is that black color is more pronounced from white stock than from brindle. I recently went into the kennels of a man who has started a comparatively short time ago, and who has been most energetic in his endeavors to produce a line of dark seal brindles, and who is much perplexed because he has a lot of stock on hand, while first rate in every other respect, are with coats as black as crows and not worth ten dollars apiece. He seemed very much surprised when I told him his mistake, but grateful to be shown a way out of his difficulty. A visit to another kennel not far from the last revealed the fact that the owner was advertising and sending largely to the West what he called black brindles, but as devoid of brindle as a frog is of feathers. His case was rather amusing, as he honestly believed that because the dog was a Boston Terrier its color of necessity must be a brindle. He reminded me a good deal of a man who started a dog store in Boston a number of years ago who advertised in his windows a Boston Terrier for sale cheap. Upon stepping in to see the dog all that presented itself to view was a dog, a cross between a Fox and Bull

"CHIEF"

Originally registered as Gyle's Little Chief, **Ch. Gyle's Ringmaster Chief** *was born in 1923 and sired by the famous Ch. Prince Conde. Chief was an outstanding show dog and he kept both his good looks and enthusiasm for the ring into his later years. At eight years of age he was still going strong and teaching the youngsters a thing or two. He was bred by M.O. Sullivan and owned by Noah E. Gyle, New York City.*

WINNA KENNELS, REG.

Mrs. William Wiechering owned a large kennel in Cincinnati, OH. Her ads appeared in dog magazines in the 1920s. This 14 lb. dog, *Invincible King, Jr.*, was one of her stud dogs.

Greatest King was billed as siring "more winning pups in 1924 than any two dogs of his breed living." This 17 lb. dog was sired by Sigourney King.

A dog that Mrs. Wiechering was showing in the late 1920s, *The Flash*.

Terrier. When the man was told of this, he made this amusing reply: "The dog was born in Boston, and he is a terrier. Why is he not a Boston Terrier?" Upon telling him that according to his reasoning if the dog had been born in New York City he would be a New York terrier he smiled. Fortunately, I had "Druid Pero" with me and said: "Here is a dog bred in my kennels at Cliftondale, Mass., that was a first prize winner at the last New York show, and yet he is a Boston Terrier." After looking Pero carefully over he exclaimed: "Well, by gosh, they don't look much like brothers, but I guess some greenhorn will come along who will give me twenty-five dollars for him," and on inquiring a little later was told that the green gentleman had called and bought the dog.

How to breed the dogs so that the brindle will not become too dark, with the bright reddish sheen that sparkles in the sun, is the important question, and I am surprised at the ignorance displayed by kennel men that one would naturally suppose would have made the necessary scientific experiments to obtain that desired shading. Only a short time ago a doctor, a friend of mine, told me he had just started a kennel of Bostons, buying several bitches at a bargain on account of their being black in color, and that he proposed breeding them to a white dog to get puppies of a desirable brindle. He seemed quite surprised when told the only shades he could reasonably expect would be black, white and splashed, all equally undesirable.

The system adopted in our kennels some years ago to obtain seal brindles with correct markings and the desirable luster and reddish sheen to the coat is as follows:

We take a rich red, or light mahogany bitch, with perfect markings, that comes from a family noted for the brilliancy of their color, and without white in the pedigrees for a number of generations, and mate her always to a dark seal brindle dog with an ancestry back of him noted for the same color. The pups from these matings will come practically seventy-five percent medium seal brindles. We now take the females that approximate the nearest in shade to their mother, and mate them to a dark seal brindle dog always. The bitches that are the result of this union are always bred to a dark seal brindle dog. The females that come from the last union are bred to a medium seal brindle dog, but now comes the time to introduce a mahogany brindle dog as a sire next time, for if these last bitches were mated to a seal brindle dog a large percent of the pups would come too dark or even black. This system is used indefinitely and desirable seal brindles with white markings can thus be always obtained. To the best of my recollection we have had but one black dog in twenty years. We have demonstrated, we trust, so that all may understand how golden, mahogany, and seal brindles are obtained, and how they may be bred for all time without losing the brindle so essential, and we now pass on to the consideration of a far harder problem, the obtaining of the rich seal brindles from all undesirable colors, and we present to all interested in this important, and practically unknown and misunderstood, problem the result of a number of years extended and scientific experiments which, we confess, were disheartening and unproductive for a long time, but which ultimately resulted in success, the following rules to be observed, known as "The St. Botolph Color Chart."

In presenting this we are fully aware that as far as we know this is the only scientific system evolved up to this date, also that there are a number of breeders of the American dog who maintain that this is an absolute impossibility, that breeding for color is as absurd as it is impractical, but we can assure these honest doubters that we have blazed a trail, and all they now have to do is simply to follow instructions and success will crown their efforts.

We will enumerate the following colors in the order of their resistance, so to speak:

No. 1. White. This color, theoretically, a combination of red, green and violet will be found the hardest to eliminate, as the shade desired will have to be worked in, so to speak, and it will take several generations before a seal brindle with perfect markings that can be depended upon to always reproduce itself can be obtained. Starting with a white bitch (always remember that the shades desired must be possessed by the dog), we breed her always to a golden brindle dog. The bitches (those most resembling the sire in color being selected) from these two are mated to a dark mahogany brindle dog, and the females from this last union are mated to a dark seal brindle dog. It will readily be observed that we have bred into the white color, golden, mahogany and seal brindle and this admixture of color will give practically over ninety percent of desirable brindles. Always see that the sires used are perfectly marked, from ancestry possessing the same correct markings. This is absolutely imperative, where the stock to be improved is worked upon is white.

No. 2. Black. This color is the opposite of white, inasmuch as there is an excess of pigment, which in this case will have to be worked out. Breed the black bitch to a red brindle dog (with the same conditions regarding his ancestry). The females from these matings bred always to a dark mahogany brindle dog. The females from the last matings breed to a medium seal brindle dog with a very glossy coat, and the result of these last matings will be good seal brindles. If any bitches should occasionally come black, breed always to a golden brindle dog. No other shade will do the trick.

No. 3. Gray Brindle. This is practically a dead color, but easy to work out. Breed first to a golden brindle dog. The females from this union

This grainy photo is of **Ch. Moran's Ohio Boy,** *who finished his championship at a Cincinnati Specialty. He was owned by Mr. & Mrs. Charles Moran, Just-Rite Kennels, Cleveland, OH.*

breed to a rich mahogany brindle, and the bitches from this last litter breed to a seal brindle dog.

No. 4. Buckskin. Breed bitch to golden brindle dog; the females from this union to a red brindle dog (if unobtainable, use mahogany brindle dog, but this is not so effective), and the females from this last union breed to a seal brindle dog.

No. 5. Liver. This is a great deal like the last, but a little harder to manipulate. Breed first to a golden brindle dog. The females from this union breed to a seal brindle. The bitches from this union breed to mahogany brindle dog with black bars running through the coat, and the females from last mating breed to seal brindles.

No. 6. Mouse color. Use same process as for gray brindles.

No. 7. Yellow. A very undesirable shade, but easy to eliminate. Breed to mahogany brindle dog as dark as can be obtained, and bitches from this mating to a seal brindle dog.

No. 8. Steel and Tiger Brindles. I class these together as the process is the same and results are easy. Breed first to a red brindle dog; bitches from this union to a dark mahogany brindle, and then use seal brindle dog on bitch from last mating.

No. 9. Red Brindle. No skill is required here. Breed first to mahogany brindles, and bitches from this union to seal brindles.

We have now enumerated practically all the less desirable shades, but let me observe in passing, in the process of color breeding that the law of atavism, or "throwing back," often asserts itself, and we shall see colors belonging to a far-off ancestry occasionally presenting themselves in all these matings. Once in a while a dog will be found that no matter what color bitches he may be mated with, he will mark a certain number of the litter with the peculiar color or markings of some remote ancestor. Just a case apropos of this will suffice. We used in our kennels a dog of perfect markings, coming from an immediate ancestry of perfectly marked dogs, and mated him with quite a number of perfectly marked bitches that we had bred for a great number of years that had before that had perfectly marked pups, and every bitch, no matter how bred, had over fifty percent of white headed pups. We saw the pups in other places sired by this dog, no matter where bred, similarly marked. We found his grandmother was a white headed dog, and this dog inherited this feature in his blood, and passed it on to posterity. The minute a stud dog, perfect in himself, is prepotent to impress upon his offspring a defect in his ancestry, discard him at once. I have often been amused to see how frequently this law of atavism is either misunderstood or ignored. Only recently I have seen a number of letters in a leading dog magazine, in which several people who apparently ought to know better, were accusing litters of bulldog pups of being of impure blood because there were one or two black pups amongst them. They must, of course, have been conversant with the fact that bulldogs years ago frequently came of that color, and failed to reason that in consequence of this, pups of that shade are liable once in a while to occur. It is always a safe rule in color breeding to discard as a stud a dog, no matter how brilliant his coat may be, who persistently sires pups whose colors are indistinct and run together, as it were.

Remember, in closing this chapter, that as "eternal vigilance is the price of liberty," so the eternal admixtures of colors is the price of rich brindles. If one has the time the works of the Austrian monk Mendel are of great interest as bearing somewhat on the subject, and the two English naturalists, Messrs. Everett and J.G. Millais, whose writings contain the result of extensive scientific experiments on dogs and game birds, are of absorbing interest also.

Chapter 14

Present Day Boston Terrier Strains

by Alva Rosenberg

It seems only logical to me that in any breed where a great degree of perfection and uniformity of type has been reached in a comparatively few years, this must in all fairness be attributed to something more than mere luck.

Take the Boston for instance—compare the evenly marked, handsomely colored and smoothly built dogs benched to-day with the many extremes in all these points we saw not so many years ago. Now the half-white, whole-white headed or splashed is a rarity at a show—then they were the rule. Surely whether they were conscious of it or not, breeders have been wise enough to follow what might be termed the lines of least resistance and have bred to dogs whose influence will be felt as long as the breed is in existence, or in other words, forever.

I shan't attempt to go back to the very early sires; in the first place, the reader has only to refer to Dr. Varnum Mott's or Edward Axtell's works on the breed and get first hand information on this score; I am not ashamed to confess my comparative youth and my knowledge of these dogs except from what I have read and heard is nil. Secondly, the blood of all these dogs have been so blended that it is difficult to find a dog who does not go back to all of them if his pedigree be traced sufficiently.

Of the modern "strains," however, and I used the word advisedly, a few stand out that have had a marked influence on the breed, each one stamping individual characteristics, faults as well as virtues on their line of descendants.

Pride of place to my mind justly belongs to the line founded by Heilborn's Raffles, a dog whose breeding might prove a shock to those whom the words "line-breeding" and "in-breeding" cause them to throw up their hands in horror, for he was the result of a union of half-brother and sister.

Raffles himself was a small dog, very appealing in head, eye and expression and teeming with quality. In color he was very dark, darker in fact than the present standard allows, and some of his descendants will be found to fail in the same respect. Surely, however, this can be condoned when we stop to consider in how many ways he proved a boon to the breed! He put "quality" in his get at a time when it was sadly needed, when type was in a chaotic state, and his very fault, color, in many cases helped modify the too prevalent washed out grey and golden brindles of the time.

His get included Champion Wampagne Prince, Croftregis, JoJo possibly the best Toy that is, under twelve pounds, ever seen and last but really most important the litter brothers, Trimount Star and Champion Dallen's Spider. Their breeding, too, might not be considered quite orthodox by some, as their dam was a white bitch! Despite that to these two dogs are the present day dogs indebted

Franz Heilborn, owner of the important dog Heilborn's Raffles, who was to have a tremendous impact on the breed. Raffles was the sire of Ch. Dallen's Spider. He helped moved the breed from the bully look to the terrier type. Raffles was a pivotal dog in the breed.

The founder of one of the modern Boston strains, the 15 lb. Heilborn's Raffles. He was smaller than most of the dogs which preceded him and was said to have been of tremendous quality, particularly in regard to head type. Those who saw him say that he could have easily won his championship, but he was very dark, almost black, in color and this was not permitted under the standard of the day. He was a prepotent dog who stamped his get with his type.

and I can't really think of a prominent winner today who does not trace back to one or both of them.

Trimount Star proved a most prepotent sire, getting such dogs as Champion Trimount Vic, Champion Dallen's Surprise, Champion Trimount Countess and Champion Trimount Lida. Others by him were Trimount Bantam, Auburn Ravello, Evergreen Progenitor and Monte Carlo Star; possibly there were many others equally worthy of mention but their names do not occur to me now.

Champion Trimount Vic was never exploited as a stud dog by his owner but what few of his get I saw were well up to standard and I feel sure that had he been used more he would have sired something of note.

Champion Dallen's Surprise sired Champion Grossi's Tansy and Aristocrat II.

Trimount Bantam was responsible for Champion Dallen's Sensation who in turn sired Champion Crystal Lady Sensation and Champion Brown's Lady Donna. Auburn Ravello with limited chances got Champion Ravenroyd Romance, Champion Heinlein's Dream Girl, Champion

Ch. Patsy Dee III

*A grainy photo of **Ch. Peter's Captain**, an important dog who sired several champions. He was owned by Corbett & Hudson, Watch City Kennels, Waltham, MA.*

The Ringmaster Bostons

The Ringmaster dogs were to become very successful in both the show ring and the whelping box. Their achievements would go on beyond the 1920s, the final date addressed in this book. Few pictures of the early Ringmasters appeared in dog magazines and publications of the time.

Patsy Ringmaster *was a successful stud dog. He is best known as the sire of Tiny Ringmaster, who went on to produce many top winning and producing champions. Patsy was owned by J.A. Hasson, Hasson Kennels, Cleveland, OH.*

The Ringmasters constituted a true strain in the breed. It all began with a dog formally registered as Sport IV, but known as "Ringmaster." Dogs from this line proved quite successful in the show ring. This is **Tony Ringmaster,** *a grandson of old Ringmaster. He was not shown because of his color. He was a very dark seal brindle, almost black, which was not allowed under early standards. He did prove to be a good producer and was the grandsire of champions.*

(On the left) **Ch. Todd Boy** *was a son of the famed old Ringmaster. A successful show dog, Todd was Winners Dog at the 1908 National Specialty. He was sold to a West Coast owner and, unfortunately, was little used at stud. He did, however, sire one champion and a number of winners.*

Alva Rosenberg poses with Canadian judge Walter H. Reeves. Born in 1892, Rosenberg fell in love with Bostons as an eight-year-old. He saw a notice of a dog show in the paper and talked his parents into taking him from their home in Brooklyn to Westminster. He fell in love with a Boston bitch priced at $800. This clearly did not fit in the family budget. On the last day of the show, father and son returned to see if the dog had sold. It was still there and they offered $300, but they were refused. Alva swore that he would get a Boston and eventually he did. In fact, he became one of the country's premier breeders and his Ravenroyd dogs were much in demand. He was to become famous as a judge. He was only 18 when he judged his first show, but he went on to join that elite group of "all-rounders." In 1946, '47 and '48, he was voted Dog Judge of the Year.

Dolly Grand and Champion Tryon's Rejoice; he also sired Donderos Freckles, the sire of Champion Arroyo Arbitrator.

Evergreen Progenitor has to his credit Champion Evergreen Evelyn III, Champion Some Boy and Evergreen Perfection possibly the best of the three; she died before attaining the championship that undoubtedly would have been hers.

Another son of Trimount Star's was Manilla Boy, the sire of Phoebe Prim, and Hanley's Cracker Boy, who sired Champion Dallen's Stutz and King Cracker Boy, one of our good present day sires.

Champion Dallen's Spider, too, proved not only a formidable ring general but a potent sire as well. He sired Champion Coastguard, Champion Boylston Prince III and, following his own sire's footsteps, a pair of famous litter brothers, Champion Trimount Roman and Champion Peter's King, although to the latter must go the greater part of the glory. The first three dogs for some reason or other never distinguished themselves in the stud, but the vast amount of good Champion Peter's King has done the breed more than makes up for their failure. "Failure" is rather a harsh word for it is very likely that they did not have opportunities to prove themselves.

A word about Champion Peter's King himself may not be in apropos before we start into what he accomplished as a sire. While Champion Trimount Roman was perfectly marked, or at least, evenly marked, Peter's King had the blot on his escutcheon of that bug-bear—half white head. When he first started to win, and win he had to in spite of his fault, for his conformation was excellent, his head the last word and he had quality to spare, some of the old breeders and many of the new ones threw up their hands in horror and vowed that putting to the top a dog so mismarked was bound to reflect on the future of the breed. It did—but not in the way they anticipated. How he practically revolutionized the breed and helped to a great degree to bring it to its present state of perfection is now history. Even as a show dog I always preferred King to Roman. Both were good in head, Roman, if anything, a bit "stronger," but King had ideal proportion of muzzle and skull and

Ravenroyd Kennels, Reg.

Ch. Ravenroyd Rounder *earned his championship in very tough competition. He took a five point Specialty win. Owned by Mr. & Mrs. D. D. Hart, Wood Vine Kennels, Reg., Los Angeles, CA.*

Born in 1925, the 25 lb. Am. & Can. Ch. Ravenroyd Rockefeller *was considered the best fronted Boston of his day. This mahogany brindle son of Ch. Million Dollar Kid sired seven champions. He was Best of Breed at the 1927 Westminster. Originally owned by Ravenroyd, he was later sold to E.H. Morse, Flint, MI*

Eisenhardt's Ravenroyd Righto *was a 14 lb. pointed dog who sired a number of winners. Owned by Mrs. George A. Eisenhardt, Cleveland, OH.*

Ravenroyd Reflection

Ch. Ravenroyd Radio *was one of the studs at Alva Rosenberg's Ravenroyd Kennels.*

The 16 lb. Ch. Rockefeller's Ace *was a son of Am. & Can. Ch. Ravenroyd Rockefeller. He was BB at Morris & Essex. Owned by W.C. Ely, Jr., Zionsville, PA.*

13 lb. Ch. Rockefeller's Progress *won three Specialties.*

The dark seal brindle **Ch. Katz's King,** *was one of the best sons of Ch. Haggerty's King. Born in 1924, King was one of the most successful show dogs of his period. This 16 1/2 lb. Group winner was Best of Winners at the 1926 Chicago Specialty and Best of Breed at the 1926 New York Specialty. He was bred by M. Gottleib and owned by Jacob Katz, Brooklyn, NY.*

Though never a champion himself, **Sigourney King** *proved to be one of the most influential stud dogs of all time. He sired six champions and was owned by Omar J. Ouellet.*

a smoothness about it that is characteristic of the strain at its best. In color Roman was a seal brindle and King a rich dark mahogany brindle. To be hypercritical King might have been just a shade closer coupled and his tail was placed a bit high to suit the ultra-critical, but he had quality and style galore.

His list of winning get reads like a page from Burke's Peerage and those that I readily recall are Champion Peter's Captain and Champion Lady Belle XVII, who were never to my knowledge ever defeated as a brace. Champion Midget King, Champion Rose Home King's Pal, Champion Joyce's Prince, Champion Queenie King, Champion Million Dollar Kid. Also Suntaug King, Bantam King, Hawke's Peter and Lillis Tip, a litter brother to Champion Peter's Captain. Strange to say, he too had a half white head, but he proved a better sire than his brother, thus bearing out the old adage that "history repeats itself."

Champion Peter's Captain sired Champion Captain's Kinsman and Woodward Captain, who is fast making a name for himself as sire, getting Champion Ramsey's Rock-a-Bye Baby and Ravenroyd Rounder, who is well on his way to championship. Champion Midget King and Champion King's Pal went west and I am not well up on their list of get, though I am sure that neither ever sired a champion. Champion Joyce's Prince went to Canada and the pups of the Million Dollar Kid are just coming out, what I have seen of them leads me to believe that he will prove himself a good sire.

Suntaug King sired Champion District Queen, dam of Champion District Boss and also sired one of New England's leading stud forces, Sigourney King. Sigourney King's get include such celebrities as Champion Vallery Belle and our latest champion, Patsy Dee, and it is difficult to find a show where some of his get are not well up in the ribbons.

Bantam King, too, proved a great stud force in getting Rattler King, Champion Rattler King II, and Keene Play Boy, who lacked but one point to championship, I believe.

Lillis Tip sired Champion Count Dee Cee and Ravenroyd Revelation, who is well on her way to championship. Count Dee Cee sired District Leader and O'Pal Midget, said to be the best young dog in Canada. District Leader is one of the leading lights in Philadelphia and has proven his mettle by siring Champion District Boss and Champion Swainson's May-Be.

Hawke's Peter, I have been told by several people, could, if he had been shown, have made his championship with ease. He was little used at stud, too, but one of his sons, Champion Mosholu Blink, has indeed "carried on" and has sired Champion Mosholu Buddy Blink, Champion Mosholu Beau, Champion Crystal Perfect Lady, Mosholu Bunkio, Ravenroyd Right o' Way, Beau Blink and Shields' Girl, all more than half way to their championship. Needless to say, Champion Mosholu Blink is regarded as one of the mainstays by the metropolitan fanciers.

Reign Count Kennels

Mrs. L. B. Daley owned the Reign Count Kennels, located in Wyandotte and Detroit, MI. An enthusiastic Boston fan, she owned nine champions. Her breeding program was in full swing when she was tragically killed in an auto accident in 1934.

Mrs. Daley took her kennel name from this dog, **Ch. Reign Count.** *It gave her instant visibility for this dog was very well known. The 10 1/2 lb. Count was a highly acclaimed show winner. His greatest victory came when he topped the Group at Westminster, in 1929.*

The dark mahogany brindle **Ch. Daley's Detroit News** *finished his championship at 13 months of age in the stiffest competition. This son of Int'l. Ch. Jab's King Tut was Best of Winners at both the Western Pennsylvania and National Specialities. It was as a special that he earned his greatest fame. He topped the Chicago Specialty, over an entry of 122, and was a multiple Best in Show winner.*

The 12 1/2 lb. **Int'l. Ch. Jab's King Tut** *was both a successful show dog and sire. He was a special favorite of Mrs. Daley and a real crowd pleaser. Those who saw him described him as a very lively and animated dog, who loved the show ring. He was the sire of several champions.*

Woodward Captain, *born in 1919, was said to be the greatest stud dog of his time. The 15 1/2 lb. dog, bred by L. Neumann, was the sire of 10 champions. What's more important, many of these followed in their sire's footsteps and proved to be notable producers themselves. He was owned by Frank Cariato, Stroller Kennels, New York City.*

The "Ringmaster" strain, so called as it traced from a dog registered as "Sport IV," but familiarly known as "Ringmaster," too, must be counted as one of principle lines of breeding and in popularity it runs the "Raffles" strain a close race; a combination of the two has produced many winners.

Notable for its extra strong heads with wide and deep muzzles, prominent dark eyes, sometimes a bit too prominent, in fact, and rich mahogany and seal brindles. It is singular but true that dogs of this strain that are short and extra strong in head sometimes run a little longer in tail than is desirable to some fanciers, but to my mind a line of breeding that can stamp the heads, fine limbs and attractive color and markings that is characteristic of it can well be pardoned if it also occasionally slips up in one point, which I have never believed is as grievous a fault as some would lead us to believe.

Old Ringmaster himself was an extra strong headed and big eyed dog, in fact exaggerated in these points; but the weak headed and small eyed bitches that were so prevalent those days just nicked with him and some "real ones" resulted. One son, Champion Todd Boy, was a rather unappealing little chap at first glance as he had just head markings but a hard one to fault seriously, save perhaps a little tendency toward legginess. He sired a number of western winners including Champion Osage Brambaletta, who was good enough to measure up to any of our eastern bitches of her time.

Ringleader was another son of Ringmaster; he was a good winner himself, well worthy of championship, although he never attained it, and sired Champion Dallen's Sport, Champion Lady Ringleader and Sister Lottie, who died before she won her final three points.

Champion Dallen's Sport sired Champion Lady Leonora, winner of the Davis Trophy for best dog or bitch at the specialty show a year ago.

A third whose influence has been great was Billy Ringmaster, a flashily marked chap who sired Champion Tony Ringmaster. Tony then sired his own duplicate in Cunningham's Ringmaster who lacked but one point of championship which he unfortunately never attained as an altercation with a cat marked his eye so badly that his show career had to be abruptly terminated. Tony Ringmaster also sired Watch City Victree who deserves a niche in canine Hall of Fame as the mother of Champion Ace of Aces and Champion Wadman's Cutie.

Another son of Billy Ringmaster was Bud B., a high quality little fellow who in turn sired Champion Dallen's Soubrette.

It is to a due of Billy Ringmaster's, however, that most of the credit for perpetuating this strain must go, Hair's Bessie Ringmaster, for she produced the famous Patsy Ringmaster.

In show dogs Patsy Ringmaster sired Champion Arroyo Anzac and Champion Arroyo Anarchist, a dog who, through one of his sons, in fact, two of them, Intruder and Tiny Ringmaster, will remain green in the memory of fanciers for years to come.

Tiny Ringmaster was no show dog, to he sure, but he proved a great sire, getting Champion Lady Harmless, Champion Haggerty's King and the full brothers, Champion Thorpe's Tiny King and Champion Tiny Teddy B.

Champion Haggerty's King sired Champion Tomlinson's Beauty and Champion Trimount King.

Intruder needs no introduction for he won special after special for best stud dog and his get. Small wonder when they include Champion Ace of Aces, Champion Headquarters Sergeant and Champion Arroyo Aztec, also Little Batice who was a big winner until she hurt her eye.

Chapter 15

Early Boston Terriers in Canada

by C. L. Mac Quillan

As far as I can trace the first Boston Terriers to be imported into Canada was about the year 1899 or 1900. These two were purchased, by Mr. Lew Thomas of Toronto, from Mr. Geo. S. Thomas of Hamilton, Mass. These gentlemen were no known relation to each other, but no doubt in the long ago they came from the same stock as they are both infected with the dog fever, which as we all know is a life malady.

The two Bostons were Tot and Stella. Of Tot we have no further record, but Stella was sent back across the line to be bred to one of the prominent stud dogs of the time and produced three puppies, two of which died young. The third was registered as Homewood Beauty. The pleasure and sport Mr. Lew Thomas got out of this bitch well repaid him for the expense and trouble in producing, raising and showing her, as she was shown at Boston, New York and the Pan-American in Buffalo, winning a first prize at each of these shows. This was a splendid start for the Canadian-bred Bostons.

About the year 1902 Mr. Lew Thomas sold Homewood Beauty to Mr. Geo. S. Thomas at Cincinnati, Ohio.

It was no doubt one of the three above mentioned Boston Terriers that the writer saw in Thomas's English chop house on King Street, West Toronto, and was attracted greatly by the screw tail, rich dark brindle and white markings, for the dog or bitch I saw at that time had all these distinguishing features of the present day Boston, just how they compared as to head and other qualities I could not say. Now, of course, there may have been Bostons in other parts of Canada during the years mentioned above; if so they did not appear at any of the shows. As a matter of fact there were very few shows outside of Toronto at that time.

After selling Homewood Beauty, Mr. Lew Thomas does not seem to have done any further showing of Bostons but reverted back to his old love, the Irish Terrier, and for the next three or four years there was nothing much doing in Bostons in Canada or Toronto. The latter city being headquarters for Bostons in Canada, but not the whole works.

About the year 1907 they began to come strong. Mr. Goebel, a jeweler, of Mitchell, Ont., imported a dog called Othello and a bitch which he named Goebel's Tess. Mr. Goebel did not stick very long, and during the year 1908 sold the two above mentioned dogs to Dr. D.C. King of Peterboro Ont. Dr. King already owned a very handsome high quality bitch, named Miss Fritz, which bitch carried off winners at the first Annual Specialty Show given by the Boston Terrier Club of Canada, on January 1st, 1909. During the years 1906, 1907 and 1908 there were a large number of Bostons imported into Canada, and the breeding became general, particularly in Toronto. Mr. J.A. Meadows being the principle importer, bringing over four stud dogs in a very short time, namely, Lord Nelson, Max Boy, Bad Boy and Combustion. Max Boy was the first Canadian Champion of record with his kennel mate, Champion Blue Bell, as first Canadian champion bitch. Mr. Meadows, who now resides in Oakville, Ont., is still going strong in Bostons and as a supporter of the shows.

Mr. T. Frank Slattery of Toronto also imported a dog called Banquo. Of the five above mentioned stud dogs Bad Boy left his mark more than any of the others with Combustion second and Banquo third. Banquo was not used much at stud but produced a dog called Bungo; this dog was bred and owned by Captain Geo. Henderson of the Toronto Fire Department and was used at stud for about ten years. Bungo did not produce any champions but his get could usually be depended upon to produce high class stock.

A great number of our present day winners can be traced to the three above mentioned dogs.

The writer's first purchase of a Boston Terrier was from Mr. A.E. Dowson; this was a bitch puppy by Bad Boy out of Bedelia, she by Champion Nugget. This puppy which I named Daisy M. proved to be a splendid brood bitch and is also ancestor to a great number of the present day winners. I also imported a 14 lb. stud dog called Happy Day by Squantum Criterion in the early part of 1908 or the latter part of 1907. This little dog proved to be a splendid producer, being awarded 1st prize for best stud dog with two of his get at five successive shows. Needless to say he was also progenitor of a large number of our present day winners. During 1908 Dr. R.S. Richardson of Toronto imported Wahnetah's Peter Pan, having purchased him from his breeder, V.E. Haywood of Buffalo, N.Y. Peter Pan proved to be one of the biggest winning Bostons ever shown in Canada. The only chance any other dog had to get winners was if Peter Pan was not there and wherever there was a show there was Peter Pan. After having won three or four championships he was retired on his laurels and lived happy ever after.

Peter Pan had the honor of taking winners dogs at the first Annual Show given by the Boston Terrier Club of Canada, January 1st, 1909. As a producer he proved a dud and never figured in very many pedigrees. During his show career the principal contenders for winners honors were the Canadian-bred Ted Shongo, bred by G.A. Beaumont and owned by W.A. Little; Lord Bell Rock, imported and owned by Gordon Smith, and Tom Boy, a son of Bad Boy, bred and owned by the late M.A. Smith, all of Toronto. The first two eventually won their championship and Tom Boy was well away. Had he been persistently shown would no doubt have been awarded this title.

Ted Shongo was, I believe, the first male Canadian-bred Boston Terrier to make a championship. He was a 13 lb. dog of extreme terrier type, very clean and trappy, and full of vim. His expression was brilliant and his markings just about ideal; in color he was a golden brindle. Although a frail puppy, Ted lived to be about thirteen years of age. He was always a prolific stock dog and his name is close up in the pedigrees of some of our most prominent dogs to-day. The other two dogs mentioned above were also good producers and left some high class breeding stock.

About 1912 Mr. W.G. Parker of Sarnia, Ont. produced the beautiful bitch, Sparkling Jewel, selling her as a puppy to Messrs. Ben Lewis and Chas. Mason. This bitch started right out to win and it was not long before she was an international champion.

After selling Jewel Mr. Parker went right back and produced Sparkling Beauty, same breeding, but a litter later. At the January 1st, 1914, Specialty Show, with John Dietschler as judge, Beauty cleaned up the works, she had everything up her sleeve, puppy, novice, Canadian-bred, limit, open, breeders, best lightweight, best in show, either sex and a whole lot of other bests.

Beauty took away a truck load of prizes at this show, or rather her owner did. Up to and including this show we had always had a good entry from the U. S. and particularly from Buffalo. But from 1914 on the United States entry dropped flat. They did not seem to care for competition; when they were reasonably sure to win they were reasonably sure to come, but when there was a chance of being beaten they held aloof.

To revert back to 1912, during this year we were shy of good stud dogs. I had lost my good dog, Gordon Delhi (afterwards recovered), a full brother to Champion Wahnetah's Peter Pan, not so good a show dog but a better stud dog, and W. A Currie had lost his good young stud and show dog, Lord Roberts, by death. Lord Roberts was a son of Gordon Delhi.

These misfortunes leaving us more or less high and dry, I took a trip over to Buffalo and paid Messrs. Pleuthner & Barr a good price for the beautiful specimen, Aristocrat. There was a vary interesting but unprofitable (to me) incident connected with this dog. I brought him home two weeks before our civic holiday. On the morning of our civic holiday I found him stark cold in death, although up to the night before he was a more than ordinarily healthy dog; and the peculiar part of it was that he was curled up as though sleeping, not stretched out as they usually are. He evidently died without a gasp. The veterinary reported indigestion as the only explanation after making a postmortem examination. We were still shy on stud dogs. So Mr. G.A. Beaumont took a trip over to Buffalo, N.Y., and purchased the best stud dog we ever owned in Canada, Onadago. The history of this dog should be a very interesting one to Canadian breeders and fanciers. Personally I think he is the most important dog ever owned in Canada, from a standpoint of improving the breed, so I will endeavor to give a short sketch of his short career. Onadago was bred by J.E. Carrol of Buffalo, N.Y.; his sire was Kintore Raffles, who in turn was by Heilborn's Raffles.

Kintore Raffles has sired a number of good dogs, but Onadago was not one of them, so the fanciers who had seen him thought Mr. Carrol had given him away or sold him as a puppy to a friend but had got him back; he had been shown once or twice to fill up, and been laughed at; it was at a show in Buffalo that I first saw him, and laughed just the same as the rest. This grubby faced little mutt had nothing to recommend him. However, when Mr. Beaumont visited Mr. Carrol during the year 1912 he saw this little dog and must have seen something in him that was invisible to others because he bought him on the spot, and brought him back to Toronto. I felt kind of sorry for Beau and felt that Mr. Carrol had put one over on him, even if he did not pay much for him; he would be only taking up the room which would be better filled by a real Boston. However, Mr. Beaumont who is somewhat of a spellbinder started right in to persuade his friends to breed to him. The first one to fall under the spell was Mr. W.T. Sommerville, who bred his nice little 17 lb. bitch, Leader's Pride. The first pup born to this mating (there being two males) was a beautifully marked dark mahogany brindle, screw tailed pup which had all the ear marks of a flyer. I had seen thousands of that kind before this and have seen tens of thousands since which were flyers at birth but never again. This pup, however, was the exception and as time went by, day by day, in every way, he got better and better, and eventually proved to be, to the best of my knowledge the first Canadian-bred male Boston to make an American Kennel Club championship. His name was Champion Clifton Star and is no doubt known to a great many of the readers of this book. I will speak of him again later.

Onadago was only at stud a matter of fifteen to eighteen months in Toronto before he died. I don't think he had ever been used in Buffalo but don't know for sure. But over here, every time he served a bitch he produced a good one, and he served a lot of bitches, and as a consequence he produced a lot of good ones. Foremost among them being Champion Ingram's Little Man, Champion Clifton Star, Champion Clifton Peach, also a number of near champions, such as Lord Lovat, a puppy sold at what was then a record price by Mr. Alex. Fraser of Toronto to that prince of good sports, the late Mr. Chas. T. McKay, of Kingston, Ont. Then there was Lord Rufas, a big winner and sire of Champion Little Miss Mack, an international winner. Onadago 2nd was also a son of Onadago and has been doing his best to carry on the good work of his sire. This dog was a good specimen but was never shown—only used as a stock dog, at which work he proved a decided success, being the sire of Onadago Don, a winner at Buffalo and a number of shows in Canada, even as late as March 30th, 1923. The

The Haggerty Bostons

The Haggerty Bostons enjoyed much success during the early period covered in this book. They were to have a continued influence after the 1920s. We present only the earliest of the Haggerty dogs here.

Born in 1916, **Ch. Haggerty's King** *was a son of Tiny Ringmaster and is considered one of the pillars of the breed. He was bred by Mrs. Dan Haggerty and purchased by Mrs. George Dresser for $2,500. He remained her lifelong companion until his death at 10 years of age.*

King was a controversial dog. Many people felt that he had almost perfect conformation, the ideal blend between the bully and terrier types. He was, in fact, hailed as "Faultless King." The 14 lb. dog finished his championship quickly taking Winners Dog at Westminster in 1918. He continued to be campaigned but, at a Boston specialty, another exhibitor made a protest on the basis of color and he was disqualified. He was a black and white dog with tan tracings and, under the standard of the time, only brindle dogs were allowed. Many feel that it was due to this incident that the standard was changed to admit black without brindle.

King was the sire of five champions. The number would, undoubtedly, have been higher, but he was never used at public stud.

Haggerty's Midget

Born in 1925, **Ch. Haggerty's King Junior's Son** *was bred by F.M. Lopardie and owned by A. Droll and B. Rosenbloom, Haggerty Kennels, New York City. The Rosenbloom's were offered the sizable sum of $1,800 for the dog, but turned it down. A successful show dog, he was a multiple Group winner. He sired a number of champions, including the well-known Ch. Haggerty Again.*

Ch. Dan Haggerty *was a Best in Show winner from the classes. This son of Ch. Haggerty King, Jr. was owned by B.F. Elgin, Bakersfield, CA.*

best in two classes of puppies under 9 months and under 12 months, twenty puppies in all, the winner in both classes was Onadago 5th, by Onadago 3rd, by Onadago 2nd, by Onadago. The mother of this puppy has also several generations Canadian-bred being by the Canadian-bred Clifton Byng out of the Canadian-bred Clifton Charm. Onadago 5th also accounted for the novice class beating a number of imported dogs, also a number of dogs bred from imported stock. This little dog is owned by J.G. Holtz of Toronto and bred by A.E. Atkinson both of whom are raw amateurs.

During the years 1913 and 1914 and part of 1915, the big four held sway. Champion Ingram's Little Man, Champion Clifton Star, Champion Prince Rexworthy and Champion Clifton Peach. Champion Ingram's Little Man was bred by his owner, Mrs. W.C. Ingram, and made his championship in a very short time. Under such well known judges as Jas. Mortimer, Chas. Mason, Alex. Fraser and J.E. Carroll. Little Man is a rich dark mahogany brindle, weighing about 12 lbs., well marked, that is even head markings, white collar, white front feet and stockings and white tips on his hind feet. He is also a sturdy, vigorous little animal, and although he is nearly ten years old he is still siring puppies. This little dog had the misfortune to have one of his eyes injured shortly after he had made his championship and although he recovered somewhat he never came just right. He was shown once or twice in the United States and although he was placed in his class was too much handicapped with the bad eye to go to the top. He was never noted as a sire of large litters but could usually be depended on to deliver good goods in small quantities. His name appears in the pedigree of a very large percentage of our well known winners and he is the sire of two champions, Champion Sweet Clover and Champion Sweet William. He is still the property of his breeder.

Champion Clifton Star was bred by W.G. Somerville of Toronto. Star was purchased by me when about seven months of age, and for the next six months had a very hard time. First there was trouble with his ears, then he had distemper; recovering from this he contracted pneumonia and as a consequence was not in sight at the shows for some time. He was awarded winners at Montreal by Ben. Lewis, Sr., and at Toronto by Vinton T. Breese. During the latter part of 1914 and the beginning of 1915, Star was used extensively at stud and produced a number of large litters. His name figures prominently in the pedigree of a great many of our Canadian-bred winners, one of his get being Captain Starlight, 2nd puppy at New York, February, 1916, and selected by Mr. John Dietschler for winners January 1st, 1918, at Toronto. Star was shown for the first time in the United States by myself at the Westminster Show, on February 22nd, 1915, and was undoubtedly the sensation of that show. He was purchased by Mr. Parker of New York, the same day, and made his A.K.C. championship in a very short time, at the largest shows in and around New York. This dog was a rich dark mahogany brindle with ideal markings. Star weighed exactly seventeen pounds at the time he was purchased by Mr. Parker.

Champion Prince Rexworthy was whelped the property of Wm. Austin of Toronto, and started right out to win, at his first show, being awarded winners at the Canadian National Exhibition in September, 1914, under James Mortimer.

Prince was more of the bully type, but was a good headed, well set up little chap, full of terrier action. He was a splendid mover and poser and also proved himself a good sire. His name is close up in the pedigree of most of our big winning Canadian-bred Bostons. One of his get a bitch named Fashion Plate, being awarded reserve winners at the Specialty Show in New York in 1917. Prince was shown at the Boston Specialty Show in Boston in 1914 and was awarded 2nd prize in the puppy class and 1st in breeders' class. In 1913, in Detroit, Mich., at the Specialty Show, he was awarded winners against a strong field. This dog was a rich, dark seal brindle with wide even face markings, white front feet but no collar. He lived to be 10 years old and was always the property of Mr. Austin.

Champion Clifton Peach was bred by H. Morrell of Toronto and was a slow finisher. He was purchased by me when about twenty months of age. His first show, after he became my property was at Chicago in April, 1915. Here he was awarded 1st novice, 1st limit and open to Champion Coast Guard. These classes were large. At the Boston Specialty Show in 1915 he won 2nd in the open class to Champion Arroyo Anarchist, (Invader) at New York in 1916 and 1917 he had also the honor of winning 2nd prizes in large classes.

Peach made his C.K.C. championship at the largest shows, having the proud distinction of being awarded winners and best in show two years in succession, at Montreal also two years in succession, at Canada's largest show, the Canadian National Exhibition, Toronto, also best in show at several other shows.

This dog was a more than ordinarily beautifully colored and coated dog being a rich dark mahogany satin finished brindle, even face markings, white collar, white front teeth and stockings and white hind feet. As a sire he was first class, siring many winners and is grandsire to a number of our most prominent winners today. He passed out accidentally by the poison route at the age of six years.

About the year 1912 Mrs. W.C. Ingram sold a very nice little bitch in whelp to Oxonian's Rex, to Mrs. Wm. Wheeler of Edmonton, Alberta. Two of the puppies turned out to be of high quality and were shown at the Western Show under Dominion Kennel Club rules. The Dominion Kennel Club was a rival organization to the Canadian Kennel Club which flourished for a short time in the West but is now extinct.

The above mentioned dogs, Major Reno and Lady Reno, made their D.K.C. championships in hot competition. Champion (D.K.C.) Major Reno was the sire of C.K.C. Champion Victoria Fosco. The latter was bred and owned by Mrs. Wheeler and was a very typical specimen. Although never shown in the East, he had the distinction of beating some of our Eastern champions at the Western shows.

During the year 1912 Mr. T.E. Milburn, who, by the way, was president of the Boston Terrier Club of Canada for about fifteen years, (and is now Hon. President), imported from Boston a dog called Totem Boy. This dog was celebrated on account of being the sire of Patsy Ringmaster. Mr. Milburn and myself also imported the good bitch, Ashland Pride. Both these dogs proved to be good show dogs and had championship points to their credit. But, as a stock dog, Totem proved to be a failure after coming to Canada. Pride, however, on the contrary, proved a veritable factory. She had about 8 or 10 litters of good puppies and as a consequence proved to be a strong factor in the improving of our stock. One of her get was sold to Alex. Fraser of Toronto. Mr. Fraser registered this dog under the name of Dominent.

Dominent's name appears in the pedigree of a large percentage of our winning Bostons.

After the passing of the big four, the importing again became general. Mr. W.S. Levack, importing in quick succession Dowd's Glory Little Pete and Count Dee Cee. Mr. Gouin of Three Rivers, Quebec, imported Yankee Speed King. Mr. H.E.C. Brennan, Derby Speed; Mr. W.G. Lewis, Joyce's Prince; Mr. R. Henderson, Yankee Sensation, and Mr. J.R. Almon of Montreal, Auburn Burly. All of the above dogs except Little Pete proved to be high class producers. The following made C.K.C. Championships—Dowd's Glory, Yankee Speed King, Derby's Speed, Count Dee Cee and Joyce's Prince. No doubt, of the lot, Count Dee Cee is the outstanding producer, having sired many winners foremost among them being the beautiful specimen, O Pal Midget. Of this latter dog I will speak later. Shortly after he was imported the Count was purchased by Mr. Harold Shaw, and was shown by Mr. Shaw practically during all of his Canadian career.

Yankee Sensation was only in Canada a short time, but left his mark on our strains, being grandsire to the famous O Pal Midget. The others mentioned were mixed in with our home-bred strains and are helping to keep Canada on the Boston Terrier map. Their progeny is spreading over the whole of Canada. We never know when some raw recruit will blow into one of our shows with a topper. Just when the above mentioned importations were going strong, Mr. H.M. Jackson of Toronto imported a beautiful pair in Jackson Paddy Dee and Jackson's Dream Girl.

These two were mated together and although they did not produce any flyers direct, they left their mark on our stock and are progenitors to a great number of our prominent winners. Both of these dogs won C.K.C. championships. Mr. Jackson was unfortunate enough to lose them accidentally by poison, while they were still young.

The Spirit having been imported by Messrs. Brown & Phillips, and now owned by Mr. J.W. Church of Simcoe, Ont., was the sire of a very beautiful bitch named Ch. Lady Evelyn. This bitch flourished during the year 1919, was bred by Mr. John Bass and was owned and shown by Mr. John Schaefer, vice-president of the Boston Terrier Club of Canada.

Champion Lady Evelyn was a rich seal brindle, with ideal markings, weighing about 18 lbs. She was sold to an American fancier for a good price. During Mr. Schaefer's ownership she was shown once at Buffalo, N.Y., winning her classes and going to reserve winners. This was a big show and competition was keen.

In the summer of 1922 I sold a very handsome high quality dog named Clifton Flash, to Mr. R.B. Carter of Assiniboia, Sask. Flash was a rich dark seal brindle with ideal markings. He was shown at the Regina, Sask., show in August, 1922, and although the competition was keen, there being a number of American bred dogs imported from Boston, New York, Chicago and other U.S. cities, Flash was chosen by the old campaigner, Mr. Frank Dole, for winners. Unfortunately for Mr. Carter and the benefit of the breed in western Canada, he contracted distemper and died in September of the same year.

There were of course a great many other Bostons imported into Canada during the foregoing mentioned period and some of them were of considerable importance in improving the breed, but as their progeny did not figure very prominently at the shows I have no way to give their record.

I have confined my article to the most prominent Canadian-bred dogs, and have done my best to record each one exactly according to its merits.

This is famous painter Louis Agassiz Fuertes' depiction of a Boston and a French Bulldog. It appeared in the National Geographic Society's Book of Dogs, *published in 1919. It is an apt coupling of the two breeds since many of the early Boston breeders were first involved with Frenchies.*

Chapter 16

Bostons in Canada Today

by C. L. Mac Quillan

The pendulum swings to and fro.

We start with imported stock; these do most of the winning, then, as our young Canadian-bred stock came along they oust the imported article, then the Canadian fancier who has not been fortunate enough to breed anything himself or herself gets real mad and forthwith proceeds to import something to beat them all. Sometimes he succeeds and sometimes he does not, in any event it all helps to stimulate the interest and also brings in new blood. These importers of good dogs are deserving of as much credit as the breeders of good ones, because after all the breeding of good ones is mostly an accident. During the years 1921, 1922 and early part of 1923, our big winners are principally Canadian-bred.

Mr. H.J. O'Neil of Hamilton, Ontario, with the trappy little 17 pound dog, Little Mickey Ringmaster being very much to the fore. Mickey is a Canadian-bred, bred by his owner and is heading towards his championship. He is a rich dark mahogany brindle with flashy white markings, and is unusually stylish and alert. This little dog is also proving himself a splendid producer, one of his get going to reserve winners at our most recent specialty show, his name being King of Ringmasters and was also bred by his owner, Dr. H.A. Thompson of Hamilton. Ont. He is a flashy marked, seal brindle of pronounced terrier type and barring accidents will no doubt earn the coveted title.

Mrs. W.C. Ingram of Mimico, Ont., is also strong with good Bostons. In addition to Champion Ingram's Little Man, she has Champion Sweet Clover—Sweet Clover made her championship at the best shows. She has been shown at a number of shows in the U.S. and held her own in the hottest company. At the Westminster K.C. show in New York, she, with her kennel mate, was awarded the special for the best pair of Bostons. Champion Sweet Marie, also owned and bred by Mrs. Ingram, is another big international winner, having held her own at New York, Buffalo, Rochester and Detroit. Sweet Marie is a daughter of Sweet Clover who in turn is a daughter of Little Man. Mrs. Ingram also owns Champion Sweetheart who is by Oxonian's Rex. Champion Ingram's Lady Bird is also another topper owned by this redoubtable fancier. Lady Bird was bred by Mr. D.D. Elder and was sired by Mr. E.E. Scott's Prince Connie. This little bitch has won first prize at New York and other A.K.C. shows. She is a lightweight, dark seal brindle with ideal markings, is dam and granddam to several of our winning Canadian-breds.

Champion Globe Sweet William was also bred by Mrs. Ingram and sold to Mr. V.G. Perry of London, Ont., while still a puppy. While this dog won a championship he was not noted as a show dog, but as a stock dog he is par excellent. Early in his career he was mated with a bitch of pronounced Boston Terrier quality named Revolo

Am. & Can. Ch. O'Glo's Midgie *was bred by E.A. Runions, of Ottawa and sold to Mrs. Hilda Ridder, of New York City. Sired by Ch. Globe League O'Nations and out of Ch. Bonnie Intruder, this bitch returned to Canada and swept the show rings. She earned her championship in four straight shows in 12 days. She won the Breed each day and captured three Bests in Show and one Reserve Best in Show. All this came after she had already had four litters. She was the foundation bitch of Holiday Kennels.*

Mazie, bred and owned by J.C. Lunan of London, Ont. This latter bitch is well worth a few words of praise, she was just about as near perfect as any Boston I ever looked at, being good dark mahogany brindle, nicely marked, well proportioned and well balanced all over, nice dark full eye, clean flat skull, nice stop, short square muzzle, not too short, free from wrinkle. She stood well on her feet and yet I have seen her, show after show, placed under very inferior specimens. I have several times asked the judges why she was set down. They would invariably mention some fault she had not. When I requested the judge to step around to her bench and verify her faults, the judge usually had important business elsewhere. She just did not catch the judges' eye. The only fault I ever saw in her was that she was of sulky disposition, but stood up all right in the ring. She, however, made up for her lack of success in the show ring by producing two champions, Globe League O'Nations and Globe Tiny Tim, both in the same litter and sired by Globe Sweet William.

Ch. Globe League O'Nations is owned by John C. Lunan and V.G. Perry of London, Ont. He was bred by Mr. Lunan. He is one of the most justly renowned Boston Terriers ever bred in Canada. Weighing about 18 lbs., is a rich dark brindle with very flashy markings, perhaps a little overdone in this respect but not splashed in any way.

Mr. Lunan and Mr. Perry formed a partnership when this dog was still young, consequently the dog became the joint property of these two fanciers. The League started right out to win and besides making his C.K.C. championship in short order at the best shows, he was a big winner across the line. At New York in 1921 he won two 1sts and two 2nds, at Rochester the same year he won two 2nds, Detroit two 1sts and winners, Rochester 1922, two 1sts and reserve winners, Buffalo 1922, two 1sts and reserve winners and Detroit 1922, two 1sts and reserve winners. The League is a real show dog. He greets the other dogs in the ring on a friendly basis, practically shakes hands with the judge and acts generally as if he was on good terms with the world. As a producer he is away to a flying start, being the sire of Nation's Little Queen, owned by A. Ship of St. Thomas, Ont. This little bitch being awarded winners at the last specialty show held in Toronto.

Champion Globe Tiny Tim is a litter brother to Champion Globe League O' Nations, is under 15 lbs., and although he is a good little dog he

Knight's Sensation *was Best of Breed at the 1927 Toronto Specialty. He was pointed in the United States for owner Stephan A. Graczyke, Buffalo, New York.*

Vincent G. Perry

Vincent G. Perry's Globe Kennels was famous in Canada as well as around the world. The kennel name came from Toronto's Globe newspaper, where Vincent was a young reporter. He also was employed as an advertising copywriter and wrote the ads for the Ford Motor Company when it announced the advent of electric lights and starters in its cars. He did his share of freelance writing, too. At 22, he was known as "Canada's Short Story King," having sold more than 300 stories to magazines.

Vincent bought his first Boston in 1918 and, until his death, was never without one of the breed. For many years, he and his wife traveled all over the U.S. and Canada showing their Bostons. He said that he put more than 100,000 miles each year on his car travelling to shows.

Born in Canada, Mr. Perry was a Director of the Canadian Kennel Club for many years and served as both President and Secretary of Canada's oldest dog club, the London Canine Association. In 1938, he moved to the U.S. and became an American citizen.

Mr. Perry was also an avid drama enthusiast, serving as both an actor and director. He was director of the Theatre Guild, in Windsor. He appeared in television and movies.

Vincent Perry was highly respected as a dog show judge. For more than 60 years, he served as an all rounder. He was known for his gentle ways with the dogs that came under him. His most lasting contribution, however, may be the books he wrote on the breed.

Ch. Rex Oxonian

does not measure up to The League in any way. He, too, is owned by Messrs. Lunan & Perry.

O Pal Midget, one of the best ever. Canadian-bred from a Canadian-bred mother but sired by the imported Count Dee Cee, Midget is a well marked, but not ideally marked dog, having even face markings and white front legs and feet. She is a rich dark brindle, weighing about 16 lbs. This dog is owned and was bred by L.L. Broley of Toronto, and at the last two specialty shows, won everything, including winners and best in the show either sex, against the hottest competition of home-bred and imported Bostons ever seen in Canada. The consensus of opinion is that barring the fact that he is a trifle high stationed he is just about the perfect Boston. His muzzle, eyes, skull, style, body, feet and legs, action, in fact, all over he is as good as they can be made. Midget has been used at stud but as he is a young dog himself it is too soon to judge his puppies, but no doubt some of them at any rate will be a credit to Canada.

King of Ringmasters, owned and bred by Dr. Harold Thompson of Hamilton, Ont., is a son of Little Mickey Ringmaster, and a great credit to his sire. At Hamilton in October, 1922, he won reserve winners to his sire. At Toronto, April, 1923, he headed the lightweight division, and went right to reserve winners to O Pal Midget. King of Ringmasters is a seal brindle weighing about 13 lbs. with full markings.

Another splendid little lightweight is Jackie Coogan, bred and owned by H.M. Jackson of Toronto. Jackie has practically accounted for all the lightweight classes around Toronto until defeated by King of Ringmasters at the last show. Still another lightweight is The Periscope bred and owned by Mr. John Schaefer of Toronto. The Periscope has won prizes at nearly all our prominent shows, was only shown in the U.S. once. That was at Rochester in 1921. He was well up in his classes there. Master Pirate, a 12 lb. son of Joyce's Prince who is another prominent dog, who holds his own at our shows. He is owned by Mr. Sam Gaston and has winners points to his credit, and if shown a little more persistently would likely make his championship.

S.D. Gus, another prominent lightweight winner, was bred by H.L. Dawson and owned by R.A.W. Rastall, both of Toronto. Gus is a handsome mahogany brindle with face markings only. His sire was the imported Ressinger's Dandy and his dam a daughter of Ch. Clifton Peach.

In middle weight dogs we have, Capricorn, sired by The Periscope and owned by Mr. William Logan of Toronto. This dog is a rich dark brindle of high quality, weighing about 17 lbs. with head markings only. He has won a great many prizes and has been runner up for reserve winners at several shows.

O Pal King is another good middle weight, bred and owned by Mr. L.L. Broley, who has won a great many prizes in the hottest competition. He is sired by The Little Welshman, who is Canadian-bred. This latter dog is not noted as a winner but, as a producer of winners, he stands well up.

The Sultan, owned by Mrs. William Evans, is a very handsome son of champion Count Dee Cee, out of a Canadian-bred bitch. He has done a lot of winning at the best shows.

Champion Banker's Beauty is a Canadian-bred who won her title at the best shows in and around Montreal. She was bred and is still owned by Mr. Painter of Montreal.

The Little Colonel is still another very high class Canadian-bred middle weight. He is owned by Mr. L. McGill of Toronto and was bred by Milo R. Logan, also of Toronto. His sire was Little Somme. The latter is by Ch. Ingram's Little Man. Colonel's dam is by Ch. Clifton Peach. The Little

Am. & Can. Ch. Little Miss Muffet II *was a hit in both American and Canadian show rings. She was a Specialty and Best in Show winner. She may have been the first female to go Best in Show. She was owned by Mrs. E.J. Dowser, Detroit, MI.*

Colonel has points towards his championship and will no doubt reach the goal. The big winning heavy weight bitch Little Princess is a litter sister to The Colonel and also has points towards her championship. Little Princess is owned by J.A. Gow of Toronto.

At the Canadian National Exhibition, September, 1924, Mrs. W.C. Ingram brought out a young dog she called Ingram's Johnny Canuck. This dog was awarded winners, defeating two A.K.C. champions. He is a Canadian-bred from a Canadian-bred sire and dam, and also has Onadaga and Oxonion on both sides.

Nation's Little Queen previously mentioned is a beautiful little lightweight bitch. She was awarded winners at our last Specialty Show. She is a flashy marked dark brindle, beautifully proportioned and will undoubtedly hold her own at any show in America.

The reserve winners bitch to Nation's Little Queen was Raffle's Soubrette, bred and owned by Mr. H.A. Chambers of Toronto. She is a dark mahogany brindle with even head markings and will always be well up when shown.

Anderson's Cupid and Anderson's Daisy are also two big winning high-class bitches. They are by the Canadian-bred Woodland Arrow. Cupid was awarded winners at the January 1st, 1923, show. She was bred by Mr. William Anderson and owned by Mr. Lorne Anderson. Daisy has gone to reserve winners at some of our shows. She is still owned by her breeder.

Fleur De Lis is a grand headed middle-weight bitch owned by Mr. A. Craddock. This bitch has done a lot of winning and has championship points to her credit. She was bred by E.A. Brown and sired by Champion Count Dee Cee.

The latter part of the year 1923 brought great honor to Canadian-bred and owned Boston Terriers. Two of these making their A.K.C. Championships. The before mentioned Nation's Little Queen being the first to attain the honor, being awarded winners at Buffalo, N.Y., Canton, Ohio, Rochester, N.Y., and Detroit, Mich., all this without one single defeat. The other one was O Glo's Beauty, owned by Mr. A.A. Ogilvie, of Toronto. Beauty scored her points at Westbury, Weymouth, Taunton, Mass., Tuxedo and the Bronx. Never once was Beauty beaten in her class, her only defeat being in the winner's class at Buffalo when she took reserve to the other famous Canadian-bred, Nation's Little Queen. Both these bitches are descendants of Onadaga and Oxonian, Little Queen being by Globe League of Nations and O Glo's Beauty, by our Bob, who is out of Cham-

Can. Ch. Highball's Just It, *owned by Earl Brown, was considered the most outstanding Canadian Boston of his day. He weighed 17 lbs.*

pion Little Miss Mack. A description of either or both the above dogs is not necessary, as they are each just about perfect. They have met four times. At Brantford, Ont., London, Ont., Buffalo, N.Y., and Toronto, Ont. Each won twice; it was necessary for the judge to decide on one or the other, as there are no tie ribbons in dog shows. If there were they would probably have been placed a tie in every case.

Western Canada seems to be taking on a new lease of life as far as Boston Terriers are concerned. Although there has been a specialty club in Winnipeg for about ten years and a great many importations of high class stock made both from the U. S. and Ontario, the breed did not make the same headway as the East, but a lot of new high-class dogs have again been brought in and the future is assured.

BOSTON TERRIER CLUB IN CANADA

The Boston Terrier Club of Canada was formed in 1908, and has been going strong ever since. Sixteen Annual Shows have been given by this club. The first was on January 1st, 1909. This club claims the distinction of being the only Kennel Club in Canada to give such a large number of shows without a single break. Cash prizes and numerous other trophies are distributed at these shows.

Never once has the club gone behind financially at one of its shows. Notwithstanding this fact, the officers do not believe in hoarding up money for posterity. Consequently any surplus over and above a reasonable amount as a reserve has been used in promoting the best interest of the Boston Terrier.

The popularity enjoyed by the great little dog to-day in Canada, is no doubt due to this club.

The Boston Terrier Club of Western Canada was formed about 1912, and although they are still going strong, have not as yet held any Specialty shows.

The Boston Terrier Club of Toronto was formed in 1920 and has given four annual Specialty Shows. This Club also gives splendid cash prizes and other trophies and are strong but friendly rivals of the old Club.

Chapter 17

The Boston Terrier Standard Simplified

compiled and edited by C.N. Grey
Secretary, Boston Terrier Club of America

This article is written to interpret and elucidate the Boston Terrier standard, and although primarily intended for the novice, it is hoped that even the critical veteran fancier will find it helpful.

The present Boston Terrier Standard was adopted by the Boston Terrier Club on October 7, 1914, as a result of a revision recommended by a committee appointed by the Boston Terrier Club. The standard as it existed before this revision had, with possibly the exception of changes in the weight clauses, been in existence since the formation of the club in 1891.

It goes without saying that the Boston Terrier was developed under the original standard from a meager beginning and against strenuous opposition to the most popular dog of the day. At the same time many differences of opinion as to the correct interpretation of this standard existed, and undoubtedly a more uniform development would have been obtained sooner had it been feasible at the origination of the standard to have made its terms more specific. While the principal breeding was done in the vicinity of Boston, where the breed originated, the necessity for an elaborately explicit standard was not keenly felt. The breed finally reached a point where it was felt that it was no longer advisable to leave so much to the personal interpretation of breeders and judges, especially in view of the fact that confusing variations in type were becoming only too apparent as the natural result of the spread of the breed over the country among breeders and fanciers not so familiar with the ideas of the original breeders around Boston as was necessary to maintain a uniform type. While the Boston Terrier breed is one of the comparatively recent breeds so far as its official history goes, the fact should be kept in mind that it is now one of the best established breeds and is no more open to experiment as to type than any of the oldest breeds. Judges in the show ring should bear this in mind and refrain from indicating personal likes or prejudices regarding type or conformation.

The standard here quoted is the only Boston Terrier Standard and is so recognized throughout the country.

GENERAL APPEARANCE: The general appearance of the Boston Terrier should be that of a lively, highly intelligent, smooth coated, short headed, compactly built, short tailed, well balanced dog of medium station, of brindle color and evenly marked with white.

The head should indicate a high degree of intelligence and should be in proportion to the size of the dog; the body rather short and well knit, the limbs strong and neatly turned; tail short; and no feature be so prominent that the dog appears badly proportioned.

The dog should convey an impression of determination, strength and activity, with style of a high order; carriage easy and graceful.

A proportionate combination of "Color" and "Ideal Markings" is a particularly distinctive feature of a representative specimen, and a dog with a preponderance of white on body, or without the proper proportion of brindle and white on head, should possess sufficient merit otherwise to counteract its deficiencies in these respects.

The ideal "Boston Terrier Expression" as indicating "a high degree of intelligence" is also an important characteristic of the breed.

"Color and Markings" and "Expression" should be given particular consideration in determining the relative value of "General Appearance" to other points. (10 points)

Ch. Blink's Fascination

The above description of the general appearance of the Boston Terrier, as given in the standard, is correct, short and definite and means just what it says, every word and punctuation mark being there for a studied purpose. It says the dog should be "compactly built." That does not mean very or most compactly built, as it is possible to get a dog too compact, but the first impression on looking at the dog should be that in details and in general he is compact, condensed, packed into moderately small space, as it were. As dogs go, his height or station should not appear especially noticeable. The Dachshund and the Greyhound are of exaggerated station. The Fox Terrier, though not a "leggy" dog, is a higher stationed dog than the "medium station" Boston. Of course, it is also entirely possible to get them too compact and too low to the ground, as in no detail should the Boston Terrier be an exaggeration.

The head is referred to as indicating a "high degree of intelligence" and "in proportion to the dog's size." The dog must not only be intelligent, but it should look to be especially intelligent. When you talk to him he should give the impression that he understands every word and that he is really of a higher degree of intelligence than the average dog of other breeds. There are other breeds of dogs just as intelligent, but the indication of a high degree of intelligence is the point brought out by the standard. The head of a Bulldog appears large in proportion to his size, but the head or no other detail of the Boston Terrier should give the impression of being out of proportion. One reason that later the standard specifies "cheeks flat" is because "cheekiness" would make the head appear larger and out of proportion.

The compact or condensed idea is still in mind in the phrase "the body rather short and well knit," carrying the idea that the impression you get should be of a short bodied dog, but not strikingly or exaggeratedly short. This distinctly means a shorter bodied, more compactly built dog than the average Terrier. "The limbs should be strong and finely turned" shows that it was not the intention that the dog should be a weakling, but should have real bone and muscle, though not to the extent desired by pugilists, and not to the extent that his strength of limb would make him coarse, but rather like the limbs of a perfectly formed, well developed athlete.

The "compactly built" dog must of necessity be sturdy, with bone and strength in proportion.

There is probably no one phrase in the standard that should be more strongly borne in mind than: "No feature being so prominent that the dog appears badly proportioned." That is the keynote which should determine whether the muzzle is too long or too short, whether the dog is too leggy or too low, or the many other similar points. Look at your dog as an architect would look at a building, and if he is well balanced and proportionately set up, with all the parts in harmony and symmetry, and if he also appears to fit the standard in these details, he will be pretty close to right—but remember, the perfect one never lived. The "impression of determination" with the "strength and activity" to carry out that determination does not mean that he should appear like a fighting dog looking for trouble, but it means that you know when you look at him that if he had just reason to attack man or beast he would fight gamely and determinedly, and further, that he has the strength and activity to win the fight were the

Thorpe's Bostons

Thorpe's North Side Kennels, in Saint Louis, Missouri, was one of the largest Midwestern breeders. They bred many puppies annually and maintained a large stud force. Below appear just some of the stud dogs housed at their kennels during the 1920s.

The Intruder son,
Ch. Headquarter's Sergeant.

Ch. Thorpe's Tiny King

Ch. Intruder Blink

Ch. Rattler King II

A very grainy photo of
Ch. Tiny Teddy B.

Ch. Out For Sport

odds not too great against him. Activity is a natural characteristic of this dog—perhaps not as fleet of foot nor as nervous or high strung as the average Terrier, but with activity combined with strength and sturdiness. His step is springy, as it were full of vim and action. Life seems worth the living to him, and he shows it in every move he makes, although he also shows that proper dignity and even disposition which befits a leader among dogs. "Style of a high order; carriage easy and graceful" is a most important characteristic of the Boston Terrier. He is an aristocrat, he looks it, and is proud of it—as stylish and graceful as the leader of a tandem park team.

The dog that is even throughout in all details is to be preferred over the dog that might score the same, but has some very good points counterbalanced by other very poor points, that is, a dog (other things being equal) with skull scoring 11 out of a possible 12 and forelegs scoring 3 1/2 out of a possible 5, but with muzzle scoring only 4 out of a possible 12 and hind legs scoring 1 1/2 out of a possible 5, should never be given the preference over the dog scoring 8 on skull, 2 1/2 on forelegs, 7 on muzzle, and 2 1/2 on hind legs, although the average is the same in both cases. Other things being equal, the judge in the ring undoubtedly does and should take into consideration the disposition of the dog. The Boston Terrier should be gentle and kind though resolute and courageous. He should not be either savage or vicious, though he should protect himself and his master when the occasion demands. He should not run away from trouble, nor should he look for it. The female of all breeds is by nature the smaller, more delicately formed, more finely turned, and in Bostons one naturally expects to see a female with a little less bone, higher rather than lower stationed, a slightly longer body and not as strongly muscled.

SKULL: Square, flat on top, free from wrinkles; cheeks flat; brow abrupt, stop well defined. (12 points)

Technically speaking, probably the skull of no Boston Terrier is absolutely "square," but, speaking in the language of the dog standards, it should be. The forehead, often called the top of the skull, and the occiput or the skull between the ears should be as flat as practicable for a dog's skull to be. Although it is, of course, appreciated that the edges must be rounding, the rounding should be of short radius curves. It is a fault for a mature dog to have the rounding start at or near the center of the forehead. This makes a round or "domey"-headed specimen. This fault is to a certain extent excusable and common in young puppies, who usually improve with age in this detail. The "domey" skull is a fault, and one which is quite prevalent in mature dogs.

No Boston Terrier is absolutely free from wrinkles, either on the forehead or between the ears when excited, as the erection of the ears causes a slight wrinkling between them. However, when he stands at attention in the show ring there should be as little wrinkle noticeable as possible.

In the early stages of the breed, wrinkled, throaty, cheeky dogs were very prevalent, however, as the breed practically has progressed, these faults have been eliminated.

Prominent cheeks not only make the head appear too large, but they take away that cleancut, trim appearance that is one of the main assets of the dog. The cheeks should be as flat as possible and parallel, similar to the sides of a nearly square box with slightly rounded corners, the top of the box being the forehead. The head, exclusive of muzzle, is very nearly equal in length, breadth and depth, and should present a square appearance, although if actual measurements were taken there probably never was a high grade Boston Terrier that did not have a slightly greater width across the skull at the ears than at the eyes. It is, however, a decided fault if the difference is enough to detract from the square appearance to the extent of even a tendency toward a wedge-shaped skull.

The brow should drop in almost a perpendicular, joining the forehead and muzzle in very slightly rounded right angles.

Between the eyes is the indentation termed "stop" which should be more pronounced at the bottom and gradually decrease to nothing at the point where it curves into the forehead. The continuation of this stop in a furrow up the forehead as in the Bulldog, is a fault, but keeping in mind the intent of the standard to avoid any extreme the stop should be merely well defined and no more.

The brow should be deep enough so that the eyes are directly in front. Some of the best dogs have too deep a brow and too much stop, but there is a larger per cent that do not have pronounced enough "stop" as the whole space between the forehead and the muzzle is often called, when the fancier is speaking colloquially and in generalities.

EYES: Wide apart, large and round, dark in color, expression alert but kind and intelligent. The eyes should set square in the skull, and the outside corners should be on a line with the cheeks as viewed from the front. (5 points)

There is little to add to this clause, if it is read and studied carefully, though it should be appreciated that the opening of the eye is in reality never actually round. They should, however, give a round appearance when the dog is at attention and they should also be most expressive. A light brown eye is a fairly frequent fault, a wall or watch eye an exceptionally bad fault, than in the opinion of many should be a disqualification. The "sunken" eye is very noticeable, even to the novice, but many novices consider the eyes practically perfect when, as a matter of fact, they are too prominent. The dog should not be "pop eyed" or have a bulging eye.

Many a dog that in head details seems almost perfect has an indescribable something lacking, which, when carefully analyzed, is due to expression or lack of expression in the dog's eyes. The Boston Terrier talks to you with his large, round, dark soft eyes, telling you he is awake; that he knows something; that he has naturally the good disposition of a "pal;" but that under the proper provocation he would defend himself. A poor expression in the eye is a fault and should be taken into account when the general appearance is scored.

The eyes should be so placed that the outside corner is "on a line with the cheeks," but this does not mean that the full eye, from corner to corner, is all in the front of the brow. The outside corners are slightly carried around on a line with the cheeks. The inside corners of the eye should be just a trifle inside of the lines of the sides of the muzzle, however, the eyeballs or eyes proper should have the appearance of being wide apart, and just between the lines formed by the sides of the muzzle and sides of the head. The horizontal line formed by the top of the muzzle should nearly intersect all four corners of the eyes. The eyeball should be large enough to practically fill the opening and the haw and white should never be noticeable.

MUZZLE: Short, square, wide and deep, and in proportion to skull; free from wrinkles; shorter in length than in width and depth, not exceeding in length approximately one-third of length of skull; width and depth carried out well to end; the muzzle from stop to end of nose on a line parallel to the top of the skull; nose black and wide, with well defined line between nostrils. The jaws broad and square, with short regular teeth. The chops of good depth but not pendulous, completely covering the teeth when mouth is closed. (12 points)

"Short, square, wide and deep and in proportion to skull" expresses a cubical or boxlike formation similar to that desired in the skull proper. The top and bottom lines and the side lines should run out straight and be parallel to each other and to the top and bottom and to the sides of the skull. The end of the muzzle should be cut off squarely. Of course, the joining of the muzzle to the head and the end of the muzzle are in slightly rounded curves, but the shorter these curves the better. There should be no tapering of the muzzle toward the end. A tapering or "snipey" muzzle or a shallow muzzle are faults. Shortness of the muzzle should not be had at the expense of other muzzle properties, however. Very short muzzles are frequently found to show "lay back" and wrinkles, both of which are faults. It is, however, seldom that one sees a muzzle too short but otherwise perfect.

Joker Mack, *owned by Frank A. Teeling, one time secretary of the Boston Terrier Club of America.*

The width of the muzzle is slightly more than the depth but they should be very nearly equal. The width is also slightly greater at the bottom than at the top, but it should also be about the same at the end as it is where it joins the head. A drop toward the end of the nose is a fault. The depth is mostly in the upper jaw, although the under jaw should be strong, with good depth, but not up swinging or protruding as in the Bulldog. An even mouthed dog is desired, but the majority are slightly undershot. A slight undershot is acceptable providing it does not deform the vertical line at the end of the muzzle. An overshot or "pig jaw" is very much worse than the same amount of undershot, as the overshot jaw invariably deforms the contour of the muzzle, making it look weak and "snipey." The teeth should be sound and strong.

The nose should be of good size, black, with well developed nostrils and straight well defined septum between them. The "butterfly," particolor, or part flesh and part black nose is a fault. Although the standard does not technically disqualify the yellow, brown or "dudley" nose, it is very objectionable.

The chops should be pendulous to the extent that they cover the teeth well, but should not hang below the bottom of the underjaw. They should also fit the lower jaw snugly and be of sufficient thickness to give the muzzle good "cushion." The muzzle should be entirely free from wrinkle, although a slight wrinkle is sometimes found in good show dogs where the muzzle joins the head. This fault is not quite as serious as one of conformation, but it nevertheless detracts from the "clean" appearance that the muzzle should have. In considering the muzzle it should be "in proportion" to the size of the skull.

EARS: Carried erect; small and thin; situated as near corners of skull as possible. (2 points)

The dog with the untrimmed ears lacks that pert, smart, stylish appearance so necessary in the Boston Terrier. If it were possible to have a narrow, thin, uncut bat ear, the question might be solved without trimming, but the rose ear of the English Bulldog does not go with Boston Terrier proportions and style, while the bat ear of the French Bulldog is too large for the smaller headed Boston Terrier.

Generally speaking, the ears of a Boston Terrier are correct when they are cropped properly and carried erect. This trimming differs slightly in length and style for different dogs, as like every other detail the ear must be in proportion to the rest of the dog. It should be done only by a person who thoroughly understands the trimming of Boston Terrier ears. Uncropped ears detract from the desired square box appearance of the head. With the dog alert and at attention the inside front lines of the ears should be parallel and perpendicular, pointing neither inward nor outward, the ears being set on the upper corners of the skull. A low placed ear is faulty as it makes the head appear too wide at the occiput.

The prevailing tendency of the day is to trim away nearly all of the base of the ear. This is unnecessary to meet the demands of the standard. If less was trimmed away at the base, there would be less necessity of collodion (a solution of pyroxylin, ether and alcohol, used as an adhesive to close small wounds; highly flammable—ed.) or any similar preparation—the use of which in the show ring is to be severely condemned.

Kingway Kennels

Ch. Kingway Blink

Kingway Kennels was located in Denver, Colorado. Owner Mrs. W. E. Porter proved to have a good eye for a dog and is noted for producing many homebred winners. She never hesitated to enter her dogs, no matter how tough the competition. Pictured here are some of her best known dogs from the 1920s. Not pictured is the outstanding Best in Show winner Ch. Kingway Connie.

Ch. Hollis' Handsome Pat

Ch. Mosholu Buddie Blink

11 lb. **Ch. Kingway K.O.A.** *was named after a Denver radio station.*

Ch. Kingway Tommy Distributer

A grainy photo of **Ch. Kingway Carina**

Dallen's Success

Ch. Kingway Tinkerbelle

HEAD FAULTS: Skull "domed" or inclined; furrowed by a medial line; skull too long for breadth, or vice versa; stop too shallow; brow and skull too slanting.

Eyes small or sunken; too prominent; light color; showing too much white or haw.

Muzzle wedge shaped or lacking depth; down faced; too much cut out below the eyes; pinched nostrils; protruding teeth; weak lower jaw; showing "turn up."

Ears poorly carried or in size out of proportion to head.

NECK: Of fair length, slightly arched and carrying the head gracefully; setting neatly into shoulders. (3 points)

The neck should be gracefully carried and be proportionate in size to the head and body.

When viewed from the side the upper line of the neck should present a slightly arched appearance and the head should be carried well above the level of the neck.

A very important point is that the neck should be "without throatiness," which means that there should be as little loose skin as possible under the throat. Judges may differ as to what are the correct proportions of the perfect dog, but they invariably want a "clean" dog and the dog with "dewlap," as the loose folds of skin under the throat are termed, cannot be called "clean."

NECK FAULTS: Ewe-necked; throatiness; short and thick.

BODY: Deep with good width of chest; shoulders sloping; back short; ribs deep and well sprung, carried well back to loins; loins short and muscular; rump curving slightly to set-on of tail; flank very slightly cut up. The body should appear short but not chunky. (15 points)

"Deep with good width of chest" is one of the most elusive terms of the standard for the novice, but again we fall back upon the language of the "general appearance" section of the standard—which is the court of the last resort in determining questions of this sort—the phrase "no feature" being so prominent that the dog appears badly proportioned.

At the same time, a "good width of chest" lends a great deal to "convey an impression of determination and strength." At the same time the chest and the whole dog must "convey the impression of...activity." Unless the chest has good breadth and depth, the ribs cannot be well rounded.

"Ribs deep and well sprung" means practically the same as well rounded ribs, giving the short back a cobby appearing dog. Occasionally a dog may be found that is too cobby, but the majority are not cobby enough. There may be a difference of opinion as to whether a dog is too cobby or not, but no interpretation of the standard could justify the shelly bodied, narrow-chested, leggy dog. The "roach" or "wheel," "sway," "hump" and "giraffe" backs are faults although a slight convex curve is preferred to a concave curve. The line from the tops of the shoulder blades to the tops of the hip joints should be very nearly level, only drooping slightly back to the hip joints to meet the low set on of tail.

"Loins short and muscular" is correct phraseology when the term "finely turned" is taken into account; this barring the beefy loined and coarse ungainly limbed dog. While each rib toward the stern should be shorter than the preceding one, the belly should not have as pronounced a tuck up as in the Bulldog, which is necessary to accentuate the latter's "roach" back.

BODY FAULTS: Flat sides; narrow chest; long or slack loins; roach back; sway back; too much cut up in the flank.

ELBOWS: Standing neither in nor out. (4 points)

"Standing neither in nor out" expresses exactly what is meant. The points of the elbows should point directly backward. The elbows should be securely bound to the shoulders by muscle, but the muscle on the shoulders should have no appearance of over development. Any looseness of elbow or shoulder is a fault.

FORELEGS: Set moderately wide apart and on a line with the points of the shoulders; straight in bone and well muscled; pasterns short and strong. (5 points)

"Set moderately wide apart." This wording should be interpreted on the same basis as the "good width of chest" is previously interpreted. Bear in mind, however, that the forelegs must not be close together any more than the chest should be narrow and shallow. The brisket, chest and legs of the Boston Terrier are very nearly proportionate to those of the Bull Terrier. The forelegs should be as straight as a plummet down to the feet and parallel, that is, the same width apart at the tops as at the bottom. The outside line is very slightly curved, owing to the muscle at the calf, but there should be no appreciable tapering toward the feet. The Boston Terrier's body is "on his legs," while the Bulldog's is between them. The Boston Terrier's forelegs should not be as close together as are the Fox Terrier's legs, which are set well under a narrow chest. Out at the elbows, that is, the elbows not in line with the point of the shoulder, is a fault that in later life comes to many Boston Terriers, but in show form neither the elbows nor the legs should be out from under the body, but rather should be just under, as are the legs at the extreme corner of a table.

HINDLEGS: Set true; bent at stifles; short from hocks to feet; hocks turning neither in nor out; thighs strong and well muscled. (5 points)

The particular point about the hindlegs is that they should "turn neither in nor out" either at stifle or hock. The hindlegs should not be so long as to make the dog higher behind than in front. By "set true" straight and parallel when viewed from the rear, and slightly closer together than the forelegs. The phrase in the "leg and feet faults" section, "hocks too prominent" is written to distinguish the formation of the hindleg as a modification of the pronounced bend of hocks in the Bulldog. Straight forward walking with good springy action of the hindlegs is most desirable. Any defect of hock formation or action is a fault.

FEET: Round, small and compact, and turned neither in nor out; toes well arched. (5 points)

The feet and pasterns of a dog are too often overlooked as unimportant. The dog "down in his pasterns" and with splay or open feet, showing space between the toes, cannot be considered entirely sound, and the dog with pasterns or feet turning in or out (the latter being the more common fault) must also be considered faulty. A long hare foot is undesirable, but not as faulty as a splay foot. A compact foot like a cat's is most desirable. The pasterns and feet are being judged very carefully of late years, and the dog not having straight or almost straight pasterns with small arched compact feet should be penalized.

He should be "up on his toes" as it were, thus precluding faults in feet and pasterns.

LEG AND FEET FAULTS: Loose shoulders or elbows; hindlegs too straight at stifles; hocks too prominent; long or weak pasterns; splay feet.

TAIL: Set-on low; short, fine and tapering; straight or screw; devoid of fringes or coarse hair, and not carried above horizontal. (5 points)

The tail is really a small detail of the dog, but it must be short, and this wording of the standard has produced endless discussion. The novice generally prefers the gnarled or screw tail, the seasoned veteran the "short, fine and tapering" straight or kinked tail. The "kinked" tail might be described as a straight tail with partial screws or slight irregularities in it and so named to distinguish it from the definite screw or pronounced irregularities. For a properly proportioned seventeen pound dog a straight or slightly kinked tail, say from a quarter to a third the distance from "set on" to hock, gives the dog a very proper finish. The tail longer than half the distance from "set on" to hock, has about reached the "too long" limit, as indicated to be preferred "under this clause of the standard." The gay tail, as a tail carried about the horizontal line of the back is called, is always objectionable. The short screw tail, sticking practically straight up for an inch or two, should never

While enroute to her championship, **Ch. Rockbound's Tangee** *earned five Bests of Breed and a Best in Show from the classes. The dark seal brindle bitch was owned by Mr. & Mrs. Charles Clark, Lancaster, OH.*

seldom "fine and tapering" as called for. First of all the standard calls for a tail "set on low, short," and these are the first essentials of a proper tail, be it straight or screw.

TAIL FAULTS: A long or gaily carried tail; gnarled or curled against the body.

(Note: The preferred tail should not exceed in length approximately half the distance from set-on to hock.)

COLOR: Brindle with white markings. (4 points)

The standard prescribes the color "brindle with white markings." This section of the standard is so worded with the deliberate intent to define the predominating color as "brindle." There had up to the time of the adoption of the present standard been more or less discussion over the relative merits of dogs of predominating brindle color and dogs of predominating white color. The public fancy finally settled the matter by practically demanding dogs of brindle color with even white markings now prescribed as "ideal markings" so that this section of the standard was accordingly made as above quoted—"brindle with white markings."

be penalized for gayness to the same extent as should the straight, very long tail (exceeding in length half the distance from "set on" to hock), sticking up at even a slight angle above the level of the back. It should be borne in mind that the tail should also be "fine and tapering," not large or coarse, nor of the same diameter throughout its length. The short screw tail, even when large and coarse, is often not penalized by a judge, when he would penalize for size and coarseness a straight tail of the same size. Strictly following the standard this is not permissible, although the screw tail is normally a coarser tail than is the straight tail.

It is argued that as the standard places the word "straight" before the word "screw," that the straight tail is the more desirable. This is true, but before either of these words are the words "fine and tapering." The extreme gnarled screw tail is

IDEAL MARKINGS: White muzzle, even white blaze over head, collar, breast, part or whole of forelegs, and hindlegs below hocks. (10 points)

The entire muzzle with the exception of the black skin on the nose end of the muzzle and lips should be white. The "blaze" should be about one-third the width of the head or a little less than the width of the muzzle and extend up and back between the ears. The collar markings should cover the greater part of the neck and chest and meet the muzzle marking under the lower jaw. The leg markings may run up to the body on the forelegs and up to the hocks on the hindlegs.

The more even the formation of the markings the better. They should be of a clean, pure white and sharply defined against the brindle. An impure or smutty white muzzle, a narrow or pencil blaze or any defects of head markings are generally considered greater faults than defects in body markings.

In connection with this section of the standard, we should refer back again to the "general appearance" section which reads "a proportionate combination of 'color and ideal markings' is a particularly distinctive feature of a representative specimen and a dog with a preponderance of white on body, or without the proper proportion of brindle and white on head, should possess sufficient merit, otherwise to counteract its deficiencies in these respects" which of course, (as set out in the "Fault" section under color and markings) simply puts a handicap on a dog "all white in color, lacking entirely white markings; preponderance of white on body; without the proper proportion of brindle and white on head; or any variation detracting from general appearance." Here again we find the standard insisting upon consistency in the Boston Terrier as to those "fancy" points such as "color and markings" and "short screw tail," etc.—but at the same time no disqualifica-

Ch. Rockbound's Bontuwyn, *a multiple Breed winner and littermate to Tangee. Owned by Mr. & Mrs. Clark.*

A posed shot of the Clark's **Ch. Rockbound's Tangee.**

tion is put upon dogs lacking any of these points beyond the penalties inflicted under the "point values."

So far as color and markings go, the standard leaves it to the judges to determine the "proper proportion" of "color and white markings," as this proportion naturally varies according to the other properties of the animal.

Of course in this breed the all white ones and the all brindle ones are necessary in the kennel for breeding purposes, but it looks as though henceforth the public demand is settled on brindle color and even markings, and it is seldom that an all-white, all brindle, splashed or solid colored dog possesses "sufficient merit" to win in the fastest company even now.

COLOR AND MARKING FAULTS: All white; absence of white markings; preponderance of white on body; without the proper proportion of brindle and white on head; or any variations detracting from the general appearance.

COAT: Short, smooth, bright and fine in texture. (3 points)

In addition to the above, it is generally understood that the coat should be close, straight, flat, smooth and glossy. It is probable that no Boston Terrier ever had too smooth or glossy a coat, and a perfect coat, also means in perfect condition. Long hairs are undesirable, and quite often indicate a lack of necessary brushing, which is more often needed in the spring to remove the extra growth provided by Nature to protect from the winter's cold. It is true that neither man nor dog should be judged too much by his coat, but a stylish dog needs a stylish, well-groomed, attractive coat.

COAT FAULTS: Long or coarse; lacking lustre.

WEIGHT: Not exceeding 27 pounds, divided by classes as follows:
 Lightweight: Under 17 pounds.
 Middleweight: 17 and under 22 pounds.
 Heavyweight: 22 and not exceeding 27 pounds.

As the specified weight is from 17 to 27 pounds, inclusive, it is fair to assume that a very acceptable weight for the average show Boston Terrier is about halfway between these two weights. The middleweight class covers this nicely and, all other qualities being even, a dog of this weight is generally preferred by experienced judges to the lightweight and heavyweight dogs.

There is probably a greater demand for the smaller dogs, as they make admirable pets and are perhaps more popular than Toy breeds on account of their short coats and other advantages. This phase of the situation, however, should never bias judgment in the show ring, as it is not the dog which is most salable, but the one which most closely personifies the standard that should receive highest honors. There is a tendency toward lack of stamina and substance in the small dogs, while the big ones are inclined toward coarseness.

The Boston Terrier is no pet for my lady's muff, nor must he be beyond the size of an ideal house dog. He must be sturdy and resolute, sound and active; in fact "all dog," according to the standard. It may be said without fear of contradiction, that during the history of the Boston Terrier the greater number of dogs typifying these characteristics have been middleweights.

DISQUALIFICATIONS: Solid black; black and tan; liver, and mouse colors. Docked tail and any artificial means used to deceive the judge.

"Artificial means" covers faking, dyeing, most methods of holding an improper ear properly, doping internally or externally and other methods of deceiving the judge. The chalking of a white blaze is technically perhaps "artificial means to deceive the judge," but is defended on the basis that white chalk is used instead of soap to take away the dirt and bring out the natural white color. Used in moderation, this is possibly true.

A "gay tail," which has been "dropped" is just as much of a disqualification as a docked tail and there can be no defense for either. A very moderate use of scissors to trim out long hairs on the body of tail may not result in giving the dog the gate, but it is not only questionable practice but is a poor substitute for needed brushing and grooming.

POINT VALUES: The standard includes a set of point values, assigned to each of the sections we have discussed. The greatest points are assigned to the body (15), skull (12), ideal markings (10) and general appearance (10). The points add up to a total of 100. The actual designation of points is listed in parentheses following each respective section.

Many have a mistaken impression as to the show qualities of their unshown pet, and it is far better for the novice to actually score his dog after a careful study of the standard than it is for him to rely on his general impression, although it is true that the judge in the ring does not actually score the dogs point for point. Experience has taught him to judge a dog fairly without a careful scoring, but nevertheless he really does or rather should mentally compare each point and the best judges will in this way arrive at the same decision as they would by scoring. In scoring keep in mind that very few ordinary dogs will score over 95% perfect in any single detail, also that the very best dogs will seldom score over 90% perfect on the average in all the details.

Chapter 18

Boston Terrier Type

by Vinton P. Breese

About twenty years ago, when associate editor on *Field and Fancy,* the writer at the behest of Mr. Fred J. Skinner, managing editor of that publication, collaborated with Mr. William H. Sawyer in compiling what purported to be and was entitled *The Boston Terrier Standard Simplified.* In lieu of the latter word, amplified, would have been the more truly descriptive expression as it was really an amplification of the then existing standard with the utmost fidelity to the same and couched in simple language. Moreover it was largely based upon the consensus of idea and opinion as gleaned and garnered from the foremost judges, fanciers and breeders of that time and our careful personal observations and investigations into the earlier annals of the breed as to what constituted correct type in the Boston Terrier. Suggestions were welcomed from all and sundry of the Boston Terrier cult and I distinctly recall among those who volunteered the same in a deeply interested manner were the late George F. Parker and James R. Waterhouse. Fast and furious were the discussions we frequently engaged in while compiling the work, until Editor Skinner would threaten to throw us all out of the office unless the racket ceased. Mr. Sawyer would go about in his persistent manner feeling the pulse of the fancy upon the matter of true type whilst I made sorties on the same subject among such experienced fanciers as Dr. Walter G. Kendall, Dr. A.F. Mount, Dr. C.F. Sullivan, Arthur Mulvey, Walter Stone, the late Thomas Kelly and Joseph M. Dale, the professional all-rounders George S. Thomas and Frank F. Dole and many others of the old brigade; all of whom had been closely associated with the best in Boston Terriers.

Mr. Sawyer and I wrote separate rough drafts on the subject and from these the finished treatise was produced. Therefore it will be seen that the work represented a composite of the idea and opinion of the leading lights of the Boston Terrier cult as to what constituted correct type in the breed at that time.

The production of this work was prompted by the extreme brevity of the standard as it then existed. Its missions were so many and its ambiguity so manifest that not only the novitiate, but the cognoscenti misinterpreted its import and frequently became embroiled in heated argument over what its precepts precisely implied. With such conditions existing it could hardly be hoped that the breed would improve in uniformity of type. Discussion was rampant as to whether the Standard should or should not be changed, amended, completely rewritten, et cetera. Some there were of the old school who vigorously objected to any tampering whatever with the document while other more progressive spirits quite as strenuously insisted that some action must be taken if the breed was to continue in its high estate of popularity.

It was at this time that the result of our efforts was published in booklet form and immediately seized upon by the latter element as an opportune weapon to utilize in carrying their contention to consummation. It proved to be just that, for shortly after its appearance the Standard was revised and enlarged by the parent club and it was learned that the treatise played an important part in the same.

Subsequent revisions have been made. Whether it was due to these or a natural inclination throughout the fancy toward a lighter, finer type of Boston Terrier the fact remains that the breed has assumed a decidedly more terrier-like conformation whereas the earlier dogs verged on a rather thick-set, bully type. Our present day dogs are cast in a finer mold. Wrinkle, lippiness and cheekiness have been largely obliterated, giving the head a classic and cleanly chiseled appearance, and the same is in evidence throughout the body. The muscular development and bony structure and in fact the very sturdy and compact build of the earlier dogs have been considerably modified. Quite naturally this transition toward a lighter, terrier-like build was accompanied by a more lively graceful action and jaunty appearance. However the limit in all of these things seems to have been reached, that is if the standard is to be adhered to and the breed preserved from degenerating into shelly, racy looking animals, of which there are far too many at the present time. But further comment will be made upon this and other details of type will be made in the amplification of the standard which will follow.

About the first of the distinctly terrier-type dogs to gain wide renown was Mr. Franz Heilborn's Champion The Demon. He appeared at the New York Boston Terrier Club's Specialty Show held in Madison Square Garden, October 7th and 8th, 1910, and in an entry of 213 dogs created a decided sensation when adjudged best of the breed by Dr. A. F. Mount. Opinion was considerably divided as to the merit of the win, many maintaining that he was not sufficiently compact in build and this was manifestly true. However, he was well balanced and absolutely sound, with the best of bone, legs and feet, a fairly shapely body, cleanly chiseled head, good neck and devoid of wrinkle or any coarseness. In view of his many excellent attributes the Doctor was thoroughly justified in rendering the decision as he did and particularly as the more compactly built contenders were quite faulty in various respects among which coarseness and unsoundness were paramount.

The Demon sallied forth into an all conquering career and the successes were largely instrumental in swerving the opinion of the fancy toward dogs of the more terrier-like type until it seemed that the compactly built Boston was doomed to oblivion. However, in 1913 there appeared two dogs which exerted quite the opposite influence upon the fancy. They were Mrs. F.A. Dallen's Champion Dallen's Sensation and Dr. C.F. Sullivan's Champion Trimount Roman, which had their initial meeting under the writer at Belmont Park in the spring of the year mentioned, and they were placed in the order named, although only by a very narrow margin of merit. Both were very high quality, compactly built dogs of ideal size. Roman held a shade of advantage in muzzle but Sensation's slightly shorter body and better hocks and hind action carried the day for him. They met on several subsequent occasions with similar results and the successes of Sensation, who was an exceptionally cobby dog, had the effect of again inclining the fancy toward that type.

This condition continued for half a dozen years or so when Sensation's influence upon the breed and cult began to wane and dogs of rather racy type once more appeared with success. The latter became more and more prevalent and upon frequent occasions of late some decidedly plain and stringy looking animals have collected championship points and changed hands at big prices. And it may be added that ballyhoo and adroit showing played no small part in their success and sale. There are individuals at the present time which may be regarded as approaching perfection quite as closely as the greatest of the past but it would be invidious to mention the names of living dogs.

Considering the breed as a whole there is perhaps a stronger tendency toward raciness in build than is altogether desirable, or as is dictated by the standard, but the breed probably shows greater uniformity of type, size and coloration than at any period in its history....

Judges and Size

...Why a heavyweight dog that scores in points over a smaller dog should be penalized for his size, is something I never could understand. Our standard gives the three weights, also that a tail shall not be over one-half the length of hock, and that the color is brindle with white markings, but that brindle must show throughout the body distinctly. Watch some of the judging. Presumably the judge does not like a large dog, also does not like a medium or light mahogany, nor a three-quarter tail, but prefers the screw tail, utterly regardless of the fact that the standard says that a tail extremely gnarled is a fault. What he likes goes up, regardless of the fact that the lighter colored dog scores the highest, and his color is absolutely correct as far as the standard specifies, the three-quarter tail penalized, and as far as putting up the heavy weight, why that is out of the question. In the past, several judges have said to me, "When two dogs are nearly equal I always put up the dog that I would rather take home with me." There is too much penalizing of the mahogany dogs, for we need them, and badly at that, either at stud or for brood matrons. If not we shall soon see more judges than ever, and it's bad enough as it is, taking the dog to the light and peering to find the brindle hairs. Personally, I prefer the short spike tail, especially in a brood female, for the twisted screw tail, is certainly no aid in whelping. If the three-quarter tail comes only half way to the back and is not carried gay, whether one likes it personally or not, it should score as high as the shorter one. As far as the heavyweight is concerned, if the judge is prejudiced against the weight, and regardless of quality would not put them to winners, then he has no right to judge those classes, unless he intends when judging the winners, to award it to the dog that scores the highest, whatever the weight and whatever his own likes or dislikes....

Mrs. F. E. Storer

April 1928

Because the supply of Mott's The Boston Terrier, which ran into several editions, has been completely exhausted and owing to the fact that the present standard differs considerably from the original one upon which Mr. Sawyer and myself had based our amplification, Editor Skinner requested the writer to cover the present standard in a similar manner.

Upon careful perusal of the original amplification it was found to apply admirably to the present standard and to describe correct type in an exhaustive manner and with much precision and detail. In fact there was too much of the latter and an excess amount of verbiage, especially as the present standard is far more comprehensive than the original one. Therefore, while the original treatise will be adhered to in its general meaning the present writing will be executed in a more brief and concise manner and with the utmost fidelity to the standard. Incidentally be it remarked that the standard of the Boston Terrier as it exists today is certainly not excelled by that of any other breed and it is difficult to see where it might be improved upon. It is couched in simple language, its phraseology is concise, and the choice of each word and placing of every punctuation mark denotes carefully studied purpose. Altogether it is one of the most comprehensive documents of its kind ever drafted.

The description of the general appearance of the Boston Terrier as given in the standard seems to be so thoroughly comprehensive that little can be said in amplification that could not better be applied to the subsequent clauses of the standard which deal directly with the various divisional parts or "points" and other desirable features of the dog. However the ensemble of build, balance,

Miss Fritz *was Winners Bitch at the first Canadian national Specialty.*

proportion, stature and contour must of necessity receive attention in connection with this paragraph as mention of such is made nowhere else in the standard. Particular attention is directed to the phraseology and its sequence, "short headed, compactly built, short tailed, well balanced dog of medium station." This means precisely what it says. Naturally a "short headed dog" must of necessity be "compactly built" and "short tailed" to be "well balanced" and were he other than of "medium station" he could not be "compactly built" or "well balanced." The "short head" must be accompanied by a "short tail" if the dog is to be "well balanced" or properly matched at both ends and certainly a short head and a long tail or vice-versa would present an odd looking Boston Terrier.

Of course station is not a matter of height as measured by inches but rather the stature of the dog in comparison with his general build and proportions. To be "well balanced" the height should be about equal to the length, exclusive of the head and neck, which will make the general body contour viewed sidewise describe a square. The standard further states "the body rather short and well knit." As the word rather modifies short the meaning is neither short nor long, therefore the only construction that can be placed upon the combination of these words is a medium length of body. As the station is described as medium, the height and length of the body must be equal, thereby describing a square, which substantiates the contentions of the writer. But aside from these technicalities it may be remarked that these are the proper proportions of the ideal Boston Terrier in actual life as observed by the writer during a period of well over twenty-five years.

Arroyo Kennels

Some confusion exists as to the record of **Ch. Arroyo Again** *because he competed under two different names. These were the days when the American Kennel Club allowed a name change. This deep rich brindle dog was originally shown and earned most of his points under the name* **Katinka Himself.** *He was bred and owned by Mrs. F.E. Storer, of Melrose, MA, who wrote the sidebar in this chapter. He was sold to Freeman Ford, of Arroyo Kennels, and finished his championship on the West Coast.*

His sire, Mrs. Storer's 14 lb. Katinka Going Up, was in much demand as a stud. He won the Stud Dog Class at the National Specialties in 1928 and 1929. It must have been quite a sight at the 1928 Specialty, when he paraded into the ring with 11 of his get. Bred in 1923, Going Up had the reputation of siring small offspring who did well in the show ring. Two of his best known get were Ch. Arroyo Again and Ch. Million Dollar Kid Boots.

Ch. Arroyo Anarchist *was one of the most beautiful of the Arroyo dogs. Said to be a spectacular show dog, he finished his championship undefeated in three straight shows in the toughest of Eastern competition. A brilliant future as a sire seemed to await him. While in the East, he sired the great top-producer Intruder, one of the pillars of the breed.*

Problems arose, however, when he was sold to a West Coast owner. It was discovered that Anarchist was deaf and probably had been so since birth. He was so intelligent and so attuned to the body language and signals of his owners that the fact had escaped notice. In California, he was retired from the show ring and seldom used at stud.

A very grainy photo of **Ch. Arroyo Ambassador,** *owned by Freeman Ford, of Arroyo Kennels, Pasadena, CA.*

An impressive show dog who also turned out to be a highly successful sire. **Ch. Introduce Me** *was the sire of seven champions. He was owned by Eunice Shuler, Walnut Hill Kennels, Canton, OH.*

A "well knit" body is absolutely essential else the dog could not be "compactly built." A shallow, shelly or long cast body is not only decidedly objectionable in itself but allows of too much open space under it, which is the very antithesis to compactness of build. "The limbs strong and neatly turned," continues the standard. Certainly the limbs must be strong to support a "well knit" body and were they otherwise the dog would not be "well balanced." "Neatly turned" describes their formation to a nicety and forestalls any misconception that heavy cumbersome bone or any appearance of massiveness or coarseness of limb is desirable. In dealing with the head the standard states it "should be in proportion to the size of the dog." This is obvious if the animal is to be "well balanced," and the same pertains to the majority of breeds. It should also be in accordance with the shape of the dog, viz., a compact dog, a compact head. Viewed in profile it should present approximately square outlines of both skull and muzzle in a similar manner to that of the body.

The remaining portions of the paragraph in general appearance will receive attention in connection with the succeeding clauses of the Standard.

The Standard states that the skull should be "square." While it does not say precisely where it should be square the natural deduction is that its several surfaces, namely, top, sides and bottom should each describe a square. Therefore, such being the case, the general formation of the skull or head proper must of necessity be that of a cube. It seems that if the word, cube, had been employed instead of, square, the meaning would have been more aptly expressed and readily understood. Technically speaking the skull of no Boston Terrier forms a cube, but in the language of dog standards it is approximately such; or at least should be. Of course, taking the cube as a basis of the skull formation, there is a rounding off of all edges and corners, but to no such extent that there should be any semblance of or approach to the form of a sphere, as is found in the Toy Spaniel and certain other breeds.

This cube conception is enhanced by the admonitions, "flat on top,...cheeks flat." Certainly if this trio of surfaces, top and sides, are "square" and "flat" the bottom one should be likewise. Such being the case the hidden surface at back and front must of necessity be "square" in contour, altogether describing the form of a cube or a skull that is of approximately the same length, depth and thickness. "Brow abrupt" further emphasizes the square or cubical idea and means that from the horizontal line of the top skull the forepart of the skull within which the eyes are set should describe a vertical drop. "Stop well defined" describes the indentation between the eyes at the juncture of muzzle and skull. This should be of moderate depth at its lowest point, extend upward in the form of a diminishing furrow and disappear entirely upon reaching the level of the top skull.

"Free from wrinkle" describes a tight skinned appearance, which should be in evidence all over the dog. No Boston Terrier is entirely free from wrinkle when unduly excited as the cocking or drawing together of the ears form tiny wrinkles on the top skull, but when standing at attention the skin should be smooth. Wrinkle is most likely to occur at the juncture of the muzzle and skull owing to the acute angle at which they join and very few Boston Terriers exist that do not show some slight corrugation of skin at this point; however the lesser the better.

In regard to the Eyes, little can be said to make this clause more comprehensive. "Wide apart" means precisely that. It may be added that they cannot be set too wide apart insofar that their outer corners do not carry around the sides of the head, which has the tendency to give them the appearance of looking outward. Their vision should be directly ahead but they should be set at the extreme outer edges of the skull with their corners on a line with the sides of the head. Their width apart should be approximately the same as that of the ears, which will give the top skull the desired "square" appearance. If they are placed closer together than the ears the skull assumes a wedge shaped appearance which is decidedly objectionable.

"Large and round" does not mean a big, bulging eye, which invariably displays the white and has a frightened, foreign expression, although there are some who seem to think such is correct. The eye should be large only in proportion to the skull, devoid of any display of white, the darker the better and neither bulging nor sunken. The eyeball is about level with the lids and although the opening is never actually round it should give the impression of roundness. Incidentally it may be remarked that there should be no falling away or hollows under or over the eyes else the skull cannot have the desired square or cubical contour.

The clause, treating the muzzle, with the exception of the one on general appearance, is the most lengthy and comprehensive of the entire Standard and gives an excellent idea of the form and proportions of the muzzle. Yet there are a few dimensions and proportions which may be more specifically furnished. It will be noted that the phrase, "short, square, wide, deep," is supplemented by, "shorter in length than in width and depth," emphasizing the fact that shortness of muzzle is highly essential. From this it may be deduced that the width and depth are approximately equal, giving the muzzle a square appearance when viewed from the front and that the length is about a third less than the width or depth. These are the perfect proportions of a Boston Terrier's muzzle, not only as based upon the wording of the standard, but according to all of the better dogs that have come under the writer's observation. It is further stated, "not exceeding in length approximately one-third the length of the skull," which is specific and correct. To this it may be added that the width and depth of the muzzle are about one-half the same of the skull. These proportions are also based upon observation of the more typical dogs.

"Width and depth carried out well to the end; the muzzle from stop to end of nose on a line parallel to the top of the skull," is a definite description. However it may be added that the unbroken under-line of skull and underjaw should also be parallel to the top lines of skull and muzzle, also that the side lines of muzzle and skull and front lines of muzzle and skull should be likewise. This will assure a full strong muzzle devoid of any taper or snipiness, also broad square jaws and even dentition. In connection with the latter it may be said that very few Boston Terriers are seen with absolutely even jaws and teeth. The majority are slightly undershot, doubtless a heritage of the early Bulldog cross, and a similar formation is found in practically all short faced breeds such as the Pekingese, English Toy and Japanese Spaniels. This is quite acceptable if it does not occur to the ex-

Ch. Introduce Me's Son *was owned by Rees L. Davies, of Anderson, IN. Mr. Davies began in Bostons in the 1920s and went on to become an all-breed judge.*

The Million Dollar Bostons

Ch. Million Dollar Kid *was born in 1920. This Ch. Peter's King son was bred by Eugene F. Shackford. He was one of the great show dogs of his time. He finished his championship in the hottest competition and then went on to ring greatness. He turned heads whenever he entered the arena. Kid was a consistent Group and Best in Show winner. It is said that he was retired only because he had beaten all comers and it was time to make room for new dogs.*

Ch. Million Dollar Kid Boots

Ch. Million Dollar Kid Boots

Few dogs have garnered as many accolades as **Ch. Million Dollar Kid Boots.** *Dubbed "The Miracle Dog of All Time" and called "incomparable," Kid Boots began his career in the late 1920s, but really reached his zenith in the early 1930s.*

From the very beginning tremendous excitement surrounded Kid Boots. The first breeding of Katinka Going Up and Kernwood Rita had produced an exciting litter which included Ch. Pomeroy's Step Up. When Rita came in season again, the breeding was repeated. One of the fans of this combination was John Harney, of Witch Hill Kennels, in Salem, MA. He purchased Kid Boots at six weeks of age and paid for an option which entitled him to first pick on any or all puppies whelped from Kernwood Rita. Naturally, the Going Up x Rita breeding was repeated a number of times.

Harney received many offers to purchase Kid Boots, but he would consider none of them, no matter the amount. Finally, when the pup was 10 weeks old, he agreed to sell an option to Eugene Shackford, of Lynn, MA, stating that should Harney ever decide to sell Kid Boots, Shackford would have first call. When he was eight months old, Kid Boots went to Shackford who turned him over for a tidy profit to Mrs. Jesse Thornton, of Maythorne Kennels, in Baltimore, MD. It was for Mrs. Thornton that Kid Boots would fulfil his potential.

The 12 lb. dog was Best of Breed at Westminster in 1930 and 1932. He was a consistent Group and Best in Show winner, thrilling crowds whenever he appeared. He proved his merit as a stud, too, siring eight champions.

Ch. Million Dollar King

The son of Ch. Million Dollar Kid, Ch. Million Dollar King was another one of the standouts from this line. Born in 1923, this dog followed in the footsteps of his sire. He was Best of Breed at Westminster in 1925 and won Groups, Best in Show and topped Specialties. He

Ch. Million Dollar King

was originally owned by Emma G. Fox, of Philadelphia, PA. In 1926, J. M. Baker paid the sum of $5,000 for the dog to head the new Ba Ro Kennels being established in Columbus, OH. Sadly, King's career was cut short when he was poisoned.

Ch. Million Dollar Blink

Born in 1925, Ch. Million Dollar Blink was bred by Bert Jones. Blink was sold to Mrs. M.C. McGlone of Mosholu Kennels. He finished his championship in short order, winning the breed and several Groups from the classes. He contributed to the Mosholu bloodlines.

Million Dollar Boy Blue

The promising Million Dollar Boy Blue was exported to England. He was purchased by Eveline, Countess of Essex who did so much to introduce the breed to Great Britain. He impressed the English audiences and did a good deal of winning in the early days. The Countess was the owner of the first Boston Terrier champion in Great Britain.

tent of giving the underjaw undue prominence or mars the perfectly perpendicular line of the muzzle. Overshot jaws are far more objectionable as they are invariably caused by a short, shallow underjaw and tend to give the muzzle a frog-faced weak appearance.

"Nose black and wide, with well defined line between nostrils," seems fully explanatory, save that the word large might have been substituted for "wide" and interpreted in the same sense that it applies to eyes. Also the word open might have been employed in connection with nostrils as the same is essential to proper respiration in any short muzzled animal. "The chops of good depth, but not pendulous, completely covering teeth when mouth is closed," may be construed to mean that their edges should not extend below the under surface of the underjaw and should fit the muzzle smoothly, but hardly so tightly or close-drawn as those of the Bull Terrier. "Free from wrinkles," means just that and has been commented upon in connection with the clause on skull.

The clause regarding the ears, while explanatory is only sufficient unto itself. No mention is made of the prevalent custom of cropping and quite rightly so, for various excellent reasons.

Born in 1925, **Ch. Fastep** *had a sensational career as a class dog. At his very first show, in 1927, he was Best of Breed at Westminster. He also took Best of Winners at a Specialty. The 16 lb. rich mahogany brindle dog earned his championship undefeated. He was bred by Warren Fitz and owned by Mr. & Mrs. A.L. Barrett, New York City.*

However as such exists it may be remarked that neatly trimmed, erect ears accentuate the cubical contour of the head and enhance the pert, smart, stylish appearance so essential in the Boston Terrier. Incidentally it should be added that under modern methods the operation can be performed without the slightest pain to the patient nor any discomfort thereafter. The placement of the ears should be at the extreme rear, top corners of the skull with the inner edges perpendicular and parallel and inclining neither forward or backward. Ambition to produce a pronounced neat and clean appearance prompts the trimming away of nearly all of the butt of the ear which is not advisable as it leaves the upper portion weak and inclined to sag or completely drop. In such cases collodion or some sort of stiffening preparation is usually resorted to; a practice to be severely condemned.

In connection with head faults, this section as well as the several other clauses throughout the standard which deal with faults only the more prevalent ones are mentioned. To include all would make far too lengthy a document. Nor will the writer attempt such as it is thought that the reader may readily distinguish the same in their many and various forms if the standard and amplification are carefully studied and borne in mind.

Medium is the preferable word to "fair" in describing the length of the neck as it coincides with the statement on station and the implication on length of body, also it is in accordance with a "compactly built, well balanced dog." Were it otherwise the dog would not be of the latter description. It should merge smoothly into both head and shoulders, showing a moderate taper toward the former, a similar arch on top and be devoid of any loose skin or throatiness. Also it should carry the head well above the level of the back which enhances the stylish, high spirited appearance of the dog.

The body clause is, in a moderate extent, contradictory to the one on general appearance, as it states, "back short" whereas the latter reads "the body rather short." They cannot be both. As it is thought that this point has been amply dealt with in the writer's comment upon the initial paragraph the reader is referred to the same, in which it will be noted that medium is the word emphasized in describing the length of the body. This contention is substantiated by the last sentence of the clause under discussion, "the body should appear short but not chunky." From this it is the logical deduction that the appearance rather than the actual existence of a short body is what is desired.

"Deep with good width of chest,...ribs deep and well sprung, carried well back to loins; loins short and muscular," can mean naught else but a sturdy, compact, capacious body devoid of any shelly, racy, narrow-fronted, flat-sided, herring-gutted appearance; which unfortunately some of our present day prize winners show. However in the matter of depth and width of chest, as viewed from the front, the Boston Terrier is comparable to none of the higher legged terriers such as the Fox and Airedale, nor to the cloddy type as exemplified in the Scottish and Sealyham. He is of about the same proportions in these respects to the Bull Terrier. In fact, except for the desired level top line from the point above the shoulder blades to that over the hip bones with a slight downward curvature toward the low set-on of tail and a trifle less length, the general contour and conformation of the Boston Terrier's body is quite similar to that of the Bull Terrier. This contention is strengthened by the phrasing, "shoulders sloping,...ribs deep and well sprung carried well back to loins, loins short and muscular;...flank very slightly cut up." An erect shoulder would make the dog's body appear too long between the fore and hind legs, and impair the desired compactness of build, besides giving the animal a stilty fore-action.

"Ribs deep and well sprung," would give a perpendicular division of the body just back of the shoulders the outline of an egg, small end down. "Carried well back to loins" means both in depth and spring of rib and in combination with, "loins short and muscular," precludes any narrow waisted or herring-gutted appearance or form. This implication is substantiated by the phrase, "flank very slightly cut up," from which it is deduced that the underline of the body should describe only a moderate upward curve upon approaching the belly and hind quarters. The correct top-line, level from withers to rump with a slight downward

With this photo of **Bob White IV,** *the last in the book, we come full circle. Here is an early dog, predominately white in color, with a squarer, more substantial type. It seems remarkable that from dogs such as these, the present day Boston Terrier sprang.*

curve to the set-on of tail, has been mentioned. When viewed from the top the body should show a slight general taper toward the rear to conform with the side view. Not the bulging fronted, pear-shaped, contour of the Bulldog, nor the narrower and rather parallel lines of the Airedale Terrier, but a medium between the two as exemplified by the Bull Terrier, although slightly lesser in length.

Pointing directly aft seems to be a terse interpretation of the elbow clause. Were the elbows to turn either out or in it would mean respectively, loose shoulders, unsoundness and an over-width of front or in-shoulders and too narrow a chest; the latter invariably being accompanied by flat ribs and a shallow body, which in turn impair compactness of build.

In writing of the forelegs "set moderately wide apart," is a confirmation of "good width of chest," the initial phrase of the body clause and may be construed as forming a front of medium width as compared between the Bulldog and the Fox Terrier or similar to that of the Bull Terrier. "On a line with the point of the shoulders," means that the outer surfaces of the fore-legs and shoulders should be flush at their juncture. Were there any extension of either the former or the latter the dog would appear thick shouldered or out at elbows, respectively. The bones of the fore-leg should be as straight as a plumb-line, preferably round in form and carrying their substance undiminished, down to the feet through the short strong and erect pasterns. A sunken, bent, long, or spindly pastern is decidedly detrimental as it indicates weakness and is apt to lower the front, thereby making the top-line of body incline toward the withers.

The forelegs should be parallel, the same width apart at the top as at the bottom, with the outer line describing a very slight convex curve near the top which is formed by the muscles of the calves.

"Set true" in the hind-legs means that the stifles and hocks or the front and rear edges of the hind-legs should point directly forward and backward. Any turning out of the former or vice-versa would be accompanied by a cow-hocked or bandy-legged formation, respectively; both of which are decidedly objectionable and border on unsoundness. "Bent at stifles" is intended to describe a well defined curve of the fore-part of the hind-leg extending downward and backward from the loins to the hock-joints, when the dog is viewed from the side. "Short from hocks to feet, hocks turning neither in nor out," is explanatory insofar as it goes, but it may be added that the hocks should be moderately well bent.

Any erect, or stilty formation at the hock joints, or in fact of any portion of the hind-legs, is decidedly detrimental, not only to the appearance of the dog but to his action, as such invariably has the effect of elevating the rump above the withers and gives the animal a stilty hind movement. "Thighs strong and well muscled," means just what it says and furthermore emphasizes the fact that a sturdy, compactly built, well-knit dog is desired.

In the vernacular the Boston Terrier has a "cat foot," which expression aptly describes its round, compact, well arched toe formation. The interstices between the toes should be so well closed that the insertion of an ordinary calling card would touch both inner surfaces. However, as the Boston Terrier is chiefly a house pet and moves on soft carpet and rugs with little opportunity of traveling about on hard pavement, digging, et cetera, his nails grow rapidly and unless kept clipped or ground down by exercise on an abrasive surface they cause splay or open feet. Many dogs' feet have been ruined by the lack of the latter attentions. In order to carry out the dog's general trim, stylish appearance and action he must be up on his toes, and such cannot be if his nails are over grown.

It is deduced from the sequence of the phrasing of the last clause, also from general observation and consensus of opinion that a tail "set on low; short, fine and tapering;" is the preferable type as it becomes the general clean, neat appearance of the dog and finishes off the rear admirably. Although a screw tail is quite acceptable, its gnarled, kinked or twisted formation is hardly so desirable as such invariably present a somewhat stubby, unfinished appearance and is apt to cause sparse and fringy in hair-covering owing to the dog's activities. In any case the tail should be set on low, be short and never carried above a horizontal position. Its length varies; however, it is thought that about two or three inches makes a very proper rear finish for the average sized dog. Should it exceed half the distance from set-on to hocks it may be considered too long.

In amplification of the word "brindle" it may be said to consist of an even and equal distribution of the composite colors. This means neither a preponderance of the light or the dark coloration of the hair. However, in the majority of dogs the latter condition exists and in some to the extent that they are only technically of brindle coloration by the saving grace of a few light hairs, usually found on the lower hind-quarters and hocks. This is doubtless due to the mistaken fetish for "dark brindles," "seal brindles," et cetera, which, unless curbed, will eventually result into the breeding out of all of the lighter brindle coloration.

That the standard states, "Brindle," and the same is emphasized by the phrase, "brindle must show throughout the body distinctly," should be borne strongly in mind in estimating the merit of a dog. As I recall off-hand two of the handsomest Boston Terriers, insofar as color and markings are concerned, that ever stepped in the ring, were Bostonia Model and Halloo Prince, yet they frequently fared badly at the hands of faddist judges who entertained the misguided idea that black with the merest interspersion of light hairs on the extremities constituted the correct coloration.

The clause concerning ideal markings is definite and descriptive and requires little comment except to say that the entire muzzle should be white and the same should extend upward between the eyes, occupying a space of about half their width apart and join in the collar marking, which in turn covers a similar portion around the neck and joins a space of like proportion on the chest. There is frequently found a small, round spot of brindle on the occiput or top skull, which is known in English Toy Spaniels and certain other breeds as the 'beauty spot" and if anything enhances the stylish appearance of the dog. No further remarks seem necessary to those of the Standard on leg markings. However, it should be stated that the white markings should be pure throughout; any presence of smudge, smut or tickings being detrimental. Also that the demarcation between the white and brindle colorations should be evenly and distinctly defined.

It may he said that the coat should be close, straight, flat and glossy, also fine and moderately stiff rather than soft in texture; else it will not fit the body closely. A Boston Terrier in perfect show condition should have the appearance of his coat fitting him after the manner of the skin on an eel.

Considering the facts that the maximum limit of weight is given at 25 pounds, that no minimum limit is mentioned, although it is an unwritten law among dog men that any canine weighing less than 12 pounds is a Toy, and that certainly the Boston Terrier is not a Toy breed, it seems that the most desirable weight would be a medium between these two limits of 12 and 25 pounds or about 18 pounds. That is about 18 pounds for males and a pound less, or 17 pounds, for females, which is the correct ratio for the differentiation between sexes in any breed of the approximate weight.

A Boston Terrier weighing 18 pounds, if he conforms with the precepts of the Standard, "compactly built" et cetera, will be encompassed in a moderately small space or one slightly lesser in length and height than the Fox Terrier, and be of ideal size for every purpose for which he can be utilized. Boston Terriers weighing upward of 20 pounds invariably are inclined toward coarseness while those under 15 pounds have a similar tendency toward shelliness, spindly legs and a generally puny build and toyish appearance, which is entirely foreign to the sturdy, well knit dog the Boston should be.

There are doubtless many who prefer the lightweights, dogs under 15 pounds, but it should be borne in mind that such seldom typify the standard to the fullest extent in its admonitions—"compactly built...well knit...limbs strong...dog should convey an impression of determination, strength and activity." Also that such smaller dogs are at a disadvantage in the show ring when competing against the sturdy, yet clean type, which is found at its best in the middleweights and that if the standard is adhered to the latter must invariably win, all other points being comparatively equal.

Appendix 1

Glossary

by Edward Axtell

On the following pages, we present a glossary dating from 1916. The terms and usages contained herein are included for your information and amusement, and to provide historical context. You will find terms here that are no longer used. In other instances you will find words whose meanings have changed entirely. Some of the meanings will surprise you and may even shock you. The idea, for instance, of administering cocaine to dogs, before going into the show ring, would seem appalling to us today.

A

Apple-headed—Skull round, instead of flat on top.

B

Beefy—Big, beefy hind quarters.

Blaze—The white line up the face.

Blood—A blood; a dog whose appearance denotes high breeding.

Brisket— The part of the body in front of the chest and below the neck.

Broken-up Face—Bulldog face, with deep stop and wrinkle and receding nose.

Broody—A brood bitch; one whose length of conformation evidences a likely mother; one who will whelp easily and rear her pups.

Bully—Where the dog approaches the Bulldog too much in conformation.

Butterfly Nose—A spotted nose.

Button Ear—An ear that falls over in front, concealing the inside.

C

Cat-foot—A short, round foot, with the knuckles well-developed.

Character—A sub-total of all the points which give to the dog the desired character associated with his particular variety, which differentiates him from all other breeds.

Cheeky—When the cheek bumps are strongly defined.

Chest—That part of the body between the forelegs, sometimes called the breast, extending from the brisket to the body.

Chops—The pendulous lips of the Bulldog.

Cobby—Thick set; low in stature, and short coupled; or well ribbed up, short and compact.

Condition—Another name for perfect health, without superfluous flesh, coat in the best of shape, and spirits lively and cheerful.

Couplings—The space between the tops of the shoulder blades, and the tops of the hip joints. A dog is accordingly said to be long or short "in the couplings."

Cow-hocked—The hocks turning inward.

Crackerjack—A first class, typical dog.

Cushion—Fullness in the top lips.

D

Deep in Brisket—Deep in chest.

Dewlap—The pendulous skin under the throat.

Dish-faced—One whose nasal bone is higher at the nose than at the stop.

Dope—A dog afflicted, usually with chorea, that has had cocaine administered to him to stop the twitching while in the judging ring.

Dudley Nose—A flesh-colored nose.

E

Elbows—The joint at the top of the forearm.

Elbows Out—Self-explanatory; either congenital, or as a result of weakness.

Even Mouthed—A term used to describe a dog whose jaws are neither overhung nor underhung.

Expression—The size and placement of the eye determines the expression of the dog.

F

Fake—A dog whose natural appearance has been interfered with to hide defects.

Flat-sided—Flat in ribs; not rounded.

Flyer—A dog capable of winning in any company.

Forearm—The foreleg between the elbows and pastern.

Frog or Down Face—Nose not receding.

H

Hall-mark—The stamp of quality that distinguishes him from inferior dogs, as the sterling mark on silver, or the hall-mark on the same metal in England.

Hare-foot—A long, narrow foot, carried forward.

Hock—The lowest point of the hind leg.

K

Kink Tail—A tail with a break or kink in it.

L

Layback—A receding nose.

Leather—The skin of the ear.

Leggy—Having the legs too long in proportion to body.

Lengthy—Possessing length of body.

Lippy—The hanging lips of some dogs, who should not possess same, as in the Bull Terrier.

Listless—Dull and sluggish.

Loins—The part of the body between the last rib and hindquarters.

Long in flank—Long in back of loins.

Lumber—Unnecessary flesh.

M

Mutt—A worthless specimen.

O

Occiput—The prominent bone at the back or top of the skull, noticeably prominent in Bloodhounds.

Overshot—The upper teeth projecting beyond the lower.

P

Pad—The underneath portion of the foot.

Pastern—The lower section of the leg below the knee or pastern respectively.

Pig-jawed—The upper jaw protruding over the lower; an exaggeration of an overshot jaw.

R

Racy—Slight in build and leggy.

Ringer—A dog shown under a false name, that has previously been shown under his right name.

Roach-back—The arched or wheel formation of loin.

Rose Ear—An ear where the tip turns backward and downward, disclosing the inside.

S

Saddle-back—The opposite of roach-back.

Screw Tail—A tail twisted in the form of a screw.

Second Thighs—The muscular development between stifle joint and hock.

Septum—The division between the nostrils.

Shelly—Narrow, shelly body.

Shoulders—The top of the shoulder blades, the point at which a dog is measured.

Snipy—Too pointed in muzzle; pinched.

Splay-foot—A flat, awkward foot, usually turned outward.

Spring—Round, or well sprung ribs; not flat.

Stern—Tail.

Stifles—The upper joint of the hind legs.

Stop—The indentation between the skull and the nasal bone near the eyes.

Style—Showy, and of a stylish, gay demeanor.

T

Terrier Type—Where the dog approaches the terrier too much in conformation.

Timber—Bone.

Tucked Up—Tucked up loin, as seen in Greyhounds.

Tulip Ear—An upright, or pricked ear.

U

Undershot—The lower incisor teeth projecting beyond the upper, as in Bulldogs.

Upright Shoulders—Shoulders that are set in an upright, instead of an oblique position.

W

Wall Eye—A blue mottled eye.

Weed—A leggy, thin, attenuated dog, bred so.

Wrinkle—Loose, folding skin over the skull.

Appendix 2

Boston Terrier Champions

Compiled by Dr. J. Varnum Mott

The following list appeared in the 1927 edition of Dr. Mott's *The Boston Terrier.* It includes a list of all champions recorded by the American Kennel Club from the date the breed was first recognized until August 1927.

A

Ace of Aces (267,497)
Agawam of By the Way (112,902)
Arroyo Adonks (160,887)
Arroyo After All (340,402)
Arroyo Adventurer (259,681)
Arroyo Aigerette (162,167)
Arroyo Angelus (190,177)
Arroyo Arbitrator (271,975)
Arroyo Audacity (177,941)
Arroyo Aviator (127,259)
Arroyo Aztec (245,125)
Aspin Hill Flapper (365,226)
Auburn Happy, Jr., (177,998)
Aulis' Happy Boy (265,256)
Aulis' Mischief (288,862)

B

Balboa Lady (382,722)
Balboa Mister Blink (520,849)
Batch (112,119)
Bayside Chauncey (72,108)
Bessie Mack (41,265)
Bestyette (265,820)
Better Luck of Manningdale (405,299)
Bierman's Judy Vee (360,070)
Bierman's Miss Victorious (400,524)
Bixie Boy II. (161,816)
Blue Princess (188,365)
Boston Jack (74,112)
Bostonia Model (148,248)
Boylston Jewel II. (118,284)
Boylston Jewel V. (137,248)
Boylston Major Noodles (126,877)
Boylston Nance (146,633)
Boylston Prince II (91,879)
Boylston Prince III. (126,878)
Boylston Reina (69,894)
Boylston Tech (80,254)
Brenda Woos II. (445,683)
Bright Eyes IV. (151,701)
Brookline Tot (65,206)
Brown's Lady Dona (216,304)
Bubble Bee (361,585)

Buddy High Ball of Rose Home (445,353)
Buffalo Again (386,162)
Bushwick Sensation (382,328)
Butte (44,020)

C

Caddy Bell (95,510)
California Poppy II. (396,284)
Captain Kinsman II. (275,635)
Captain Moody (482,699)
Cedarwold Peter Punch (249,379)
Chink II. (109,958)
Chip Chase (111,866)
Classy (134,745)
Clearcut Intruder (419,763)
Clifton Star (188,980)
Coast Guard (197,631)
Colebert's Dolly (329,592)
Col. Monte (59,722)
Commodore Flash (179,794)
Connell's Pretty Bumbles (278,956)
Croakins' Peggy (318,236)
Crystal Hard Boiled Egg (356,474)
Crystal Lady Sensation (224,652)
Cupid's Duchess (134,516)

D

Dailey's Detroit News (541,500)
Dallen's Sample (173,941)
Dallen's Sensation (168,123)
Dallen's Sentinel (345,405)
Dallen's Soubrette (177,802)
Dallen's Speedster (257,498)
Dallen's Spider (110,362)
Dallen's Sport (139,811)
Dallen's Stutz (211,507)
Dallen's Surprise (149,399)
Dandy Pat II. (257,197)
Dan Haggerty (564,204)
Day Dreamer (472,927)
Dean's Stanzalone (550,661)
Del Rey Rexona (183,277)
DeMar's Dream Girl (319,757)
Derby Boy's Gift (109,185)
District Queen (290,777)

Dolly Grand (239,275)
Dork Burma Girl (162,320)
Dougrey's Queenfull (345,523)
Druid Vixen (44,371)
Dunkel's Miss Perfection (219,641)

E

Eastover Lancelot (64,986)
E. Delilah (537,730)
Ellsworth Fifi (88,684)
El Mundo Dolly Varden (106,721)
Endcliffe Toby (37,931)
Endcliffe Topaz (113,172)
Endcliffe Totora (91,627)
Endle's Alice June (459,973)
Endle's Georgette Roman (387,250)
Endle's Speed King (525,734)
Etah (133,936)
Evergreen Evelyn III. (155,215)

F

Fairlawn Pollyanna (321,036)
Fairlawn Talk o' The Town (308,246)
Fangmann's Sandra (528,690)
Fastep (572,638)
Flash of Sunnyhill (383,178)
Folcroft Rebel (130,226)
Fosco (88,800)
Freezer (40,219)
Full Dress (286,162)

G

Gaudette's Little Boy (117,794)
Glenwood Enchantress (82,724)
Gloria Grand (307,473)
Glynn's Dotty (392,191)
Governess (10,370)
Graeber's Lady Cheerful (68,847)
Graeber's Maxinna (187,684)
Gregg's Queen O' Queens (372,715)
Grossi's Gloria (286,972)
Gyle's Ringmaster Chief (435,288)
Gyp's Beauty (248,756)

H

Haggard's June (218,279)
Haggerty's King (226,344)
Haggerty's King, Jr. (467,549)
Haggerty's King Junior's Son (496,166)
Haloo Prince (137,793)
Hammil's Bit O' Honey (420,754)
Hammil's Minstrel Boy (477 218)
Hammil's Wonderful Lady (414,714)
Hanley's Babe Boy (109,792)
Haynes' Midgie (482,095)
Headquarters Sergeant (267,037)
Heinlein's Dream Girl (22,287)
Henderson's Nifty Toss
Hickman's Mischief (264,023)
Highball Let's Go (437,232)
High Point Toddles (377,155)
Highway Boy (292,569)
Hollis' Handsome Pat (381,116)
Hygrade Sweet and Pretty (393,599)

I

I Am Damfino (404,793)
Idlewood's Invader (358,789)
Illahee Brilliant (125,951)
I'm The Guy (412,651)
Impressionable Lady (328,564)
Innis Arden (110,111)
Introduce Me (487,530)
Intruder III. (547,885)
Intruder Blink (322,471)

J

Jab's King Tut (366,703)
Jackson's Marchetta (465,568x)
Jenning's Caesar (301,807)
Joy O' Valentine (514,461)
Junior II. (85,268)

K

Katz's King (439,515)
Kenilworth Pickpocket (83,124)
Kenilworth Yankee Doddle (103,660)

Ketoson's Worthy Maid (393,944)
Kielway's Little Dreams (438,573)
King's Pride III (293,416)
King's Romance (375,783)
Kingway Blink (427,224)
Kingway Charlotte (350,410)
Kingway Cheerie (377,872)
Kingway's Connie (427,221)
Kingway's K. O. A. (498,842)
Kingway Tommy Disturber (301,387)
Kinsman Belle (72,327)

L

Laddy Babbie Forbes (411,097)
Lady Anthony (83,340)
Lady Belle XVIII. (207,962)
Lady Careless (114,118)
Lady Dainty (71,617)
Lady Dilham (225,062)
Lady Harmless (204,141)
Lady Highball (82,795)
Lady Johnston (289,314)
Lady Leonora (230,213)
Lady Margaret Jane (301,634)
Lady Muffit IV. (291,630)
Lady Nu Nu (358,064)
Lady Ringleader (159,823)
Lady Tameless (265,874)
Lencon Beauty (458,377)
Lento's Handsome Boy (340,613)
Little Bo-Peep Forbes (328,400)
Little Jack Horner II. (520,068)
Little Miss Muffit II. (535,875)
Little Tommy Tucker II. (351,419)
Little Tony Wagner (193,700)
Lord Brilliant (462,597)
Lord Derby (63,146)

M

Mabel Trask (207,483)
Major Dilham (306,851)
Major Raffles (163,191)
Marshall's Intimate (371,966)
Master Perfection (189,558)
Master King III. (292,761)

Matteson's Little Queen
Mecca's Gloriana (484,390)
Midget King (185,752)
Million Dollar Kid (301,881)
Million Dollar Kid, Jr. (340,555)
Million Dollar King (439,091)
Miss Bunch (64,050)
Miss Fortune Ring (368,231)
Miss Kinsman (74,940)
Miss Phyllis (45,840)
Miss Punch II. (181,083)
Miss Rosasano's Beauty (463,755)
Miss Sporty Toss (187,118)
Mister Jack (108,555)
Misty Morning (343,152)
Montclair June Day (340,760)
Monte (39,414)
Mosholu Bambino (385,767)
Mosholu Beau (281,608)
Mosholu Billy Boss (452,391)
Mosholu Blink (243,321)
Mosholu Brigand (220,215)
Mosholu Buddy Blink (296,638)
Mosholu Tommy Blink (514,431)
My Rockabye Baby (488,868)

N

Nation's Little Queen (391,258)
Noboska II. (63,272)
Noel's Bebe (491,464)
Novelty Girl (282,870)

O

Oakcliffe Polly-With-a-Past (263,077)
Oakmont Gent (97,114)
Oarsman (73,073)
Ogden's Rolls Royce (342,670)
O Glo's Beauty (380,735)
On Time (352,274)
Onstadt's Tom Tucker (240,137)
Opal (55,650)
Osage Brambelette (134,666)
Our Sammy (246,615)
Out for Sport (347,600)

P

Paramount Keteson (292,571)
Paramount Nioda (326,122)
Patsy Dee II. (370,116)
Patterson's Teddy Buster (326,144)
Per Capita Max (478,827)
Peter's Captain (187,881)
Peter's King (167,232)
Picktime Glencoe (149,652)
Playfair's Let's Go (449,162)
Preston Fairy (119,439)
Prince Conde (265,072)
Princess Iris (171,502)
Princess Lou II. (220,717)
Profile Lady of the Lake (346,342)
Profile Real Select (425,607)

Q

Queenie B. (282,124)
Queenie King (243,804)
Queenie VI

R

Raffle's Lady Bug (242,131)
Ralby's Beautiful Girl (184,790)
Ramsey's Rockabye Baby (347,594)
Rattler King II. (233,500)
Ravenroyd Radio
Ravenroyd Revelation (339,941)
Ravenroyd Rockefeller (497,232)
Ravenroyd Rock 'n Rye (427,689)
Ravenroyd Rolls Royce (271,423)
Ravenroyd Romance (212,231)
Ravenroyd Rounder (348,314)
Remilik Bonnie (64,488)
Revillo Beauty (133,203)
Revillo Peach (72,425)
Revillo Tomah (91,649)
Rexcella Tomah (91,649)
Rexonian King O' the Avenue (450,625)
Roach's Honey Boy (142,742)
Rockbound's Bontuwyn (513,493)
Rockbound's Tango (540,215)
Rockcliffe Beautiful Doll (155,465)

Rockcliffe The Joker (149,912)
Rocks (93,061)
Roop's Step Out (369,473)
Rose Home Blue Princess (285,003)
Rose Home Fair Play (344,380)
Rose Home King's Pal (219,070)
Rose Home My Own (386,322)
Rose Home Queen of All (331,213)
Rose Home Speed (410,582)
Rose Home Trickey Trixie (231,635)
Roxie (49,346)

S

Sanborn's Stutzette (350,429)
Sands of Pleasure (406,626)
Selwonk Beauty (60,294)
Sergeant's Gleaming Silk (436,802)
Silk Hat King (479,281)
Simmon's Little Buster (248,356)
Sir William (102,053)
Sister Carrie (131,630)
So Big of Sunny Hill (425,851)
Some Boy (175,800)
Sonnie Punch (210,539)
Some Fascinator's Surprise (30,982)
Sparkling Jewel (163,261)
Spider (40,220)
Sportsman (71,215)
Spotlight Girl (28,197)
Sunlight II. (120,366)
Sunny Blink (428,463)
Surprise (60,802)
Sweet Susanne (485,552)
St. Louis News (484,733)

T

Tansy (39,409)
The Bat of Buffalo (303,913)
The Demon (133,661)
The Jolly Widow (133,658)
The Painted Lady (421,221)
The Pink Lady (163,924)
The Whistler (183,101)
Thorpe's Tiny King (262,697)
Thwaite's Keto (222,521)

Tiny Raffles (209,360)
Tiny Teddy B. (265,949)
Todd Boy (114,309)
Tomlinson's Beauty (288,718)
Topsy Ringmaster (158,233)
Topsy (37,060)
Trimount Countess (142,476)
Trimount Fairy (132,892)
Trimount Harper (496,876)
Trimount King (336,451)
Trimount Lida (179,332)
Trimount Roman (168,711)
Truxton Queen (139,122)
Tyron's Dianette (447,166)
Tyron's Doreen (447,165)
Tyron's Heads Up (413,667)
Tyron's Queen's Adele (216,212)
Tyron's Queen Diana (354,426)
Turnstile Victory Boy (251,184)

V

Valla Verde Boy (428,222)
Van Velsor's Virgie
Victory Belle (254,073)
Viking (81,448)
Vivillo Dandy (109,816)
Vuelta Glory (102,322)

W

Wadman's Cutie (296,211)
Walnut King (346,982)
Wampagne Delight (139,075)
Wampagne Prince (149,406)
Whisper (71,718)
Who Cares II. (382,134)
Who Knows Me (423,929)
Wildwest Sparkle (185,035)
Worthwhile Dottie Dae (401,046)

Y

Yankee Doodle Darling (133,469)
Yankee Doodle Pride (137,979)
Yankee Spider (151,510)
Yankee Doodle Dick (138,268)
Yankee Doodle Rip (124,996)

Appendix 3

First Annual Dog Show

Boston Terriers Only

Boston Terrier Breeders' Club

Wednesday, Thursday, Friday

November 23, 24, 25

1898

Officers of the Boston Terrier Breeders' Club

Joseph O. McMullen, President
A. M. Tyner, Vice President
F. E. Danker, Secretary
T. Benson, Treasurer

Executive Committee

T. Benson   F. J. Munson
Dr. F. A. Locke   H. E. Belmont
P. H. Clarke   P. Brickley
G. S. Haliwell

Judge

H. W. Lacy, of Boston

Dr. G. B. Foss, Veterinary Surgeon
C. F. Sullivan, Superintendent

Rules

A dog suffering from any hereditary, contagious or objectionable disease shall be disqualified, and forfeit the prize which may be awarded to it, and shall be at once removed from the show building. A regularly appointed veterinary surgeon shall alone decide as to the condition of the dog, and his decision must be given in writing.

Full discretionary power is given to the judge of each class to withhold any or all prizes for want of merit. The judge's decision will be final in all cases affecting the merits of the dogs, and appeals can only be entertained where misrepresentation or breach of the rules is alleged.

A judge shall disqualify a dog which, in his opinion, has been improperly tampered with, subject to the decision of the veterinary surgeon. Should the judge's disqualification not be sustained, the class must be rejudged.

Classes

I. The Puppy Class shall be for all dogs over six months and under twelve months of age. No entry can be made or accepted of one under six months of age, or whose date of birth is unknown.

II. The Novice Class shall be for all dogs never having won first prize at any recognized show, wins in the Puppy Class excepted.

III. The Open Class shall be for all dogs of any age over six months.

1. No special prizes can be accepted or offered by a Show Committee after the show has opened.

2. The age of a dog shall be calculated up to and inclusive of the day preceding the show; for instance, a dog whelped April 30th shall not be eligible on May 1st of the following year to compete for dogs under twelve months of age.

3. Entries made in the name of a kennel must be accompanied by the name of the actual proprietor or proprietors, but not necessarily for publication. The partners in a kennel shall be deemed equally culpable in the case of fraud perpetuated in their name.

4. The person presenting the identification ticket shall be recognized as the agent of the owner in the latter's absence, and his receipt of prize money shall be binding on the owner, unless notice to the contrary is indorsed (sic) on the identification ticket.

5. The Secretary of the Boston Terrier Breeders' Club must cancel all wins when he is satisfied himself that these rules have been violated by the exhibitor, in the following instances:

When an entry has been made after the advertised date of closing of entries.

When a dog has been pronounced deaf by a competent authority.

When a puppy is entered, being under six months of age, or as date of birth unknown.

List of Special Prizes

J.H. Horrigan offers Silver Cup for the best Stud Dog judged by two of his get. Also offers Silver Cup for best Brood Bitch judged by two of her get.

J. McMurray offers Silver Cup for the best Headed Dog or Bitch in show.

Mrs. E. Deffley offers Silver Cup for the best Dog or Bitch sired by Banker.

Mr. J. A. Boutelle offers Silver Cup for the best Light Weight Bitch.

A.M. Tyner offers Silver Cup for the best Heavy Weight Bitch. Also offers Silver Cup for the best Puppy Bitch.

T. Benson offers Silver Cup for the best Heavy Weight Dog.

C.F. Sullivan offers Silver Cup for the best Dog sired by Sullivan's Punch. Also Cup for the best Bitch sired by Punch.

J.O. McMullen offers Silver Cup for best Dog or Bitch. Also Silver Cup for the best Dog or Bitch sired by Sullivan's Punch.

Mr. F.J. Munson offers Silver Cup for the best Kennel of four or more.

P.J. Brickley offers Silver Cup for the best Dog or Bitch sired by Lord Nelson.

G.S. Haliwell offers Silver Cup for the best Dog or Bitch sired by O'Connell's Ned.

A Friend of the Club offers Silver Cup for the best Dog or Bitch sired by Plant's Tom Sayers.

Mrs. T. Benson offers Silver Cup for the best Puppy Bitch sired by Punch, owned by Lady exhibitor.

Educator Cracker Company offers for best Puppy 1 Box of Dog Biscuit.

L. Hitchcock offers a $15.00 Prize for best Dog and Bitch owned by one exhibitor.

Dr. F.A. Locke offers Silver Cup for the best Puppy Dog.

Mr. John O'Connor offers Silver Cup for the best Dog or Bitch sired by Monte. Also Silver Cup for the best Dog or Bitch sired by Conspirator.

James Forgie & Son offer Fancy Collar for the best Light Weight Bitch in Show.

Entries

CLASS 1—PUPPY DOGS

First Prize, $3.00. Second Prize, $2.00   Third Prize, Medal

1. Joseph McMurray. **Cameron.** November 22, 1897. Breeder, Dr. Henderson. By Peko—Peggy. Price, $500

2. Joseph McMurray. **Richard.** January 30, 1897. Breeder, M.F. Tierney. By O'Connell's Ned—Tierney's Liz. Price, $100

3. Joseph McMurray. **Jim.** February 28, 1898. Breeder, J. McMurray. By King—Nell. Price, $50

4. John F. Gillespie. **Mickey Duffy.** April 15, 1898. Breeder, T. Arahill. By Senator—Nancy. Price, $100

5. John F. Gillespie. **Whiskey.** April 15, 1898. Breeder, T. Arahill. By Senator—Nancy. Price, $100

6. T.S. Connelly. **Buster, Jr.** March 2, 1898. Breeder, T.S. Connelly. By Punch—Muggins. Price, $75

7. John Howard. **Punch II.** Price, $100

8. J. O'Conner. **Davy.** May 9, 1898. Breeder, J. O'Conner. By Punch—Peggy. Price, $100

9. J.J. Gilman. **Prince.** May 20, 1898. Breeder, J.J. Gilman. By Hickey's Teddy—Budge. Price, $50

10. J.J. Gilman. **Colonel.** May 20, 1898. Breeder, J.J. Gilman. By Hickey's Teddy—Budge. Price, $50

11. J.F. Murray. **Broker.** Dec., 1897. Breeder, J.F. Murray. By Buster—Floss. Not for sale

12. W.J. Scott. **Leo Boy.** May, 1898. Breeder, W.J. Scott. By Dandy Boy—Bessie. Not for sale

13. R. Roach. **Muggins.** April 1, 1898. Breeder, R. Roach. By Punch—Jenny.

14. R. Roach. **Ben.** April 1898. Breeder, P. Dolan. By King 3rd—Topsy.

15. Waban Kennels. **Pepper.** May, 1898. Breeder, Waban Kennels. By Midget—Bonner.

16. R. Travers. **Dewey.** March 8, 1898. Breeder, R. Travers. By Arahill's Bob—Judy. Price, $150

17. G.S. Haliwell. **Aladdin.** March 5, 1898. Breeder, G.S. Haliwell. By Ned—Bess.

18. M.F. Mulcahey. **Banquo.** April 1, 1898. Breeder, Mrs. Skelly. By Pat G.—Nellie.

19. Esther B. Deffley. **Roosevelt.** May 1898. Breeder, Mrs. F.A. Young. By Banker—Peggy.

19a. W.H. Carroll. **Rake.** January 3, 1898. Breeder, J. McCabe. By Tony Boy, Jr.—Nance. Price, $100

19b. C. Carroll. **Davy.** Seven months. Breeder, C. Carroll. By Punch—Trilby.

CLASS 2—PUPPY BITCHES

First Prize, $3.00. Second Prize, $2.00   Third Prize, Medal

20. John F. Gillespie. **Bessie.** March 8, 1898. Breeder, R. Travers. By Bob—Judy. Not for sale

21. T. Benson. **Judy.** May 9, 1898. Breeder, T. Benson. By Punch—Vick. Price, $100

22. George F. Cudahy. **Trouble.** May, 1898. Breeder, Mr. Lawton. By Lord Nelson—Lawton's Bitch.

23. J. McMullen. **Bessie.** March, 1898. Breeder, McMullen. By Punch—Corinne. Not for sale

24. Benjamin L. Jones. **Princess.** January 12, 1898. Breeder, F.G. Calhoun. By Buster—Empress. F.G. Calhoun, Agent.
    Winnings: First Prize, Providence, 1898. Second Prize, Braintree, 1898

25. C. Cabot. **Grit.** February 12, 1898. Breeder, F. Ross. By Kenyon's Punch—Emma.

26. J.F. Gilman. **Topsey.** December 25, 1898. Breeder, Mr. Patterson. By Buster—Nellie.

27. John Lawler. **Peggie.** January 3, 1898. Breeder, John Lawler. By Tom Sayers—Gypsey. Price, $100

28. P. Donahue. **Lady.** December, 1898. By Buster—Floss.

29. R. Roach. **Rosie.** April 1, 1898. Breeder, R. Roach. By Punch—Jennie. Price, $100

30. Mrs. H.M. Stone. **Peggy S.** February 12, 1898. Breeder, H.M. Stone. By Punch—Sadie S.

31. H.M. Stone. **Lady Spotty.** January 30, 1898. Breeder, H.M. Wolf. By Jocko—Bess.

32. Dr. Locke. **Carrie.** March 5, 1898. Breeder, G.S. Haliwell. By O'Connell's Ned—Bess.

33. Dr. Locke. **Peggie.** March 5, 1898. Breeder, G.S. Haliwell. By O'Connell's Ned—Bess.

34. P. Brickley. **Floss.** May, 1897. Breeder, M. Lawton. By Lord Nelson—Mollie.

35. Mrs. H. Sullivan. **Caprice.** March, 1898. By Punch—Corinne. Price, $200
Winnings: First Prize, Providence, 1898

36. F.B. Grout. **Patrice.** April 1, 1898. Breeder, Mrs. Skelly. By Pat G.—Nellie.

37. Esther B. Deffley. **Mahala.** November, 1898. Breeder, Esther B. Deffley. By Banker—Jessie.

37a. Miss Mattie O'Brien. **Polly.** March 18, 1898. Breeder, C. Richardson. By Max—Dolly.

37b. D. Manley. **Venice.** By Bixby's Tony Boy—Flossie.

CLASS 3—NOVICE DOGS

First Prize, $3.00.   Second Prize, $2.00   Third Prize, Medal

[1.] **Cameron.** Entered in Class I.
[2.] **Richard.** Entered in Class I.
[3.] **Jim.** Entered in Class I.
[17.] **Aladdin.** Entered in Class I.
[13.] **Muggins.** Entered in Class I.
[14.] **Ben.** Entered in Class I.
[11.] **Broker.** Entered in Class I.

38. J. McMurray. **McMurray's King.** AKCSB, 42,756. Breeder, P. Dolan. By Old Sport—Dolan's Chester. Price, $250

39. T. Arahill. **Bob II.** AKCSB, 41,512. Breeder, Owner. By Monte—Nancy.

40. R. Robbins. **Jingo.** AKCSB, 47,856. Breeder, Mr. Greeley. Price, $1,000
Winnings: First Puppy, Boston, 1897

[4.] **Mickey Duffy.** Entered in Class I.
[5.] **Whiskey.** Entered in Class I.

41. John F. Gillespie. **The Alderman.** February 26, 1897. Breeder, E. Rogers. By Buster—Beauty. Not for sale

[6.] **Buster, Jr.** Entered in Class I.

42. T. Benson. **Jem Mace, Jr.** Breeder, T. Plant. By Jem Mace—Nellie. Price, $350

[7.] **Punch II.** Entered in Class I.

43. John Howard. **Sham.** July, 1896. By Baldwin's Bob. Price, $100

45. J. O'Connor. **Little Billee.** January 4, 1896. Breeder, R. Travers. By Tom—Nell. Not for sale.

[8.] **Davy.** Entered in Class I.
[9.] **Prince.** Entered in Class I.
[10.] **Colonel.** Entered in Class I.

46. John Shepard. **Skip.** 1887. Breeder, J. Shepard. By Grip—Lady. Not for sale

47. P. Donahue. **Donahue's Vic.** 1896. Breeder, Owner.

48. P. Donahue. **Donahue's Grit.** 1896. Breeder, Owner.

49. P. Donahue. **Doctor.** April, 1896. Breeder, Owner. By Bob—Donahue's Nancy.

50. P. Donahue. **Alpine.** Breeder, owner.

51. R. Roach. **Trix.** November 13, 1896. Breeder, Mr. Wadell. By Tony Jr.—Beauty.

52. J. Hildebrand. **Mike.** August 19, 1897. Breeder, G.S. Haliwell. By Prince—Bess.

53. G.S. Haliwell. **Ben.** August 19, 1897. Breeder, G.S. Haliwell. By Punch—Bess.

54. G.S. Haliwell. **Nobby Boy.** August 19, 1897. Breeder, G.S. Haliwell. By Punch—Bess.

55. P. Brickley. **Lord Nelson.** November 18, 1896. Breeder, Mr. Sims. By Buster—Tot.

56. P. Brickley. **Governor.** May, 1897. Breeder, P. Brickley. By Turk—Peggy.

57. P. Brickley. **Bob.** May, 1897. Breeder, Mr. Topham. By Punch—Flirt.

58. P. Brickley. **Bingo.** 1894. Breeder, P. Brickley. By Judge—Floss.

59. P. Brickley. **Sandy.** 1896. Breeder, Mr. Collins. By Dick—Fuse.

60. Mrs. T. Plant. **Tom Sayers.** (Imported)
    Winnings: Second, Boston; Second, Providence; Second, Manchester; Second, C. Club

61. Mrs. B. Pope. **Chappie.** June 17, 1897. Breeder, Mrs. B. Pope. By Punch—Wag.

62. Dr. Kendall. **Dabster.** June, 1895. Breeder, J. Sullivan. By Ned—Rose.
    Winnings: Second, Brooklyn, 1897; First, Providence, 1897; Third, New York, 1898

62a. C.F. Sullivan. **Nixie S.** Breeder, H.M. Stone. By Buster—Hazel.

CLASS 4—NOVICE BITCHES

First Prize, $3.00.   Second Prize, $2.00   Third Prize, Medal

62b. Esther B. Deffley. **Favorite.** Breeder, Esther B. Deffley.

63. G.H. Fisher. **Cissy Fitzgerald.** 1894. Breeder, McClough. By Tony Boy, Jr.—Rooney. Price, $100

[24.] Benjamin L. **Princess.** Jones. F.G. Calhoun, Agent. Entered in Class 2. By Buster—Empress.
[25.] C. Cabot. **Grit.** Entered in Class 2.
[26.] J. Gilman. **Topsey.** Entered in Class 2.

64. J.F. Gilman. **Bridge.** September 5, 1894. Breeder, T.J. Kenny. By Tom Sayers—Tug.

65. J.F. Brown. **Mab.** January 11, 1893. Breeder, J.F. Brown. By Ben—Rose.

66. J.F. Brown. **Dinah.** August 27, 1897. Breeder, E. Linnett. By Tom—Meta.

67. George Lally. **Topsey.**

68. John Shepard. **Nellie.** 1895. Breeder, Mr. Tayler. By Dandy—Nell.

69. J. Shepard. **Lady.** September, 1896. Breeder, J. Shepard. By Dixie—Nell.

[28.] P. Donahue. **Lady.** Entered in Class 2.

70. P. Donahue. **Lucy.** 1896. Breeder, P. Donahue. By Teddy—Fanny.

71. D. Roach. **Cissy Fitzgerald.** November, 1896. Breeder, J. McMurray. By Old Sport—Fanny Mack. Price, $500
Winnings: Second, Manchester, 1897.

72. R. Roach. **Jenny.** November, 1896. Breeder, J. Roach. By Punch—Jennie. Price, $150

73. Mrs. O'Neil. **Nancy.** April, 1897. Breeder, O'Neil. Pedigree, unknown. Price, $50

[32.] Dr. Locke. **Cassie.** March, 1898. Entered in Class 2.
[33.] Dr. Locke. **Peggie.** March 5, 1898. Entered in Class 2.

74. D. Manley. **Flossie.** June, 1898. Breeder, D. Manley. By Judge—Rose.

75. J. Gussen. **Queenie.** October, 1897. Breeder, J. Gussen. By Kearn's Tony Boy—Liz.

76. C.F. Sullivan. **Rosemary.** June, 1896. Breeder, Mr. Fields. By Pilot—Beauty.

77. C.F. Sullivan. **Betsey.** August, 1896. Breeder, Owner. By Spider—Debbie.

78. C.F. Sullivan. **Trixie S.** 1896. Breeder, H.M. Stone. By Spider—Debbie.

79. C.F. Sullivan. **Buttons.** 1896. Breeder, H.M. Stone. By Spider—Debbie.

80. R.B. Jewett. **Cinders.** February, 1898. Breeder, J. Marra. By Buster—Whitey.

81. J. Stewart. **Elenoir.** September, 1897. Breeder, Mr. Jarvis. By Tony Boy—Hazel.

82. G.S. Haliwell. **Della Fox.** 1896. Breeder, Mr. Moriarty. By Burrell's Dog—Moriarty's Bitch.

83. G.S. Haliwell. **Mollie.** August, 1897. Breeder, Owner. By Punch—Bess.

84. G.S. Haliwell. **Melba.** August, 1897. Breeder, Owner. By Punch—Bess.

85. G.S. Haliwell. **Diana.** 1897. Breeder, Owner. By Punch—Bess.

86. J. Hildebrand. **Lucy.** October, 1897. Breeder, Mr. Lynch. By Ned—Fanny.

87. G.S. Haliwell. **Bess.** 1893. Breeder, G.S. Haliwell. By Boxer—Daisy.

[34.] P. Brickley. **Floss.** Entered in Class 2.

88. P. Brickley. **Topsy.** August, 1897. Breeder, Mr. Topham. By Punch—Flirt.

89. Charles O. Hart. **Clotilde.** February, 1896. Breeder, Charles O. Hart. By Commissioner II—Topsy.

90. J.J. McBride. **Wrinkles.** 1897. Breeder, J.J. McBride. By Dan—Beauty.

91. D. Manley. **Sting.** 1898. Breeder, P. Brickley. Pedigree, unknown.

92. T. Arahill. **Nancy II.** July, 1897. Breeder, H. Reed. By Tom Sayers—Mollie. Price, $1,000

93. H. Reed. **Mettie.** February, 1897. Breeder, H. Reed. By Tom Sayers—Mollie. Price, $150

94. P. Clark. **Beauty.** April, 1894. Breeder, P. Brickley. By Mike—Mollie. Price, $500

95. P. Clark. **Betsy.** Breeder, E. Reedy. By Tom Sayers—Judy.

96. P. Clark. **Daisy.** Breeder, P. Clark. By Tip—Nell. Price, $300

[20.] F. Gillespie. **Bessie.** Entered in Class 2.

97. George H. Fisher. **Melba.** 1897. Breeder, G.H. Fisher. By Woogle—Nellie. Price, $100

98. T.S. Connelly. **Rags.** October, 1896. Breeder, Owner. By Monte—Kit. Price, $250

99. T.S. Connelly. **Judy 2nd.** September, 1897. Breeder, Owner. By Turk—Kit. Price, $100

100. T.S. Connelly. **Cyrene.** January, 1898. Breeder, Owner. By Bonnie—Kit. Price, $100

101. T.S. Connelly. **Judy.** February 18, 1898. Breeder, P. Boyd. Tom Sayers—Gypsy. Price, $100

102. T.S. Connelly. **Muggins.** May, 1897. Breeder, P. Boyd. By Lord Nelson—(—). Price, $125

103. T. Benson. **Bo-Peep.** 1897. Breeder, Mr. Weeks. By Buster—Bessy. Price, $100

[21.] T. Benson. **Judy.** Entered in Class 2.

104. T, Benson. **Queen.** Breeder, Mr. Hartford. By Monte—Fannie. Price, $500

105. J.O. McMullen. **Dolly.** July, 1897. Breeder, Owner. By Punch—Corinne.

106. J.O. McMullen. **Gyp.** July, 1897. Breeder, Owner. By Punch—Corrine.

[23.] J.O. McMullen. **Bessie.** Entered in Class 2.

107. J.O. McMullen. **Corrine.** July 30, 1896. Breeder, G.S. Haliwell. By Turk—Bess.

108. John Howard. **Gypsy.** June, 1897. By Jingo—(—). Price, $100

108a. H.J. O'Brien. **Bijou.** August 12, 1896. Breeder, unknown. By Tom Sayers—Woods.

CLASS 5—LIGHT-WEIGHT DOGS

First Prize, $7.00.   Second Prize, $5.00   Third Prize, $3.00

[1.] **Cameron.** Entered in Class 1.

109. J. McMurray. **Richard.** January, 1897. Breeder, Owner. By Ned—Liz.

[40.] **Jingo.** Entered in Class 3.
[4.] **Mickey Duffee.** Entered in Class 1.
[5.] **Whiskey.** Entered in Class 1.
[41.] **Alderman.** Entered in Class 3.
[6.] **Buster, Jr.** Entered in Class 1.
[7.] **Punch H.** Entered in Class 1.
[8.] **Davy.** Entered in Class 1.
[9.] **Prince.** Entered in Class 1.
[10.] **Colonel.** Entered in Class 1.
[3.] **Jim.** Entered in Class 1.
[47.] **Vic.** Entered in Class 3.
[48.] **Grit.** Entered in Class 3.
[11.] **Broker.** Entered in Class 1.
[46.] **Skip.** Entered in Class 3.

108b. J. Shepherd. **Dixie.** 1892. Breeder, unknown. By Leland's Dandy— (—).

109. Joseph Murphy. **Pat.** September, 1897. Breeder, J. Shepherd. By Dixie—Nellie.

110. F.H. Speed. **Ben Butler.** June, 1895. Breeder, F.B. Seavy. By Buster—Stella.

111. F.H. Speed. **Milo.** August, 1897. Breeder, F.H. Speed. By Doctor—Topsy.

[50.] **Alpine.** Entered in Class 3.
[51.] **Trix.** Entered in Class 3.
[52.] **Mike.** Entered in Class 3.
[53.] **Ben.** Entered in Class 3.
[54.] **Nobby Boy.** Entered in Class 3.
[17.] **Aladdin.** Entered in Class 1.
[56.] **Governor.** Entered in Class 3.
[57.] **Bob.** Entered in Class 3.
[59.] **Sandy.** Entered in Class 3.
[61.] **Chappie.** Entered in Class 3.

112. C.F. Sullivan. **Punch.** July, 1896. Breeder, Mr. Belmont. By Ned—Peggy. Winnings: First, Providence, 1897; First, Providence, 1898.

113. C.F. Sullivan. **Major.** Price, $75

[62a.] C.F. Sullivan. **Nixie S.** Entered in Class 3.

114. Dr. Kendall. **Shawmut.** November, 1897. Breeder, P. McDonald. Tom Sayers—Fan. Winnings: First, Puppy, Braintree, 1898; First Novice, Limit, Open, Winners, Danbury, 1898.

115. Richard Hickey. **Lord Randolph.** By Dixie—Juno Mack. Not for competition.

115a. Fred. McLaughlin. **Binkie.** July 16, 1887. Breeder, Tim Walsh. Pedigree unknown. Price, $1,000

CLASS 6—LIGHT-WEIGHT BITCHES

First Prize, $7.00. Second Prize, $5.00   Third Prize, $3.00

[68.] **Nellie.** Entered in Class 4.
[69.] **Lady.** Entered in Class 4.
[70.] **Lucy.** Entered in Class 4.
[72.] **Jennie.** Entered in Class 4.
[29.] **Rosie.** Entered in Class 2.
[27.] **Peggy.** Entered in Class 2.
[32.] **Cassie.** Entered in Class 2.
[83.] **Mollie.** Entered in Class 4.
[84.] **Melba.** Entered in Class 4.

[85.] **Diana.** Entered in Class 4.
[82.] **Della Fox.** Entered in Class 4.
[96.] **Daisy.** Entered in Class 4.
[95.] **Betsy.** Entered in Class 4.
[20.] **Bessie.** Entered in Class 2.
[98.] **Rago.** Entered in Class 4.
[100.] **Cyrene.** Entered in Class 4.
[99.] **Judy II.** Entered in Class 4.
[101.] **Judy.** Entered in Class 4.

116. T. Benson. **Vick.** August, 1896. Breeder, Mr. Carroll. By Lord Nelson—Bessie. Not for competition. Price, $500

[104.] **Queen.** Entered in Class 4.
[105.] **Dolly.** Entered in Class 4.
[106.] **Gyp.** Entered in Class 4.
[23.] **Bessie.** Entered in Class 2.
[108.] **Gypsy.** Entered in Class 4.

116a. Esther B. Deffley. **Pauline.** September, 1896. Breeder, B. Deffley. By Banker—Florence. Winnings: First, New York, April, 1898.

[63.] **Cissy Fitzpatrick.** Entered in Class 4.
[26.] **Topsy.** Entered in Class 2.
[165.] **Mab.** Entered in Class 4.
[66.] **Dina.** Entered in Class 4.
[88.] **Topsy.** Entered in Class 4.

117. Volney Poore. **Miss Phyliss.** Breeder, F.J. Bixby. By Tony Boy, Jr.—Princess. Winnings: First Novice, Open, and Winners, New York, April, 1896.

[75.] **Queenie.** Entered in Class 4.
[76.] **Rosemary.** Entered in Class 4.
[77.] **Betsy.** Entered in Class 4.
[78.] **Trixie S.** Entered in Class 4.
[79.] **Buttons.** Entered in Class 4.

118. Dr. Kendall. **Pig Wig.** Breeder, Owner. By Tom Sayers—Mora. Winnings: Providence, 1895.

118a. C. Carroll. **Bloaks.** 1896. Price, $100

[108a.] **Bijou.** Entered in Class 4.
[74a.] **Jess.** Entered in Class 4.

CLASS 7—HEAVY-WEIGHT DOGS

First Prize, $7.00.   Second Prize, $5.00   Third Prize, $3.00

[38.] **Jos. McMurray's King,** Not for Competition. Entered in Class 3.
[1.] **Cameron.** Entered in Class 1.
[39.] **Bob, 2nd.** Entered in Class 3.
[42.] **Jem Mace.** Entered in Class 3.
[23.] **Sham.** Entered in Class 3.

119. Jos. McMullen. **Boxer.** Not for Competition.

120. Esther B. Deffley. **Banker.** September, 1895. Breeder, Mr. Kernan. By Tony—Nell.
   Winnings: First, Danbury, 1897; First, New York, 1895; First, New York, 1898.

[44.] **Mark Hanna.** Entered in Class 3.
[45.] **Little Billie.** Entered in Class 3.

121. J. Donahue. **Jim Corbett.** 1897. Breeder, J. Manley. By Tony Boy—Queenie. Price, $300

122. George Lally. **Pilot.** Breeder, C. Kammerer. By Trimount King—Countess
   Winnings: Third, New York, 1894; Third, New York, 1895; First and Special, Providence, 1895.

123. M. Murphy. **Doctor.** 1896. Breeder, unknown. By Tony—Musty.

[49.] P. Donahue. **Doctor.** Entered in Class 3.

124. J.J. Doleni. **King II.** AKC 45,346. Breeder, unknown. By King—Crusty. Price, $2,000.

125. T. Digman. **Jerry.** September, 1896. Breeder, J. Gunley. By Dan—Specks.

[55.] **Lord Nelson.** Entered in Class 3.
[58.] **Bingo.** Entered in Class 3.
[60.] **Tom Sayers.** Entered in Class 3.

126. Mrs. J. P. Belcher. **Billie.** 1897. Price, $25.

127. W. Lynch. **Ben Harvard.** September, 1896. Breeder, W.W. Lynch. By Rennie—Browni.

128. Mrs. Benjamin Pope. **Casey.** September, 1895. Breeder, Mr. Wells. By Quinn's Ben—Well's Ciler.

129. C.F. Sullivan. **Ned.** 1895. Breeder, unknown. By Tom—Maher's Bitch.
   Winnings: First, Providence, 1897.

130. Dr. Kendall. **Buck.** Breeder, owner. By Kenyon's Punch—Stella.
   Winnings: First, Providence, 1898; First, Danbury, 1898.

131. R. Hickey. **Teddy.** Breeder, W.H. Carroll. By Rosse Richards—Jennie.

132. R. Hickey. **Duke.** Breeder, J. Sullivan. By Teddy—Oteo. Not for Competition.

132a. C.J. Megan. **Billy Boy.** September, 1897. Breeder, J. Devens. By Tom—Mollie. Not for Competition.

132b. H.J. O'Brien. **Towser.** Breeder, T. Plant. By Tom Sayers—Plant's Lillie.

CLASS 8—HEAVY-WEIGHT BITCHES

First Prize, $7.00.   Second Prize, $5.00   Third Prize, $3.00

[73.] **Nancy.** Entered in Class 4.
[93.] **Mettie.** Entered in Class 4.
[94.] **Beauty.** Entered in Class 4.
[102.] **Muggins.** Entered in Class 4.

133. F.J. Munson. **Kate.** March, 1897. Breeder, F.J. Munson. By Ben Butler—Nix. Not for Competition.

[103.] **Bo-Peep.** Entered in Class 4.
[64.] **Budge.** Entered in Class 4.

134. M. Murphy. **Rose.** 1895.

[63.] **Cissy Fitzgerald.** Entered in Class 4.
[87.] **Bess.** Entered in Class 4.
[62.] **Favorite.** Entered in Class 4.

135. Mrs. T. Plant. **Queenie.** April, 1895. Breeder, Owner.

136. M. O'Brien. **Mugsie.** April, 1897. Breeder, M. O'Brien. By Grizzle—Granlee's Specks.

[91.] **Sting.** Entered in Class 4.
[107.] **Corinne.** Entered in Class 4.

137. Dr. Kendall. **Famous.** 1895. Breeder, Mr. Stewart. By Dean—Famous. Price, $250
   Winnings: First Open, Pawtucket, 1897; First Open, Danbury, 1898.

138. Dr. Kendall. **Fan Tan.** Breeder, Mr. Massey. By Davis' Ned—Lady.
   Winnings: First, Manchester, 1897; First Open, New York, 1897; First Novice, New York, 1897; First Novice, Washington, 1897.

139. R. Hickey. **Duchess.** Breeder, J. Sullivan. By Teddy—Oteo.

140. H. De Ford. C.F. Sullivan, Agent. **Miss Nancy.** Breeder, Mr. Hickey. By Ben Butler—Hickey's Bitch.
Winnings: First Novice, Second Open, Braintree, 1898.

140a. F.J. Munson. **Topsey.** March, 1897. Breeder, F.S. Munson. By Ben Butler—Mix.

118b. F.J. Munson. **Trouble.** Breeder, G.H. Webster. By Kenyon's Punch—Maggie.

CLASS 9—OPEN DOGS

First Prize, $7.00. Second Prize, $5.00   Third Prize, $3.00

[2.] **Richard.** Entered in Class 1.
[38.] J. McMurray's **King.** Entered in Class 3.
[1.] J. McMurray's **Cameron.** Entered in Class 1.
[39.] **Bob II.** Entered in Class 3.
[40.] **Jingo.** Entered in Class 3.
[6.] **Buster, Jr.** Entered in Class 1.
[42.] **Jem Mace, Jr.** Entered in Class 3.
[43.] **Sham.** Entered in Class 3.
[44.] **Mark Hanna.** Entered in Class 3.
[120.] **Banker.** Entered in Class 7.
[44a.] **Banker.** Entered in Class 3.
[45.] **Little Billee.** Entered in Class 3.
[122.] **Pilot.** Entered in Class 7.
[3.] **Jim.** Entered in Class 1.
[49.] **Doctor.** Entered in Class 3.
[50.] **Alpine.** Entered in Class 3.
[51.] **Trix.** Entered in Class 3.
[52.] **Mike.** Entered in Class 3.
[53.] **Ben.** Entered in Class 3.
[54.] **Nobby Boy.** Entered in Class 3.
[17.] **Aladdin.** Entered in Class 1.
[55.] **Lord Nelson.** Entered in Class 1.
[56.] **Governor.** Entered in Class 3.
[57.] **Bob.** Entered in Class 3.
[58.] **Bingo.** Entered in Class 3.
[59.] **Sandy.** Entered in Class 3.
[60.] **Tom Sayers.** Entered in Class 3.
[112.] **Punch.** Entered in Class 5.
[114.] **Shawmut.** Entered in Class 5.

141. L.H. Topham. **Yankee Boy.** AKCSB, 44,504. Breeder, J. McMurray. By Old Sport—Juno Mac.

[120.] **Ned.** Entered in Class 7.

CLASS 10—OPEN, BITCHES

First Prize, $7.00.   Second Prize, $5.00   Third Prize, $3.00

[92.] **Nancy.** Entered in Class 4.
[93.] **Mettie.** Entered in Class 4.
[94.] **Beauty.** Entered in Class 4.
[95.] **Daisy.** Entered in Class 4.
[96.] **Melba.** Entered in Class 4.
[98.] **Rags.** Entered in Class 4.
[99.] **Judy.** Entered in Class 4.
[100.] **Cyrene.** Entered in Class 4.
[101.] **Judy.** Entered in Class 4.
[102.] **Muggins.** Entered in Class 4.
[103.] **Bo Peep.** Entered in Class 4.
[104.] **Queen.** Entered in Class 4.
[106.] **Gypsey.** Entered in Class 4.
[105.] **Dolly.** Entered in Class 4.
[107.] **Corinne.** Entered in Class 4.
[20.] **Bessie.** Entered in Class 4.
[63.] **Cissy Fitzgerald.** Entered in Class 4.
[26.] **Topsy.** Entered in Class 4.
[64.] **Budge.** Entered in Class 4.
[69.] **Lady.** Entered in Class 4.
[70.] **Lucy.** Entered in Class 4.
[85.] **Diana.** Entered in Class 4.
[72.] **Jennie.** Entered in Class 4.
[65.] **Mab.** Entered in Class 4.
[87.] **Bess.** Entered in Class 4.
[83.] **Mollie.** Entered in Class 4.
[62a.] **Nixie S.** Entered in Class 4.
[34.] **Floss.** Entered in Class 2.
[73.] **Nancy.** Entered in Class 4.
[75.] **Queenie.** Entered in Class 4.
[91.] **Sting.** Entered in Class 4.
[117.] **Miss Phillis.** Entered in Class 6.
[140.] **Miss Nancy.** Entered in Class 8.
[76.] **Rosemary.** Entered in Class 4.
[77.] **Betsy.** Entered in Class 4.
[116a.] **Pauline.** Entered in Class 6.
[95.] **Betsy.** Entered in Class 4.
[78.] **Trixie S.** Entered in Class 4.
[79.] **Buttons.** Entered in Class 4.
[138.] **Fan Tan.** Entered in Class 8.
[74a.] **Jess.** Entered in Class 4.

Appendix 4

Reliable Breeders of Boston Terriers

ALLENA KENNELS (Mr. and Mrs. A. J. Allen), 15 Academy St., Skaneateles, N Y.

ANTHVALE KENNELS (A. J. Heckelman), Broadway and Merrick Rd., Rosedale, L. I., N. Y., R. F. D. No. 4, Hempstead, L. I., N. Y.

ARISTOCRAT KENNELS (J. L. Underwood), 308 So. Beech St., Syracuse, N. Y.

ARROYO KENNELS (Freeman Ford), Pasadena, California.

ASPIN HILL KENNELS (Mr. and Mrs R. C. Birney), Rockville, Md.

AUVERN KENNELS, Reg. (Harry G. Cain), 1227 Springfield St., Dayton, Ohio

BA-RO KENNELS (J. M. Baker), 1143 N. High St., Columbus, Ohio.

BAGMORE KENNELS (Dr. H. P Bagley), 306 E. Main St., Galesburg, Ill.

BERKSHIRES KENNELS (Sullivan, Mrs. T. H.), Lee, Mass.

BERKSHIRE TRAIL KENNELS (Mrs. Alice Simpson), Haydenville and Florence Rds., Northampton, Mass

BLAZEAWAY KENNELS (C. Latunda), 36 Havre St., East Boston, Mass.

BROOKHOUSE, JOHN (No Kennel Name), 391 Central Park West, cor 99th St., New York N. Y.

BRYNTEG KENNELS (Miss Katherine Underhill), South Ashfield, Mass.

BUCKLEY, JOHN J., Jr. (No Kennel Name), 809 Glen Terrace, Chester, Penn.

CANOBIE KENNELS (Ed. F. Joyce), 13 Bunkerhill St., Lawrence, Mass.

CLARK, RETA A., 4206 Rosemont Ave., Drexel Hill, Delaware Co., Penn.

> ### Editor's Note
>
> This list of breeders comes from Dr. Mott's book. We do not know if the list constitutes Dr. Mott's assessment of the breeders of his day or if those listed paid to be included in the book. It is apparent that several well-known breeders, with very large kennels, are not included in this list although they advertised in many dog magazines and newspapers of the time.

CLIX ROSEBUD KENNELS (H. V. Clickenger), Chatham, New Jersey.

COOKSTONS-STAR KENNELS (M. C. Cookston), Brownwood, Texas.

DALLEN KENNELS (Mrs. F. A. Dallen), 1735 East 13th St., Brooklyn, N. Y.

DALTON, J. M. (No Kennel Name), Chattanooga, Oklahoma.

DELMAR KENNELS, Reg. (Joseph F. Potts), 528 Revere St., Revere, Mass.

DEVOINE KENNELS (Mrs. C. C. Crook), Catonsville, Maryland.

DOGDOM (F. E. Bechman, Pub.), Battle Creek, Michigan.

DROLL AND ROSENBLOOM, 9 Delancey St., New York, N. Y.

DWILLARD'S KENNELS, Route 2, Kalamazoo, Michigan.

EVANSTON KENNELS (W. J. Sullivan), 1830 Duck Creek Ave., Cincinnati, Ohio.

EVERGREEN KENNELS (Dr. Norman T. Harris), 25 Revere Beach Parkway, Chelsea, Mass.

EXCEL KENNELS (Mr. and Mrs. C. E. Eckenberg), 213 Kilgore Ave., Muncie, Indiana.

FASCINATION KENNELS (Mrs. Edw. J. Graves), 2421 Ferry Park, Detroit Mich.

FIRESTONE KENNELS (Mrs. H. P. Mallison), 58 Hamilton St., Rochester, N.Y.

FORRESTER HILLS KENNELS (Mrs. C. C. Glase), Dauphin, Pa. Breeder of Boston Terriers, Smooth Fox Terriers, and Pekingese.

FRISKIE KENNELS (Mrs. J. Ra!ph Hess), Gap, Penn.

GLENWAY KENNELS (Theo. Mohrbacher), 606 S. 18th St., Cedar Rapids Iowa.

GOLDEN RULE KENNELS (J. J. Briggs), 33 Monastery Road, Brighton, Mass.

GRANDVIEW KENNELS (A. N. Bengel, Prop.), Pomeroy, Ohio.

GRAYMAR KENNELS (Allen P. Kirby), Care of Kirby Davis Company, Wilkes-Barre Pa.

GREENE, N. M., 126 Ocean Boulevard, Atlantic Highlands, N. J.

GRISWALD KENNELS (John Dietschler), 870 Clinton St., Buffalo, N. Y.

GYLE, NOAH E., 122 East 87th St., New York.

HARKNESS KENNELS (M. Soulman), 1829 E 90th St., Cleveland, Ohio.

HASSON KENNELS (J. A. Hasson), 13833 Euclid Ave., Cleveland, Ohio.

HENDERSON KENNELS (A. Henderson), 1823 South Wabash Avenue, Chicago, Ill.

HIRSCH, ED. (No Kennel Name), 1805 W. Madison St., Chicago, Ill.

HI-TEST KENNELS (V. C. Winsor), Excelsior, Minn.

HUDSON KENNELS (F. L. Bradford), 65 River St., Hudson, Mass.

JAB KENNELS (Mrs. J. E. Benjamin), 3635 Washington Ave., Cincinnati, Ohio.

JOY KENNELS (Mrs. B. B. Burdge), Leonard Ave., R. F. D. 1, Asbury Park, N. J.

KEEWAYDIN KENNELS (Godfrey J. Hodges), 4101 Blaisdell Ave., Minneapolis, Minn.

KIELWAY KENNELS (E. Kiel), R. F. D. No. 2, Box 363, San Antonio, Texas.

KINGWAY KENNELS (Mrs. W. E. Porter), 869 Vine St., Denver, Colo.

KRUGER KENNELS (L.B. Seguin), 5 Ste Julie St., Montreal, Que.

KUETTEL KENNELS (Mrs. C. W. Kuettel) 234 West Olive Avenue, Fresno, Calif.

LAWRENCE, MRS. NELLIE Y. (No Kennel Name), 281 South Ohio St., Columbus. Ohio.

LLANERCH KENNELS (Dr. D. A. Bolard), Llanerch, Pa.

MAHASKA KENNELS (Dr. F. L. Barnes), Oskaloosa, Iowa.

MARGATE KENNELS (Raymond M. Ziegler), 9633 Pacific Ave., Margate City, N. J.

MASSASOIT KENNELS (Fred A. Bearse), 1075 Boston Rd., Springfield, Mass.

MAYTHORN KENNELS (Mrs. Jesse Thornton), 202 W. 28th St., Baltimore, Md.

MESSING, A. (No Kennel Name), 1010 East 172nd St., New York, N.Y.

McGIFFIN KENNELS (Robert McGiffin), 1917 Doll Way, N.S., Pittsburgh, Pa.

MILL STREET KENNELS (Frank Dondero), 121 Mill St., Abington, Mass.

MINERVA KENNELS (Mrs. Wayt), 161 Franklin St., Astoria, L. I., N. Y.

MINNETONKA KENNELS, Reg. (L. E. Taylor), 312 S. Sixth St., Minneapolis, Minn.

MOBLEY'S KENNELS (M. R. Mobley), Haverhill, Mass.

MONBAR KENNELS (Mr. C. A. Latham), 807 East 24th St., Los Angeles, California.

MONTE CARLO KENNELS, Reg. (Julius M. Fangmann), Rochelle Park, N. J.

MOSHOLU KENNELS (Mrs. M. C. McGlone), 1439 Bronx and Pelham Parkway South, New York, N. Y.

MOUNT GREYLOCK KENNELS, Reg. (R. Knowles), 47 Summer St., Adams, Mass.

MT. JOY KENNELS (A. E. Littig), R. F. D. No. 3, Davenport, Iowa.

MYERS, MRS. FRANK H. J., 62 Chester St., Rochester, N. Y.

NAST, MRS. WILLIAM, 36 North Landon St., Kingston, Pa.

NOSREDNEH KENNELS (Milton H. Henderson), Bloomville, N. Y.

NUGENT, THOMAS, 370 W. 43rd St., New York, N. Y.

OAK KLAN KENNELS (Mrs. J. M. Rodgers), 2011 Tremont St., Taunton, Mass.

ONSTADS KENNELS (Mrs. A. L. Onstads), 1038 Westchester Place, Los Angeles, California.

PARAMOUNT KENNELS (Chas. F. Grosse), 4750 Lorain Ave., Cleveland, Ohio

PARDNER KENNELS (Wm. M. Eberhardt), 517 Humboldt Parkway, Buffalo, N. Y.

PEERMONT KENNELS (M. A. Durney, Mgr.), 5552 Market St., Philadelphia, Pa.

PENTUCKET KENNELS (Dr. C. Bricault), Haverhill, Mass.

PERFECTION KENNELS (F. B. Van Ry), Holland, Mich.

PICKTIME KENNELS (Edward J. Bernhard), 724 Jefferson St., Buffalo, N. Y.

RAVENROYD KENNELS (Alva Rosenberg and Fred H. Mealia), 75 Columbia Heights, Brooklyn. N. Y.

RHODIUS KENNELS (Mr. and Mrs. H. U. Rhodius), 340 Carolina St. San Antonio,

RICH'S KENNELS (Rich C. Paul), 1210 13th St., Canton, Ohio.

RIDDER, MRS. H. M. (No Kennel Name), Bellclaire Hotel, 77th St. and Broadway, New York, N. Y.

ROLLS ROYCE KENNELS (E. M. Beaty), Central City, Nebr.

ROOP, A. H., 164 W. Main St., Norristown, Pa.

ROSE HOME KENNELS (B. M. Rosenheim), Hammond, Ind.

ROSELAWN KENNELS (A. A. Haley), Old Mystic, Conn.

ROSENBERGER, MILTON (No Kennel Name), 66 West 130th St., New York.

RUH'S KENNELS (V. J. Ruh), 280 Park Ave., San Jose, Cal.

RYZON KENNELS (Mrs. M. F. Belleher), 19 Monroe Road, Brighton, Mass.

SCHWENINGER, MRS. E., 6208 Cortelyou St., Pleasant Ridge, Cincinnati, Ohio.

SEMLOH KENNELS, Reg. (Wm. B. Holmes), Bridgeton, N. J.

SHENANDOAH KENNELS, Reg. (Mrs. William Lynn Irwin), 806 South Stewart St., Winchester, Va. See Picture Shenandoah Pal.

SHRINE CITY KENNELS (William Turner), 3 Steams St., Lackawanna, N. Y.

SIGOURNEY KENNELS (Mr. O. J. Ouellet), 3532 Lake Pk. Ave., Chicago, Ill.

SILVER CITY KENNELS (John H. Quinn), 47 State St., Meriden, Conn.

SOCIETY KENNELS (J. Schrall), 1621 Freeman Ave., Cincinnati, Ohio.

SOUTH SIDE PARR KENNELS (Mrs J. M. McLarney), 10 Tremont Ave., Binghamton, New York.

STANIFORD KENNELS, 121 Staniford St., Boston, Mass.

STANLEYS KENNELS (Frank F. Stanley), Northeast Harbor, Maine.

ST. BOTOLPH'S KENNELS, Reg. (Edward Axtell), Cliftondale, Mass.

STROLLER KENNELS, 244 W. 34th St., New York, N. Y.

SUNNYCREST KENNELS, Hogsett, West Virginia.

SUNNY HILL KENNELS (Mrs. E. A. Rine), 34 Crane St., Caldwell, N. J.

TAFT, MINA L. (No Kennel Name), 355 West 34th St., New York, N. Y.

THE ENDLE KENNELS, 13304 Hartford Road, East Cleveland, Ohio.

THE HERBERT KENNELS (H. Claud Clayton), Pittsburgh, Texas.

TRAFORD, T. B. (No Kennel Name), 42 West 58th Street, New York City.

TRIMOUNT KENNELS (Dr. C. F. Sullivan), 74 Harbor View St., Dorchester, Mass.

TURNSTILE KENNELS (H. N. Bulger), 34 Sanborn St., S. Lawrence, Mass.

TYRON KENNELS (Mrs. F. M. Tyron), 2071 Dracena Drive, Hollywood, Calif.

WALNUT HILL KENNELS (Eunice V. Shuler), 909 Walnut Ave., N.E., Canton, Ohio.

WATCH CITY KENNELS (John R. Hudson), Prospect St., Waltham, Massachusetts.

WELLINGTON KENNELS (C. J. Derrick), 653 Rockaway St., Tottenville, Staten Island, N. Y.

WHEATLAND KENNELS (H. E. Cooke), Lancaster, Pa.

WICHERING, MRS. WILLIAM. (No Kennel Name), Rosemont and Andrews Ave., Cincinnati, Ohio.

WILBER'S LYRIC KENNELS (M. A. Wilber), 516 W. 28th St., Richmond, Va.

WINSTON, C. (No Kennel Name), 4217 Lewis Ave., Toledo, Ohio.

WOLFRAM KENNELS (John S. Trotzke), 1530 Wolfram St., Chicago, Ill.

WOOD, W. L. (No Kennel Name), 1307 Hutchins Ave., Portsmouth, Ohio.

WORTHWHILE KENNELS (Mrs. W. R. Bollard), P. O. Box 705, Willard, Ohio.

ZIEGLER, R. M., 167 Virginia Ave., Atlantic City, N. J.

ZIZEL KENNELS, P. O. Box 703, Youngwood, Penn.

Index of Bostons Appearing in This Book

Amulet Bobbie 96
Ch. Arroyo Again 155
Ch. Arroyo Ambassador 155
Ch. Arroyo Anarchist 155
Atkinson's Toby 12
Ch. Auburn Happy Jr. 71
Ch. Autocrat 24

Bantam Ace of Aces 70
Barnard's Tom 12
Ch. Bayside Chauncey 77
Ben Butler 13
Bixby's Tony Boy 38
Ch. Blink's Fascination 140
Bob White IV 161
Ch. Boylston Reina 34
Bramello Skeeter 87
Brewer's Marionette 111
Broker 82

Ch. Caddy Belle 67
Ch. Captain Kinsman 36
Ch. Captain Monte 24
Ch. Captain Moody 76
Ch. Colonel Monte 34
Ch. Crown Prince III 102

Ch. Daley's Detroit News 123
Ch. Dallen's Spider 21
Dallen's Success 145
Ch. Dan Haggerty 128
Ch. Deanhurst Stanzalone 64
Ch. Dean's Lady Luana 82
Dick Turpin 29, 83
Druid Merk 110
Ch. Druid Vixen 110

Ch. E. Delilah 103
Eisenhardt's Ravenroyd Righto 121
Ch. Ellsworth FiFi 29
Escape 97
Excel Glenwood King 79

Ch. Fangmann's Sandra 57
Ch. Fascination 15
Ch. Fascinator 71
Ch. Fastep 160
Ch. Flash of Sunny Hill 78
Ch. Forsythe's Velvet 107
Ch. Fosco 70
Ch. Friendship 91
Fuzzie Dee 62

Ch. Gloria Silk 87
Goode's Buster 34
Gordon Boy 32
Greatest King 114
Ch. Gyle's Ringmaster Chief 113

Ch. Haggerty's King 128
Ch. Haggerty's King Junior's Son 128
Haggerty's Midget 128
Ch. Halloo Prince 62
Hall's Max 13
Ch. Hamill's Minstrel Boy 95
Ch. Haynes' Midgie 94
Ch. Headquarter's Sergeant 141
Heilborn's Raffles 118
Can. Ch. Highball's Just It 137
A/C Ch. Highball's Let's Go 79
Highball's Sensation 79
High Hat 76
Ch. High Point Toodles 96
Ch. H.M.S. Kiddie Boots Son 54
Hollander's Peter 26
Ch. Hollis' Handsome Pat 145
Hook's Punch 17

I'm The Boy 102
Ch. Introduce Me 156
Ch. Introduce Me's Son 157
Ch. Intruder Blink 141
Invincible King, Jr. 114
Ittsawood Direct 83

Int'l. Ch. Jab's King Tut 123
Joker Mack 144
Ch. Joy O'Valentine 70

Ch. Katz's King 122
Ch. Ketoson's Worthy Maid 88
Ch. Kingway Blink 145
Ch. Kingway Buddie Blink 145
Ch. Kingway Carina 145
Ch. Kingway K.O.A. 145
Ch. Kingway Tinkerbelle 145
Ch. Kingway Tommy Distributor 145
Knight's Sensation 134

Ch. Lady Babbie Forbes 64
Ch. Lady Dainty 21, 35
Lady Dimple 31
Ch. Lady Sensation 77
Ch. Lento's Handsome Boy 111
Ch. Little Bo Peep Forbes 64
Ch. Little Miss Muffet II 137
Ch. Little Tommy Tucker 59
Ch. Lord Derby 35
Ch. Lord Direct 25
Ch. Lyon's Gold Top 94

Ch. Million Dollar Blink 159
Million Dollar Boy Blue 159
Ch. Million Dollar Kid 158
Ch. Million Dollar Kid Boots 158
Ch. Million Dollar King 159
Minqua's Spark 100
Miss Fritz 154
Ch. Mister Jack 67
Ch. Monte 34
Monte Carlo Billy 57
Moody's Play Boy 107
Ch. Moran's Ohio Boy 115
Ch. Mosholu Bad Boy 59
Ch. Mosholu Bearcat 59
Ch. Mosholu Beau 58
Ch. Mosholu Blink 59
Ch. Mosholu Brigand 58
Ch. Mosholu Buddie Blink 59, 145
Ch. Mosholu Little Tommy Tucker 59
Ch. Mosholu Tommy Blink 59

Ch. Noel's Bebe 97

Ch. Oakmont Gent 25
Ch. Oarsman 36
Oarsman's Anthony 79
O'Brien's Rossie 31
Ch. O'Glo's Midgie 91, 134
Ch. Opal 35
Ch. Our Sammy 101
Ch. Out For Sport 141

Ch. Patsy Dee II 118
Patsy Ringmaster 119
Ch. Patterson's Ted Bustler 102
Peggy IV 30
Ch. Peter's Captain 118
A/C Ch. Playfair's Let's Go 72
Pomeroy's Trimount Billy 82
Ch. Prince Conde 73
Prince Lutana 70
Prince Walnut 76

Rajah's Premium 95
Ch. Rattler King 141
Ch. Ravenroyd Radio 121
Ravenroyd Reflection 121
Ch. Ravenroyd Rockefeller 121
Ch. Ravenroyd Rounder 121
Ch. Reign Count 123
Remember 32
Ch. Remlik Bonnie 36, 37
Rex Americus 27
Ch. Rex Oxonian 136
Rickenbacker Kid 96
Ch. Ringmount King O'The Avenue 96
Ringmount Tiny Tim 96
A/C Ch. Rockabye Dempsey 91
Ch. Rockbound's Bontuwyn 149
Ch. Rockbound's Tangee 148, 149
Ch. Rockefeller's Ace 121
Ch. Rockefeller's Progress 121
Rockydale Junior 62
Rossie Richards 88
Ch. Roxie 79

Shenandoah Pal 107
Sigourney King 122
Ch. Silk Hat King 80
Ch. So Big of Sunny Hill 78
Ch. Sonnie Punch 63
Ch. Sportsman 21, 36
Squantum Criterion 66
Squantum His Nibs 66
Squantum Punch 66
Squantum Rags 66
Squantum Shawmut 66
Squantum Squanto 66
St. Botolph's Mistress King 94
Ch. Stubbie 25
Sunlight 31
Ch. Suni Blink 100
Sunny Boy Beck 111

Tannery Town King 95
Teddy IV 29
Ch. The Bat of Buffalo 65
The Flash 114

Ch. Thorpe's Tiny King 141
Ch. Tiny Teddy B 141
Ch. Todd Boy 119
Tony Ringmaster 119
Trimount King 20
Ch. Trimount Roman 21
Ch. Trimount Tad 20
Ch. Tryon's Doreen 111

Ch. Vallery Belle 111

Ch. Wampagne Buddy Boy 100
Weiner's Bessie 26
Well's Eph 17
Ch. Whisper 20, 31
Ch. Willowbrook Glory 80
Woodward Captain 124
Worthwhile Watchme 64

Ch. Yankee Doodle Pride 77

Zizel's Hold 'Em 26